UNAPOLOGETIX

Right-brained Reasons for Christian Faith

BARTLEY SAWATSKY, M.DIV.

Copyright © 2017 by Bartley Sawatsky, M.Div.
All rights reserved. This book or any portion thereof may not be reproduced or used in any manner whatsoever without the express written permission of the publisher except for the use of brief quotations in a book review.

This title is also available in ebook. Visit www.**amazon**.com
Printed in the United States of America

First Printing, 2017

ISBN 0692737413
ISBN 13: 9780692737415
Library of Congress Control Number: 2016909797
Go2, Telford, PA

Published by:
Go2 Network
320 N. 3rd Street
Telford, Pa. USA 19438
info@go2minitries.org

Unless otherwise noted, Scripture quotations are taken from the Holy Bible, New International Version ®, NIV ®. Copyright © 1973, 1978, 1984, 2011 by Biblica, Inc. ® Used by permission. All rights reserved.

Please visit Bartley's website: www.bartleysawatsky.com

Thank you, Dr. Tim Boal, for your help in producing this book. You have been a true friend and mentor.

*Dedicated to my wife, Sarah,
for daring to be my life partner
and for always keeping
things interesting.*

TABLE OF CONTENTS

	Introduction: Are we overthinking things?	xi
Chapter 1	The scientific evidence is good enough	1
Chapter 2	I can't explain it all	18
Chapter 3	Whether you believe the Bible literally or not, its message makes sense	25
Chapter 4	The problems of beauty and pleasure	31
Chapter 5	Love is the central theme of the universe	39
Chapter 6	It should be about a person, not a religious system	48
Chapter 7	The message of the Bible is inclusive	54
Chapter 8	Faith puts the smackdown on logic	59
Chapter 9	I like being a person of faith	71
Chapter 10	Grace – The best thing in life is free	80
Chapter 11	Humility is greater than intellect	88
Chapter 12	I like doing "good" more than doing "wrong"	98
Chapter 13	Alternative philosophies don't ring true	106
	Neo-Darwinian Evolution	108
	Sexual Libertarianism	118
	The Pursuit of Happiness	127
	Materialism	131

	Humans are Basically Good	137
	All Roads Lead to God	139
	Individualism	144
	Humans As the Measure of All Things	148
	We Are All God	150
	Relativism	151
Chapter 14	The arguments against faith aren't as strong as you've been told	155
	Creationism is laughable	157
	Hell	161
	God is bloodthirsty	167
	All other religions are wrong	171
	God allows such suffering	177
	Most of the trouble in the world has been caused by religion	186
	Christianity is out of touch	189
Chapter 15	Justice Must be Had	194
Chapter 16	The Bible is the most resonant book of all time	199
Chapter 17	Certain Bible prophecies pique my interest	206
Chapter 18	The Bible's depiction of end-time events is eerily believable	212
Chapter 19	My Christian faith gives me hope	218
Chapter 20	The teachings and life of Jesus inspire me like none other	225
Chapter 21	I need God	231
	Conclusion	241
	About the Author	245
	Endnotes	247

*What you don't have you don't need it now
What you don't know you can feel it somehow*

–U2, *Beautiful Day*

Introduction

ARE WE OVERTHINKING THINGS?

Have you ever noticed? Some things just resonate with you and some things just don't. Some things make sense to you the moment you encounter them, and some things will never make sense. Not to me, anyway.

Electric fireplaces. Soy milk. Plastic flowers. The AMC Pacer. The mullet. Spray butter. The Kardashians.

Then there are things that strike a chord with a lot of people, but not all of us. Macintosh computers. The ocean. Old train crossings. Pumpkin spice lattes. 80's music. Autumn. Feta cheese.

But then, in a final category, there are things that resonate with all of us. If we deny that they do, we're simply lying. They have universal appeal. I'm talking about things like kindness, grace, beauty, honor and redemption.

In most cases, we have never taken the time to really understand why something resonates with us or not. We probably could if we sat down and thought about it: cars shouldn't look like spaceships; fire, milk and flowers are natural and can't be imitated. The Kardashians... where do I even begin?

The fact is, as much as we like to think of ourselves as careful and calculating in our assessments, much of our decision-making is instantaneous and intuitive. We size up people, situations and ideas effortlessly and in an instant, and often our instincts are right. According to Malcolm Gladwell, author of the bestseller, *Blink*, they are right more often than not! But in a world where we've been taught to evaluate everything scientifically, we've been conditioned to suppress these perceptions in favor of cold, hard data. Is it possible that we place too much emphasis on rational argument and not enough on simple intuitive perception?

> *Is it possible that we place too much emphasis on rational argument and not enough on simple intuitive perception? Are we overthinking things?*

Are we overthinking things?

You may never have considered it, but many of the activities we engage in on a daily basis depend on much more than simple science for success, particularly complex activities. Take sports for instance. There is a lot of explainable science that goes into the highly complex activities of shooting a basketball, stopping a puck, throwing a pitch or sinking a putt, but science alone doesn't make these things happen at an optimum level. Factors impervious to science like inspiration and courage and hope come into play. On those rare occasions when athletes "get in the zone" and perform at a peak level, their brains seem to bypass normal cognitive functioning to a point where we say the athlete is "unconscious." In their best moments, they're *feeling* it.

POSTMODERN BRAIN SHIFT

I was born in 1970. It's a great birth year because it makes remembering your age a lot easier, something for which an absent-minded person like me has a disproportionate appreciation. God knew I needed all the help I could get. Besides being an easy year to remember, 1970 (or somewhere in that vicinity)[0.1] has also come to be regarded by many as the end of the modern era – the age of reason, dominated by the scientific method. Many books have been written over the past few decades trumpeting the decline of modernity and the rise of postmodernity. But in all honesty, "postmodernity" more accurately describes a wide-scale shift in perspective rather than an abandonment of reason or science. (No one seems to be giving up on their iPhones or refusing modern medicine.) The real discussion is how those of us born since the decline of the modern era view the world differently than it has been viewed for many generations prior.

From the time I was young, most of my interaction was with what I would call "modern" people – logical, authority-loving folk who were raised to see science as the answer to life's problems. They were optimistic, institutional in their relationships and believers in objective truth. This group would include my parents, pastors and teachers, both pre- and post-secondary. It included my coaches and music teachers, and just about everyone who had the opportunity to meaningfully influence my life. Consequently, I was raised to view the world as a modernist.

As I grew older though, I noticed a new spirit emerging among many of my friends and newfound acquaintances, one that challenged authority and was unimpressed with well-developed, logical arguments. It was almost as if the entire world (or as much as I could see of it) began to think with the more creative and intuitive right side of their brain instead of just the analytical left side. While people of the new generation still appreciated the scientific method and modern technology, I found them more adventurous and creative in their approach to life. This was something I found very refreshing, having always been an artistic type – but also something that made me understandably cautious. After all, while the lines in the modern world were clearly drawn, there seemed to be fewer set rules in the postmodern world.

One area of concern for this Christian-raised boy was that of Christian apologetics. In the modern world, Bible-believing Christians had to be able to explain their faith in rational, scientific ways. Entire libraries have been filled with books written to defend the historicity of the Bible and a literal 6-day creation. Scores more have attempted to render supernatural biblical accounts more logical, more palatable to the modern mind. Despite our transition into postmodernity, the onslaught of secular modernists against biblical supernaturalism continues to intensify today. Well-spoken Christian authors like Josh McDowell (*Evidence That Demands A Verdict*) and Lee Strobel (*Case for Christ, Case for Faith*, etc.) have done well to defend their faith with well-constructed, left-brained arguments, and I am extremely thankful for their work.

Oddly enough, however, as postmodern thinking continues to replace modern thought, I continue to notice a shift in the way people – believers and non-believers alike – approach faith. I have noticed the shift in my own thinking. In my experience as a pastor, I have witnessed firsthand that fewer and fewer people are looking for the left-brained explanations for faith that once seemed so essential. Today's generation is more *pragmatic* and *intuitive*. Let me explain.

By *pragmatic* I mean that we are not so interested in the scientific or factual underpinnings of things as we are the function of them. Today's generation isn't beginning with the question, "Did God really write the Bible?" but rather, "Does the truth that the Bible presents really work?" It's not that the first question isn't valid or that today's generation never thinks in such a left-brained way, it's just that the second question holds much more appeal. Postmoderns (particularly Millennials and Generation Z) intrinsically believe that if something works in their world, it must be true somehow at its root. They employ a right-brained function that connects truth with beauty, a shortcut to truth that cuts through layers of argument. In an age where information is piled upon information, this type of "thin-slicing" (a brilliant term popularized by Malcolm Gladwell in *Blink*) is a very useful means of decision-making.

> *Postmoderns... intrinsically believe that if something works in their world, it must be true somehow at its root. They employ a right-brained function that connects truth with beauty, a shortcut to truth that cuts through layers of argument.*

By *intuitive* I mean we do not rely upon the five senses for confirmation of truth as much as on a sixth sense that combines the five senses with the broader perspective of experience and a sort of emotional intelligence. Today's generation "feels" their way through life much more than their parents did. We talk, not so much in linear arguments, but in nonlinear pictures, with story and parable as the preferred vehicles for understanding. As a result, we may not always be able to build neat and tidy reason-upon-reason arguments for our beliefs, but we are deeply convinced of them and defend them passionately.

Many modern-thinking people make the mistake of interpreting this difference in communication on the part of many postmoderns as a sign of shallow thought. The opposite is often true: the postmodern's thought processes are often so complex and so right-brained that they are difficult to express – similar to the difficulty an artist might have in answering why she adds a particular brushstroke to her work. It just *feels* right.

RIGHT-BRAINED APOLOGETICS

When it comes to matters of faith, it has long been my desire to articulate a more postmodern perspective on Christian apologetics. This book is my attempt at doing just that. For the modern reader, many of the "arguments" (hopefully we won't really argue) may seem fluffy and of little worth. They may seem self-centered. Some may even appear to downplay the importance of well-developed logic and doctrine upon which moderns have based their entire faith, experience and practice for generations.

Rest assured that I still appreciate left-brained, rational thinking. My goal here is simply to engage the other side of the brain in the process. I believe it is something that will strengthen the faith of many younger believers and that will resonate with many who are contemplating faith.

The premises I present are largely right-brained. They deal with that side of the brain that appreciates beauty, feeling and emotion.[0.2] Take a moment to see the different approach each side of the brain takes.

Left-Brain	**Right-Brain**
• uses logic	• uses feeling
• detail oriented	• big-picture oriented
• facts rule	• imagination rules
• math & science	• philosophy & religion
• knowing	• believing
• acknowledges	• appreciates
• forms strategies	• presents possibilities
• practical	• impetuous
• safe	• risk-taking

As you can see, the right brain leans more on intuition and experience than it does fact and reason. Although the contributions of the right brain have been subjugated to the left brain in the modern era, you can see how essential they are in forming a balanced perspective in all areas of life, including faith.

Unfortunately, even the church has largely failed to recognize this, and this despite ancient texts that encourage us to *taste* and *see* that God is good (Psalm 34:8). God himself encourages an experiential approach to faith. I suppose that many conservative Christians fear that allowing intuition to play a greater part in their faith would be to embrace dangerous "new-age" subjectivity. The end result would have people replacing the objective truth contained in the Bible with personal feelings.

I understand and appreciate this concern and in no way espouse ignoring the objective truth found in the Bible. My concern, however, is that people of faith have long ignored an entire hemisphere of the brain that was designed to be intricately involved in the faith process. Failing to engage the right brain is akin to walking on one leg or only using one hand. And in a day when a growing majority of people are approaching things from a right-brained perspective, failing to understand and express faith at a more intuitive level will leave people of faith speaking a different language from the people they are trying to influence. As I heard Christian author and futurist Leonard Sweet intentionally overstate it at a conference in April, 2008: "The church only has half a brain, and it's the wrong half!"

> ...people of faith have long ignored an entire hemisphere of the brain that was designed to be intricately involved in the faith process. Failing to engage the right brain is akin to walking on one leg or only using one hand.

If the church (which flourished in the modern era) does not learn to understand and express its faith in more right-brained ways, the divide between people on both sides of faith will only continue to grow. Adherents to Christianity will go on wondering why nobody seems interested in their rich and compelling faith and non-adherents will remain oblivious as to why so many Christians are passionate about their faith.

Perhaps you are a person on the fringes of faith, trying to get a better grasp on God and the Christian perspective, but the traditional rationales for the Christian faith are unappealing to you. Surely if Christianity (as the Bible defines it) is so great, its greatness will be apparent in a variety of ways beyond the typical arguments over the deity of Christ and the veracity of the Bible. True greatness, it would seem, should emanate from every part of something that is of exceptional quality. It should resonate with the one who experiences it and impress itself upon both mind and heart.

Over my past twenty-three years of pastoring and teaching, I have had lots of time to contemplate the intuitive and experiential reasons for Christian faith that you are about to read. Because they are right-brained, they have taken some time to draw out and express, but they are strong and valid motivations for faith in God, Jesus and the Bible. For me, they make being a follower of Jesus *feel* right, and I can say with all honesty that they are some of the most powerful reasons behind my faith. I suspect many will resonate with you too.

Chapter 1

THE SCIENTIFIC EVIDENCE IS GOOD ENOUGH

I'm not listening to you! You only believe in Science. That's probably why we never win!

We never win because you are fat!

– Nacho and Esqueleto, *Nacho Libre*

Science has sometimes been said to be opposed to faith, and inconsistent with it. But all science, in fact, rests on a basis of faith, for it assumes the permanence and uniformity of natural laws – a thing which can never be demonstrated.

–Tyron Edwards (American theologian and compiler of *New Dictionary of Thoughts*)

"Good enough" is really annoying to perfectionists like myself. Maybe you're a perfectionist too. By nature of their personalities, many scientists and theologians are perfectionists. They are driven to search out

1

every uninvestigated lead, to tie down every loose end and to make sense of everything they encounter. Everything should be resolved, categorized and cataloged.

Unfortunately, life is not kind to perfectionists, because in life nothing is ever fully resolved. Having kids was a real revelation of this fact in my own life. My wife and I have four children. In my ideal world, I would love to see my home in a state of constant order and cleanliness. That's how I always dreamed it would be prior to marriage. You know – you see the catalogs and picture your living room looking like something from Crate & Barrel. The dining room table is always set and ready for entertaining guests. The entire house is neat and orderly at all times. Whenever one of us uses a towel or a toothbrush, we immediately put it away and restore the house to its perfect state.

In my twenty-plus years of marriage, this has yet to happen, and I've given up holding my breath. My wife is a stay-at-home mom of four who cleans homes and waitresses part-time. She does an amazing job. But my vision of the perpetually perfect house is totally unrealistic. The house was unfinished when we moved into it, so we've always been behind the curve. Life happens, and we try to keep up. We paint one room and our youngest son marks on the walls of another one. We rush out the door to hockey practice unable to leave the house perfectly clean, so we make a frantic effort to blitz on Saturday morning and make up for lost time. We never fully get there.

And then there's the basement. Let's not even go there. I feel a wave of depression come over me every time I descend the stairs.

Whether it's the state of our homes, our businesses, our scientific research or our pursuit of truth, we will never reach a place of perfectionistic bliss and static resolve. Not in this life. We are always moving, always being acted upon by forces much larger than ourselves. We manage. We try to keep up. Through the chaos we learn to embrace some greater ideals and we hold onto them, at least until someone convinces us of a better way of operating. We crave perfection, but we are forced to live with "good enough."

As a parent and homeowner, I have come to embrace "good enough." As a follower of Jesus and a pursuer of truth, I have come to embrace "good enough."

Good *enough*? Doesn't a Christian have to be able to prove beyond the shadow of a doubt that God exists, that the Bible is true, that God created the earth, that Jesus was virgin-born and that the miracles described in the Bible actually happened? Well, I believe all of these things, and I think they're at the heart of Christian belief. But I don't feel the need to prove them to anyone. In fact, none of them can be empirically proven, so the best anyone can do is to be personally convinced of their truth.

The need to be "right" about personal beliefs has resulted in endless debate between supernaturalists and naturalists on every front, including the fields of textual criticism and archeology. While this battle is of utmost importance to the left-brained, the right-brained tend to seek more philosophical reasons for believing in the supernatural. After all, no amount of empirical thinking is ever going to fully prove or disprove God, who is not accessible to our five senses. Instead of fretting over the dearth of evidence of God in the universe, we'd be better off considering if there might be reasons for his apparent distance from his creation – reasons that have some innate appeal. I've given it a lot of thought over the years.

GOOD ENOUGH REASONS FOR FAITH IN GOD

If God is God (as we traditionally define God – personal and omnipotent), he could easily prove himself to us. He could leave us with no doubt whatsoever. But to be honest, I find God's choice *not* to absolutely prove himself to mankind to be masterful. Think about it: if true belief is all about a relationship based upon faith and trust, then isn't God wise in requiring us to believe in him by deeper means than simply cold facts? Isn't he wise in not overwhelming us with his own greatness?

You may never have considered it, but he could very well do this if he is the God the Bible describes. I'm convinced this is why he never fully reveals himself. He always shrouds his glory, appearing in light, or cloud, or smoke. Yet even in the shroud of a human body God's glory leaked through. Take, for example, the transfiguration[1.1] or people being healed by merely touching his clothing.[1.2] Jesus was the fullest unveiling of God mankind has ever witnessed.

If God is as magnificent and "beyond" us as the Bible says, then we would not want him to reveal himself fully to us. If he gave us even a glimpse of his utterly otherworldly glory, we would have no choice but to love him and embrace him, thus eliminating any true, voluntary relationship – the one thing that God has always wanted in relation to mankind. Our inability to fully prove God, then, is absolutely essential to a real and free relationship.

Søren Kierkegaard addresses this very concept in his *Philosophical Fragments* when he recounts a parable of a king trying to win the love of a peasant girl that had captured his affection. Resolved to find true love and not infatuation, he disguised himself as a peasant before approaching the girl. He veiled his glory in favor of developing real trust and relationship. (It's a pretty powerful metaphor for how God veiled his glory in the incarnation.) But the concept that God should somehow hide himself from us is very frustrating for some people. The notion that some leap of faith is required to experience God does not sit well with these people at all.

An article by Gary Wolf in the November 2006 issue of *Wired* magazine (a personal favorite) probes the depth of the religion of "New Atheists" – defined by Wolf as unapologetic, even militant in their stance that God and faith are not only irrelevant but even damaging to mankind. Men like Richards Dawkins, Sam Harris and Daniel Dennett "condemn not just belief in God but *respect* for belief in God" (emphasis mine).[1.3] Their goal is to make faith not merely unfashionable, but downright embarrassing.

In reading Wolf's article, I couldn't help but ask myself the question, "Why are some people so insistent on eliminating faith?" Would these same people eliminate trust as well? (They are essentially the same thing.) And what of true relationships, seeing that true relationships are all based upon trust? Would they prefer video-monitoring all of their relationships 24-7, just so nothing was ever in doubt? Do they trust their spouse when they say that they just returned from the store? Surely they are not opposed to *all* faith, but one wonders at what point faith becomes okay.

At what point is their understanding of things *good enough*?

This rudimentary question of God's self-disclosure is just one example suggesting there are deeper philosophical reasons for faith in God, reasons that beg for some additional perspective and imagination. The more you think about it, to simply write off God because you can't experience him with your five senses is a gross overreaction.

GOOD ENOUGH REASONS FOR FAITH IN THE BIBLE

The historicity of the Bible is another hot topic for the scientifically inclined. For centuries both scholars and laypersons have questioned the Bible's accuracy and reliability. Here again the debates are endless. (As a sidebar, people need to understand that the Bible is the most consulted book of antiquity when it comes to comparing the archeological record with recorded history – hands down.) Understandably, Christian archeologists will be motivated to identify their finds with biblical references and unbelieving archeologists will be motivated to connect their finds to other-than-biblical reference points. Nonetheless, much of what we know from ancient history comes as a result of the biblical record.

The real question comes down to whether or not one's confidence in the Bible in this area is good *enough*. (There's that word again.) Has archeology ever dealt the Bible a knockout blow – a finding that indisputably showed the Bible to be false or unreliable? Or has the Bible shown a general consistency with the archeological record?

A fair degree of research would be worthwhile, and is possible thanks to the internet. But I would contest that the experiential approach is far more favorable to testing the Bible's veracity than the archeological approach. In other words, instead of trying to dig up objective facts that prove the truth of the Bible, maybe try asking, *When I live in keeping with the Bible's teachings, does my life get better? Does the Bible's explanation of life resonate in my heart of hearts?*

> **The scientific debate at hand will surely outlive all of us. The experiential approach can render answers now.**

The scientific debate at hand will surely outlive all of us. The experiential approach can render answers ***now***.

GOOD ENOUGH REASONS FOR FAITH IN GOD AS THE CREATOR

On February 4, 2014, the eyes of the scientific community turned to the Creation Museum in Petersburg, Kentucky, where evolutionist Bill Nye (a.k.a. the Science Guy, whom many of us watched on PBS growing up) faced off against Ken Ham, a creationist and the founder of the creationist non-profit organization *Answers in Genesis*. Some three million viewed the event live via the internet while millions more have watched the footage after the fact. While it's impossible to measure how much the debate might have changed anyone's opinion on the topic of evolution and creation, it did reinforce one unfortunate belief – that is, that science and faith are somehow diametrically opposed to one another. Once again, faith and science are shown on opposite sides of the floor, launching missiles back and forth in an attempt to blast a big enough hole in the opposition's platform to sink them once and for all.

But Christianity and science are by no means on opposite playing fields. This is a perception held by people on both sides of the issue, but one that isn't even close to being true. Many of history's most influential scientists were driven to understand the universe based on the presupposition that the world was made by a purposeful creator, and this foundational belief drove them to discover the laws that God built into the universe. I'm talking about people like Kepler, Galileo, Descartes, Pascal, Boyle, Leibniz, Newton, Faraday, Mendel, Kelvin, Marconi, Fleming and Planck. Even today's scientists don't necessarily view faith and science as incompatible. Far from it. According to *100 Years of Nobel Prizes*, a review of Nobel prizes awarded between 1901 and 2000, 65.4% of Nobel Prize Laureates over the past century have identified Christianity in its various forms as their religious preference.[1.4]

Christian faith and science are by no means incompatible. In fact, when it comes to the origins of the universe, both camps agree that the physical cosmos began at a point of singularity and has been expanding ever since. (Almost 100 years ago astronomers observed that virtually all clusters of galaxies appear to be moving away from all other clusters, giving strong indication that the universe is expanding.) The scientific community refers to the point of singularity as the *Big Bang* – the explosion of subatomic particles that gave birth to the universe. Christians refer to it as God speaking the universe into existence, as it says in Genesis 1:1 – "In the beginning, God created the heavens and the Earth."

Obviously, Christians and scientists have widely varying opinions in relation to how long ago that event took place, but the basic understanding is one and the same. Moreover, many are surprised to learn that the one who proposed the theory of the expanding universe and what became known as the *Big Bang* theory was a Christian man – a Belgian priest named Georges Lemaître. In 1927 he was the first to derive what are today known as *Hubble's Law* and *Hubble's Constant*, publishing his findings two years before the renowned Edwin Hubble himself. Lemaître found no inconsistency between his findings and scripture, the ancient language of which aligns very neatly with modern scientific discovery, referring to the "circle of the earth" and how God "stretched out" the heavens (Isaiah 40:22).

Lemaître's understanding of the origins of the universe were similar to the understanding I now embrace – that a great mind and purpose were at work in the creation of the cosmos. I cannot help but lose respect for men like Richard Dawkins who talk in circles in an attempt to disconnect the origins of the cosmos from any kind of intelligent design. In essence, he claims that the cosmos was somehow pre-programmed and that it has simply unfolded over billions of years – similar to how a seed grows into an oak tree. Forgive us in the creationist camp for asking how that information might have gotten programmed in the first place! I understand scientists' ongoing battle with the Intelligent Design camp and their fear that opening the door on that discussion will result in crazy creationists taking us back into the dark ages. But at a certain point my right brain starts screaming foul when scientists have to work so hard to avoid any inference of mind, will and purpose connected with the cosmos. As we've discussed already, we're basically on the same page when it comes to the inception of it all.

Of course, arriving at a consensus on how life has developed since the Big Bang will be difficult to impossible, even with the advances of science. This is true because even new scientific information in this regard is built upon philosophical presuppositions that naturalists and supernaturalists still argue over. For example, naturalists have almost entirely accepted Darwinian evolution as the model for the development of life on earth, and so any new discoveries will be explained in relation to that system of thinking, while supernaturalists will be more apt to give credence to the Bible's creation and flood accounts. Having grown up hearing convincing arguments from both sides has led me to integrate some philosophy in my quest for understanding in this area as well.

To be honest, my faith in Darwinian evolution took a hit shortly after high school. I remember my Grade 11 biology teacher in 1987 stating as fact that the coelacanth (a.k.a. "mud puppy") was a missing link between fish and animals with legs that had lived about 400 million years ago and became extinct some 66 million years ago. A few years later in college I was a tad perturbed to come across an article (I believe in *Reader's Digest*) that announced the finding of a live coelacanth off the coast of Madagascar.

After a bit more research, I discovered that people have been finding them for years. In 1997 a man on his honeymoon in Indonesia was visiting the local market. Incidentally, he happened to be a marine biologist who recognized that the fish someone was trying to sell him was a coelacanth! (Guess he confirmed the suspicion that you can find just about anything at an Indonesian market!)

Scientists still regard the coelacanth as a missing link, but in fairness, live missing links aren't that sexy. In fact, scientists are baffled as to how a species that was labeled as living during the Devonian period to the end of the Cretaceous period could have survived so long without evolving. Kind of makes you wonder how many other species never really evolved either. According to Wikipedia, "this situation is still under investigation by scientists."[1.5]

The blind acceptance that today's students (and teachers) often give to the evolutionary theory would be disturbing to me had I not grown up in the middle of it. I get it that most students are not that interested in combing through the mountains of data necessary to arrive at solid convictions, and I realize that many of those who teach the material haven't formed solid convictions either. Unlike most people, I have studied the theory in considerable depth and remain unconvinced of the greater tenets of it. It is certainly possible that humans are the product of a long line of infinitesimally improbable accidents (a.k.a. natural selection), but I'm just not convinced.[1.6] I prefer the idea that I am a descendant of human beings of my same species. I also prefer the biblical explanation that plant and animal species reproduce after their own kind, that they always have, and that they will continue to do so. (I must point out, that's exactly how it works today and the only way recorded history has ever shown it to work. Simple observation. Simple science.)

Sure, the creation story has its challenges as well. I'm well aware of that. But I guess what I'm saying is that it's *good enough*. I asked myself a long time ago, "How will my life be different if someone can prove to me that evolutionary theory is true rather than creationism?" Regardless of who is right in the evolution debate, it doesn't eliminate the question of God's part in creating and sustaining the world, and to me that's the bigger question in play.

WHILE WE'RE ON THE TOPIC OF SCIENCE...

I think it's important that people recognize the difference between various scientific fields. Some are more evidentiary; other fields are more philosophical. For instance, physicists and chemists have the luxury of dealing with science that can almost always be tested in the here and now.

However, as we move into biology and then evolutionary science (the latter of which has to wrestle with huge periods of time in past history), we have to be aware that we are talking about something very different. There is a lot of very good science going on, but it is fraught with large information gaps that need to be filled with estimates, guesses and narratives. It is in these gaps, which require greater philosophical and "big picture" thinking, that I find myself losing faith in modern scientific thought.

Perhaps there's a reason why Gary Larson (the creator of the *Far Side* cartoons we read growing up) picks on scientists so mercilessly. (For a good time, google "Gary Larson scientist" and take a browse.) Scientists are a brilliant lot, with minds that handle detailed data in ways mine never will. Problem is, they are prone to delve so deeply into the details of things that they often lose sight of the big picture. (That's why it takes the jingle of the popsicle truck bell to get their attention!) If science existed in a vacuum, where only known formulae applied, all would be well. But there's so much about science that we don't know, where the voices of epistemology, philosophy and morality need to come into play – right-brained disciplines that help temper the left-brained scientific process.

Scientists are routinely wrong. They propose theories, and many of those theories prove to be wrong. Admittedly, experimentation is a big part of the scientific process, but meanwhile, half of the population has to clean out their fridge and medicine cabinet every six months when the newest scientific studies come out. The sun is bad. The sun is good. Milk is good. Milk is bad. Milk is good again.

Furthermore, scientists are people with motivations that can be improperly influenced like the rest of us. If politicians can be corrupt, and preachers can be corrupt, why can't scientists? Pharmacists are great scientists, but anyone who believes that pharmaceutical companies and doctors (scientists in their own right) never make deals to get us using certain drugs is a little naïve. Everyone has their own motivation. Keep in mind that every new beauty cream and weight-loss program comes certified by "scientific" studies. Keep in mind that the entire population is swayed by people like Dr. Oz.[1.7]

All of this is to say that the *carte blanche* affirmation we often give to scientists today scares me a little. And particularly that which we give to evolutionary scientists, who are forthright in their disbelief in God. I, on the other hand, find myself trusting the Bible's explanations for the development of life on planet Earth based on greater, more right-brained ideals.

The idea that God created the universe *ex nihilo* is distasteful to many scientifically minded folk, but I don't see how it's any more problematic than a complex universe forming itself out of an explosion, disconnected from any mind or intent. I can understand how the Bible's six-day creation story is challenging to people, but for the record, many Christians even wrestle with how literally we should take the six-day account, and that's okay. The problem is that we're short on options. I've spent a lot of hours chewing on Darwinian evolution and I just can't appreciate the flavor. There's something screwy with the recipe. More evolution discussion later on.

For now it should be noted that while both science and faith have questions, neither is incompatible with the other. Most Christians I know love science, and most scientists I know are people with sincere religious faith, including a brilliant childhood friend of mine who I consulted in writing this book. Today he is a respected chemistry professor at a prominent Canadian university, and I admire his ability to hold faith and science in tension.

GOOD ENOUGH REASONS FOR FAITH IN MIRACLES

So what about miracles? Can I find "good enough" reasons to believe in those too?

When it comes to the virgin birth and other miraculous events, I sympathize with today's scientifically-minded skeptics.[1.8] I agree that it's most difficult to justify today's seeming void of the miraculous with the numerous wonders of the Bible, and to be honest, I doubt most of what I hear from religious zealots today who claim to have seen or performed miracles. (For example, I've never seen the Virgin Mary's face appear on my grilled cheese or, much less, wrestled with the moral implications of biting into her face.) I have some left-brained reasons for believing that the miracles described in the Bible actually took place, but again, I lean more to my right brain on this one.

Since I've already made the leap toward a purposeful Creator, I guess I choose to see life as being thoroughly purposeful. In other words, I see life like a story, or movie – not one of these new movies that appeal to people who have watched far too many movies and are bored with good endings. You know – where everybody dies and you feel like joining them. I mean a good, purposeful, poetic, resolved movie, complete with twists and intrigue. A movie like one from the *Lord of the Rings* trilogy.

Taking the miracles out of life is like taking magic out of *Lord of the Rings*; I suppose you could make the movie without it, but where's the fantasy in that? Where's the ecstasy and imagination? *Lord of the Rings* has moments that are punctuated with the supernatural, but also long stretches that lack any miraculous flare. Evidently, J.R.R. Tolkien decided to write it that way for artistic reasons.

For some reason (undoubtedly connected back to the Enlightenment), when it comes to life's biggest questions, here in the West we tend to look at the world as a scientist would. But is it somehow less legitimate to look at life through the eyes of an artist or a movie director? I see the course of history in the same way as I see a *Lord of the Rings* movie. Have you ever considered that we may just be 45 minutes into a 105-minute movie that has most of its action at the beginning and the end? If the biblical account is right about the unprecedented fury and wonder of the end times, isn't it brilliant strategy on the part of the Director to prepare the stage with a good long dry spell prior to it? Students of the Bible may note that even the advent of Christ was preceded by 400 years of prophetic silence. As far as we know, there were no visions from God, no miracles, no *nothin'*. (Again, students of the Bible may recall that in the end times people will mock believers in regard to the delay in God's promised coming. [1.9]) Isn't it entirely possible that God is just setting us up for a juicy ending?

For sure, I'd love to see more miracles happen today as well. But the fact that I don't doesn't mean they can't happen, that they haven't happened or that they won't in the future. [1.10] This is another instance where I must ask if my faith in God as a whole and in the revelation of himself that he has left us in the Bible is bigger than this issue. For me it is. At every turn, life is full of the mysterious and the miraculous. Some choose to believe that it is only a matter of time until humankind comes up with answers to all of these questions, but I just can't envision it. Actually, I'm not even sure I'd prefer it.

THE LIMITATIONS OF SCIENCE

As time goes on, I think that people are coming to terms with the limitations of science. Don't misunderstand me; we still place a lot of stock in science, and rightly so. But in our postmodern world we are recognizing the inherent limitations of equating truth merely with what can be studied between microscope slides. Not all realities within our universe are logical, as we'll discuss later.

As a pastor, I deal extensively with the concepts of hope and faith, neither of which are completely "logical." While science deals exclusively with the use of the five senses, the Bible proposes a powerful concept called faith – "the substance of things hoped for, the evidence of things not seen."[1.11] By definition, it's an unscientific approach, but boy, does it work. The story of Terry Fox illustrates this beautifully.

Terry Fox is Canada's most beloved hero, even though he never lived to see his 23rd birthday.

When Terry was just 18 he was diagnosed with a cancer known as *osteosarcoma* that led to the amputation of his right leg along with chemotherapy treatment that would promise him only a 50% chance of survival. Within three weeks of the amputation he had learned to walk on an artificial leg. Inspired by the first amputee to complete the New York City Marathon, Terry secretly embarked on a 14-month training program, and then in August 1979, he competed in a marathon in Prince George, British Columbia. He finished dead last, a full ten minutes behind the second last runner, but his effort was met with a powerful outpouring of tears and applause from the other participants.

Frustrated at how little money was being given to cancer research, Terry devised a plan, and on October 15, 1979, he sent a letter to the Canadian Cancer Society to inform them about a special marathon that he would be running. Terry's "Marathon of Hope" began on April 12, 1980, when he dipped his artificial leg in the icy Atlantic Ocean near St. John's, Newfoundland. His goal was to run across the entire country of Canada – the world's second largest nation – on his artificial leg. He would do so by running a marathon *every day* – 42 kilometers per day until he reached Vancouver.

Many thought he was straight up crazy.

Before he left Newfoundland, 10,000 residents showed up to meet him in Port aux Basques with $10,000 to donate. Word began to spread, but not as fast as Terry's body began to deteriorate. Shin splints, inflamed knees and cysts on his stump caused excruciating pain, but barring a few exceptions, he refused to take a day off. As the news media caught wind of his story, young kids across Canada (including me) began to imitate Terry's awkward running gait on our school playgrounds.

By the time Terry got to Montreal, he had raised $200,000 in donations. Momentum was building. Soon, famous athletes and celebrities (including Prime Minister Pierre Trudeau) began to meet him on his path. Large crowds showed up to hear his speeches in every town and many people started to run along with him. By the time he got to Toronto, he was a nation-wide hero. For a few months, he was not only the lead story in every news broadcast – he was the *only* story.

But on September 1, outside of Thunder Bay, Ontario, intense coughing and chest pain forced Terry to stop his marathon. The next day, without shedding a tear, he announced to the nation that his cancer had not only returned, but spread to his lungs, and that he would be forced to end his run – a run that had lasted 143 days and covered 5,373 kilometers. He had raised an amazing 1.7 million dollars by that time.

Terry died early in the morning on June 28, 1981.

I was a 10-year old kid sitting in my little white Baptist church in Pleasantville, Nova Scotia, when our pastor delivered the news. The church fell silent for what seemed to be several minutes and then we all wept and prayed and thanked God for his incredible life and sacrifice.

Every September in Canada, people everywhere run in Terry's name. Even the kids in school do it, and a few, after watching movies of him, still imitate his gait. The Terry Fox Run is the world's largest one-day fundraiser for cancer research, and to date over 600 million dollars has been raised in Terry's name. Today, cancer treatment is effective in ways that Terry could only have imagined, in ways that likely could have saved his own life.

This is a rather long story to demonstrate a rather simple point.

Had someone decided way back in 1980 that they wanted to devise a scientific solution for overcoming cancer, it would have looked *nothing* like this. Nor could it have produced the same result. Cancer had been beating us for years, killing our loved ones and baffling our scientists. Logic was not turning the tide on cancer. The financial boost that our scientists needed was fueled by something that science itself could not provide – namely, inspiration, faith and hope. In more recent years, science has been able to benefit cancer research because a boy with an amputated leg had the faith and courage to do something ridiculous.

Placing confidence in what is unseen or unproven so as to obtain a more favorable outcome is a concept that works on a different plane than science. The powers of faith and hope are known to be real, and should work hand-in-hand with science. Yet many people today, our scientists included, default to working from a strictly empirical model. They insist on being logical. To this I say, "Why be merely logical when you can be smart?"

If you haven't already, someday you are going to realize that science alone can't provide all of the answers you need for life, and you will be forced to broaden your search. At first you may be disappointed, but give it some time and you will embrace a new and better perspective. It's a perspective I call "good enough."

> *Placing confidence in what is unseen or unproven so as to obtain a more favorable outcome is a concept that works on a different plane than science.*

Chapter 2

I CAN'T EXPLAIN IT ALL

The most beautiful thing we can experience is the mysterious. It is the source of all true art and all science.

–Albert Einstein

Mysticism keeps men sane. As long as you have mystery you have health; when you destroy mystery you have morbidity.

–G.K. Chesterton

Doubt is uncomfortable, certainty is ridiculous.

–Voltaire

What is the greatest TV comedy of all-time?

The debate will rage on, but in the Sawatsky household, the decision was made a long time ago. It's *The Office (U.S. Version)*, and although it left the air in 2013, my kids and I still watch random episodes almost daily on Netflix. No joke. It makes us laugh like no other show we've ever seen.[2.1]

Michael Scott (played by Steve Carell) is the most brilliantly concocted, delightfully awkward character in TV history; the fictional boss of the Dunder Mifflin paper company that we all swear we've met before. When Carell left the show at the end of Season 7, many expected it to dissolve into obscurity, but the brilliant cast (bolstered by various cameo appearances) carried on for two more successful seasons, largely in part to the acting of Rainn Wilson, a.k.a. Dwight Schrute.

Schrute is the know-it-all, sycophant and assistant to the regional manager, Michael Scott. Raised on a beet farm, Schrute is famous for spouting his "wisdom" throughout the office on a daily basis. There is absolutely nothing about which he does not have a solidly formed opinion.

Dwight Schrute on decision-making...

"Before I do anything I ask myself, 'Would an idiot do that?' and if the answer is yes, I do not do that thing."

Dwight Schrute on heroes...

"No, don't call me a hero. Do you know who the real heroes are? The guys who wake up every morning and go into their normal jobs, and get a distress call from the Commissioner and take off their glasses and change into capes and fly around fighting crime. Those are the real heroes."

Dwight Schrute on tipping...

"Why tip someone for a job I'm capable of doing myself? I can deliver food. I can drive a taxi. I can, and do, cut my own hair. I did however, tip my urologist, because I am unable to pulverize my own kidney stones."

When it comes to *The Office*, Dwight's know-it-allness is hysterical. But have you ever met a real-life know-it-all?

At first glance, know-it-alls are impressive. When you meet them they speak confidently about their area of expertise, and they grab your initial respect. But over time you begin to notice that they speak with the same confidence on every subject that they address. Eventually you conclude that they can't be experts in everything. The respect they gained is lost as you realize that they likely weren't even very knowledgeable in their own field of expertise. Blowhards.

Unfortunately, many Christians have fallen into what I consider a trap when it comes to "know-it-all-ness." In a world that is daily steered by investigative reports and the latest scientific studies, Christians have largely come to believe that they must be able to explain every last detail of their faith in order to be considered legitimate.

I am not saying here that I believe traditional apologetics to be of no value. I am extremely grateful to have studied under some of the best Christian minds in North America and to have learned to defend my beliefs from the left side of my brain. Part of my seminary training involved walking onto the University of Maryland campus and engaging in friendly debate with students. On such occasions I was happy to have some left-brained answers to share.

But the truth is, a large part of what I have studied about God and the Bible is still very confusing to me. There was a day when my inability to sound the depths of every subject, to wrap my mind around every theological notion, was frustrating. But over time I have come to appreciate the many mysteries of my faith. I have embraced the fact that I can't explain it all.

EMBRACING THE MYSTERY

We all know that the best things in life are inexplicable: Love, the development and function of the human body, the power of forgiveness, and so on. There's a definite mystique about the inexplicable. The mystique of the inexplicable is what drives scientists toward new discoveries and men toward mysterious women. And never is the mystery a deterrent to discovery! On the contrary, it fuels the research.

> *The mystique of the inexplicable is what drives scientists toward new discoveries and men toward mysterious women.*

That's how I see my faith. I teach my theology students that God is *knowable*, but not *comprehensible*. That is, we can know God as we know another person, but we will never be able to fully wrap our minds around him. Such a reality drives me to want to understand God more.

Maybe I'm just the stubborn type, but doesn't your inability to understand God make him more awesome to you? I don't know about you, but watching the Discovery Channel can be a powerful worship experience for me. One time while on vacation outside of Ottawa, my wife, Sarah, and I watched a show on the development of human life inside the womb. How every little cell somehow knew what to do at precisely the right moment was beyond imagination. We can't begin to explain it, but we're all fascinated by shows like that.

I don't understand God. I believe I'm made in his image, meaning that in some fundamental way I must be like him, but he is largely confusing to me. For example, the Bible asserts that God, who is one divine spiritual essence, exists in three personalities. I accept that as a fact, but I can't wrap my mind around it. And that's okay. Some people may be put off by it, but there are lots of times and places in life where we need to trust that clarity will come later on. Kind of like doing trigonometry in high school!

For a long time, sines, cosines, and tangents frustrated the snot out of me, because to me, it was all merely knowledge in a vacuum. My teachers, for whatever reason, were unable to show me any tangible application of trigonometry to life, and back then I didn't have the internet to run to. I've since come to discover many tangible applications, but at the time I just had to take their word for it and blindly use their formulas to solve pointless problems. (It was not a good time.) My point is, when I finally just accepted that I had to work out equations using sines, cosines and tangents, I managed and made it through. [2.2] The fuller understanding would come later on.

I don't understand prayer particularly well. I tell my parishioners that prayer is just communicating with God, which is accurate, but exactly how God answers my prayers is very much a mystery. How my requests can move the hand of the Almighty and change things in this universe without screwing up the course of events is beyond me. But isn't the idea captivating? It sure makes you want to give prayer a try.

I don't have the foggiest idea how to explain a lot of what takes place on this globe. I believe that miracles have happened. (I don't even believe you can be a true Christian without belief in miracles. After all, Jesus' resurrection – an absolute miracle – is the defining event of Christian faith. So anyone who claims allegiance to Christ and denies a literal resurrection makes Jesus a fraud when you really think about it.) I do have left-brained reasons for believing that more miracles used to happen. I won't get into that now. The truth is that there are still things that happen in our universe for which I don't have a logical explanation. But why do I need to be able to explain everything? Life can't be very complex if my little mind needs to be able to figure it all out.

People ask me all of the time if I believe God still does miracles. Well, I've seen some amazing things, but I don't know if any of them fit the true definition of a miracle. I say that God can do whatever the heck he wants. Who am I to say what God can or can't do in his universe? Maybe God doesn't show me miracles because I already believe. Maybe he doesn't show me because he knows I'd try to explain them away.[2,3] Just because I haven't seen them doesn't qualify me to discount them from ever having happened.

As a trained theologian, I don't even understand lots of things about the Christian faith. I've studied church history and spiritual gifts, but I don't know why some Christians still speak in tongues; I have never done it, but I love and respect people who do. I can't relate to some of the incredible experiences people in my own church have shared with me. One man, who attended my church for years, once recounted a story of how an angel appeared when he was lost deep in the woods as a young child. The angel allegedly held him by the hand, soothed him and protected him until help arrived. (Or until *just before* help arrived; angels seem to have this thing of leaving before the crowds arrive, kind of like Superman.) I've never seen an angel before, but I don't have any reason to believe this man was lying to me. He was an able-minded man who had never lied to me about anything else; I've even read the newspaper article telling the story of him being lost. There's so much I can't explain.

As much as I don't understand the past or the present, I surely can't claim to understand the future. I don't know how God is going to accurately judge this huge and complex world; I'll leave that up to him. Nor can I understand the vastness of his universe. I don't know if there's life on other planets. I'm positive that God could handle the workload, but he's never told us anything about it, so I just figure he didn't want me wasting a whole lot of time worrying about it. I can appreciate someone's fascination with it. It has made for some really cool movies. Sometimes when I think about how big God's brain is, I can't imagine him *not* having created life in other universes.

Much about God and Christian faith is confusing to me, but there are a couple of concepts that make great sense. Their resonance outweighs the hundreds of unanswered questions.

The Bible's explanations of sin and redemption make incredible sense. The theory that something like "sin" has messed up our world seems obvious to me. The theory that God alone could come and make it right makes sense when I see humanity's perpetual inability to fix it. The theory that God came to us in the helpless form of a human baby is off the charts in terms of artistic resonance, and his sacrifice on the cross humbles me to the core. It establishes love as the central theme of the universe, and nothing else I've heard of compares with that narrative for the universe.

That's what I've chosen to believe. It would feed my ego to be able to explain it all, but I can't.

You can lose a lot of sleep over your inability to understand it all. Or you can dream about it. As theologian G. K. Chesterton once said, "the riddles of God prove more satisfying than the solutions of man."[2.4]

I couldn't agree more.

Chapter 3

WHETHER YOU BELIEVE THE BIBLE LITERALLY OR NOT, ITS MESSAGE MAKES SENSE

*I've done everything the Bible says – even the
stuff that contradicts the other stuff!*

–NED FLANDERS

*The trick to forgetting the big picture is
to look at everything close-up.*

–CHUCK PALAHNIUK, AUTHOR OF *FIGHT CLUB*

Here's another area where supernaturalists and naturalists argue. Is the Bible literal or not? Well, first of all, even the majority of Christian literalists don't take *all* of the Bible literally. Like any book, the Bible makes use of similes, metaphors, parables, and so on. Some of the dreams and visions it contains, such as those found in the book of Daniel, are explained within the text as being figurative. Heck, apart from instruction manuals and legal documents, does anyone actually take *any* writing or speech as *entirely* literal? Similarly, when Christians refer to interpreting the Bible literally, they usually mean it in a "natural" sense. But some Christians are definitely more literal than others.

To be honest, I avoid wearing the label "literalist" because of the baggage it tends to carry; but I definitely take the Bible at face value. Unless the text gives me a good reason for not taking the passage as being literal, then I take the story as having really happened that way. (But isn't that the way we read any book?) The Bible definitely makes use of metaphor, and when it comes to apocalyptic literature, I think most of us agree that there is ample room for interpretation of those images. But unlike many Christians I know, I don't waste time fighting with people who default to more figurative interpretations. In general, I think people who automatically look for non-literal explanations are on a slippery slope that can lead them to discrediting the Bible entirely – including incontrovertible elements like the resurrection of Jesus – and that obviously concerns me. I take the time to explain to these skeptics, from the right side of my brain, how I am able to take certain passages literally and still call myself logical. Some of my critics see my point; some don't.

I have come to believe that people who constantly avoid a face-value interpretation of scripture have issues with the Bible that go way deeper than whether or not Jonah could have survived for three days in a fish's belly. Theirs is a fundamental problem of disbelief.

Let me explain it in more common terms. When I meet a person, it is not normal behavior for me to be looking for faults in their personality. On a few occasions, when I have been forewarned about someone's character, I might take such an approach, but in general, this type of outlook is unattractive to me. I think it only fair and right to give someone I meet the opportunity to carve their own impressions on my mind. Unless they give me reason to believe otherwise, I think it is most admirable to assume the best on the part of that person.

Similarly, when people approach the Bible with a predisposition for finding fault, I try to encourage them in a different line of thinking. Their bent is symptomatic of deeper issues they hold in regard to God and faith. (In fairness to these people, many of them have been so warned about the Bible's character that their caution is only natural.)

I believe people should take the Bible at face value after personally investigating it. *As a whole, does the Bible make sense?* This is the question people need to begin with. Do its historical passages accurately recount history? Does its explanation of good and evil mesh with what I see and experience? Does the picture it paints of God and the relationship he has with his creatures make sense? Does the concept of redemption (God's intricate plan of rescuing fallen mankind through Jesus) resonate within us?

I think I can look past my bias enough to say that the Bible makes terrific sense. In fact, I'm convinced that most people who have a decent understanding of it know this to be true. Generations of people from all different cultures have lived by this book, and with success. It has inspired more artists and musicians than any other book. Even today, in a generation whose information and technology far surpass that of even fifty years ago, honest, well-informed people continue to attest to the Bible's wisdom and relevance to today's biggest issues.

The lack of miracles we see today in comparison with what the Bible claims could be a challenge for many people, as I discussed in the previous chapter; things today are obviously different for some reason. Yet this shouldn't be reason to reject the Bible altogether. Think about it: the fact that we see no dinosaurs today doesn't cause us to disbelieve that they ever existed, even though no one is exactly sure what happened to the great lizards. In the same way, the Bible should be evaluated on a grander scale.

How about the Bible's description of right and wrong? Even with modern religions and religious syncretism, people everywhere still adhere to the basic concept of right and wrong. You've likely witnessed documentaries that describe a hierarchy of "sinfulness" that exists even in our federal penitentiaries. Child molesters are deemed more sinful than, say, thieves – and as a result are treated much more harshly, even brutally, by their fellow inmates. The measuring stick varies with the context, but make no mistake – even among hardened criminals, there is always a measuring stick. This meshes with the Bible's defense of an innate sense of morality.

Mankind also generally shares in the biblical idea that judgment awaits us all. Even though evolution has indirectly taught us that chaos rules the universe, few of us cast off restraint in consequence. Nor does adopting an impersonal view of God ease our inner angst in regard to eventual judgment. The biblical concept of giving account to our Maker is powerful within us, no matter where we come from or what religious background we have come to embrace.

Probably most impressive, to my mind, is the Bible's explanation of what's wrong with the world. Here we have this beautiful world, replete with beauty and intricate design. It follows its cycles with unequaled precision while remaining thoroughly original at every moment. And yet, at least at a surface level, we sense that something is desperately wrong. Our apples have spots on them and weeds invite themselves into our gardens. Animals prey on other animals and humans live selfishly, waging wars and living in extravagance while other humans starve. Solutions to our problems seem so simple and at the same time remain so unsolvable.

The Bible's explanation of sin as the cause of these "aberrations" is the best explanation I've encountered for what's wrong with the world. Not only does the Bible fully describe sin as the problem, but it also clarifies the way in which sin operates and how God is overcoming it. When sin is juxtaposed with the love of God, it renders a very sensible, very useable paradigm of the world. It works.

I also appreciate the fact that the Bible's explanation of reality goes beyond the physical. Atheistic scientists present compelling arguments to explain the physical universe, but their research barely scratches the surface of the many moral and spiritual questions that we wrestle with every day. The Bible goes there.

One last right-brained defense. It is very right-brained because it is based entirely upon experience. I don't expect those who have never had the experience to understand, but I still must share this last point: *Those who embrace the Bible and the God it describes are convinced that it makes sense.* Like I said, if you haven't tried to live in keeping with the Bible, I don't expect you to get all tingly upon reading this. All I can say is that I have spent my entire life comparing the Bible's claims with everything else. From the time I entered elementary school I was already comparing what the Bible said to other philosophies for life (even though I didn't know the word "philosophy" at that point). As I grew older, I looked at the lives of people who embraced the Bible and put it into practice and compared them with those who did not. I compared not only the way their life seemed to work on the surface, but I also probed deeper to see what kind of peace and hope and joy these people had. I watched to see how parents raised their children and saw how they responded to their parents. As the son of a pastor, I got an inside look at how people's lives changed in relation to the truth they embraced or rejected. I came to see how God's laws work irrespective of one's status or occupation. (Trust me, I've seen a lot of messed up Christians as well, but without fail I could see that the problem was the *application* of God's laws, not the laws themselves.)

Suffice it to say that the lessons I learned prior to college and seminary were among my most valuable. I was so convinced of the Bible's truth when I left high school that I turned my back on some great scholarships (and the advice of my teachers) in order to study the Bible's claims further. Some may suppose that I was just a brainwashed kid, but it really wasn't like that. The things I could understand about faith were so powerful and true to life that I was compelled to look deeper.

If someone told you a story about someone you knew, and the people and events described in the story were largely consistent with what you knew to be true about that person, you wouldn't disregard the entire story because of a few confusing details. You would presuppose that the major parts of the story had truth to them and then look into what was confusing. Yet so many people today throw out the Bible with the bath water. There is still so much about my faith that I can't explain, but the larger brushstrokes work to perfection, and I won't let some confusing details ruin the whole picture.

> *If someone told you a story about someone you knew, and the people and events described in the story were largely consistent with what you knew to be true about that person, you wouldn't disregard the entire story because of a few confusing details.*

I attended seminary just outside Washington, D.C. On many occasions my friends and I would hop on the train in New Carrolton and go into the city to visit the Smithsonian museums. One of my favorite places to visit was the National Art Gallery. My father-in-law is a big Claude Monet fan, so I always took some time to look at the numerous Monets on exhibit. If you've ever had the chance to witness any of Claude Monet's paintings you will see how your eye gets lost in the painting when you are too close to it, but back up 10 or 15 feet and suddenly all of the accented brushstrokes blend into a beautiful and lifelike image.

The Bible itself, with all of its loose ends, admits: "now we see but a poor reflection as in a mirror."[3.1] For now, the clarity I lack in areas of my faith I use to fuel my imagination. And for the time being, I like the image the Bible presents, fuzzy as it may be.

Chapter 4

THE PROBLEMS OF BEAUTY AND PLEASURE

For every beauty there is an eye somewhere to see it. For every truth there is an ear somewhere to hear it. For every love there is a heart somewhere to receive it.

–Ivan Panin, Russian mathematician

It struck me, after reading my umpteenth book on the problem of pain, that I have never seen a book on "the problem of pleasure." Nor have I met a philosopher who goes around shaking his head in perplexity over the question of why we experience pleasure…

We Christians… look for ways to explain the origins of suffering. But should not atheists have an equal obligation to explain the origin of pleasure in a world of randomness and meaninglessness?

–Philip Yancey, Christian author

The human body is amazing. Did you realize that our eyes can differentiate between up to 10 million different shades of color? The human tongue has around 10,000 taste receptors and can distinguish about 500 different tastes. The human nose can recognize up to 10,000 different odors. Our ears can hear vibrations ranging from 15 or 16 per second to 20,000 per second, and can distinguish a vast array of sounds based on their pitch, volume, phase and timbre. Direction and distance also play a part in sound recognition. (Maybe you've seen that YouTube that shows a blind boy who is able to navigate like a bat simply by listening to his own echo. Amazing!) Human bodies are also covered with skin, most of which is full of receptors that enable us to sense cold, heat, pressure and pain.

People, for whatever reason, have an incredible ability to interact with their environment. We seem to be made to experience and appreciate. Despite all of the ugliness we sometimes complain about in the world, no one I know considers blindness or deafness a blessing. On the contrary, we consider these sensory capacities to be the most basic privileges of human existence. They are the gateways to experiencing pleasure and beauty.

PLEASURE AND BEAUTY

Pleasure and beauty are huge problems for people who reject faith – huge right-brained problems. It was in reading Philip Yancey's book, *Soul Survivor*, that I was first introduced to G.K. Chesterton's thinking on this subject. Chesterton, an Englishman who became a renowned journalist, theologian and philosopher (among other things) was first an atheist who converted to Christianity because it provided an answer to questions rarely asked – questions such as, "Why does pleasure exist?" Chesterton set out to explain pleasure by atheistic means, but eventually confessed, "I did try to found a heresy of my own; and when I had put the last touches to it, I discovered that it was orthodoxy."[4.1]

Having grown up in the Christian faith, I would never have even thought to ask the question that Chesterton raised about pleasure. To me it always made perfect sense that God, who I understood as being loving and kind, made mankind with great capacities for enjoyment and tailored the world around us so as to accentuate that pleasure.

Some of my fondest childhood memories are of playing next to the ocean in the tiny seaside village of West Berlin, Nova Scotia. There I would spend entire days clambering on the rocks and playing "chicken" with the waves of the incoming tide. I would touch and smell (and sometimes taste) a million different shells, rocks and pieces of driftwood. I would lay on the hot beach rocks in the summer sun or huddle between massive boulders during a storm, watching the violent surf crash and scramble to within inches of my feet. I would breathe in deep the salty air or the irresistible smell of the piles of peat moss that would cover the beach the morning after a storm.

West Berlin was a wonderland. As an 8-year old, I could see no limits on how much there was to discover. Looking back, I suppose that this early experience made a believer out of me as much as anything I ever learned in Sunday school. The notion that everything so amazing could have come from anywhere other than a loving, creative God never once entered my mind – not a single electrical surge in a single synapse of my brain. Perhaps someone in an inner-city environment, hemmed in from witnessing the beauty of the natural world, could be convinced of the non-existence of a creator. But for me, there was no question that God exists.

Today I live in the concrete jungle, but I still am amazed at the beauty of the world: the vines that climb the front of my house; the sunset; the design of a leaf; the delicacy of a flower; the loveliness of the human body (the female variety being of particular interest); the way water reflects light and the way smoke wafts upward. Even the city can't hide the splendor of it all.

And then there's pleasure. Maybe it's a symptom of living in such a decadent culture as ours, but rarely do we consider just how much pleasure we enjoy in the run of a day. This truth was highlighted for me recently in watching *The Diving Bell and the Butterfly* (*Le scaphandre et le papillon*), a sobering but must-see film based on the memoir of the same name by Jean-Dominique Bauby.

After suffering a major stroke at the age of 43, Bauby, *Elle* Magazine's editor-in-chief, was left with "locked-in" syndrome, a rare condition that left him entirely paralyzed but for the ability to move his eyes and blink his eyelids. The film, much of which is presented through the eyes of Bauby, forces the viewer to feel firsthand the desperation that he experienced. In order to communicate, a speech therapist would recite the alphabet, stopping at the first letter to which Bauby would blink. The therapist would then recite the alphabet again in search of the second letter of the first word of the sentence. Simple phrases like, "I am hungry," took agonizing minutes to form. Director Julien Schnabel did a masterful job in making the audience feel Bauby's torture, and nothing in recent years has so effectively jolted me to notice just how routinely I disregard even the most basic pleasures of communication and mobility.

Since watching that movie, I've taken notice of just how many pleasures I take for granted: the taste and texture of a blueberry as it crushes between my teeth; the smell of a baby's skin; the refreshment of a cool breeze against my cheek. We experience pleasure at a rate far more quickly than we can even register it. Perhaps this is why we all tend to take it for granted.

Beauty and pleasure are problems because they beg us to answer a very basic question: Is the world predominantly a good and planned and purposeful place, or is it a random, chaotic, hostile place? When I'm sitting on a sunny

> *Beauty and pleasure are problems because they beg us to answer a very basic question: Is the world predominantly a good and planned and purposeful place, or is it a random, chaotic, hostile place?*

beach, it's all good. When I'm lost in the mosquito-filled woods at night – not so good. Obviously, there are arguments to consider on both sides. But from my perspective, beauty and pleasure are definitely foundational and point to the existence of a loving and creative source.

DESIGNSPIRATION

If the world were intrinsically chaotic, there'd be no way we would see the natural order and design that we do in the quantities in which we see them; every tree, every blade of grass is an architectural masterpiece. Scratch that. Every *cell* in every blade of grass is an architectural masterpiece. Let alone the fact that every blade of grass can be eaten and ingested by animals which in turn assimilate the elements and nutrients into their own bodies. The interplay of the different aspects of the natural world (the food chain, the water cycle, etc.) suggest not only an architect or multiplicity of architects, but a *master* architect who coordinated all of this design.

A number of years ago I developed a friendship with one of my congregants who worked for SPAR Aerospace. SPAR was an ongoing participant in the development of some of the world's greatest aviation, military and space equipment, and was famous for its development of the *Canadarm* that long adorned NASA's space shuttles. Upon getting to know this gentleman better, he invited me to come and tour his workplace. After thorough screening and preparation, I walked through the vast building and peered through windows where huge sections of aircraft were being constructed. I saw complex robotics in action like I had never witnessed before, and my friend explained to me the immensity of some of the projects under development.

He detailed how in every aerospace endeavor, hundreds of companies like his all over North America and the world received contracts to produce very specific components. These companies took years to create and fine-tune the pieces, often requiring the projects to survive the changing of the guard in Washington. Eventually, all of the parts (each one a masterpiece of architecture) would be shipped to a common destination for assembly – sometimes requiring entire highways to be shut down in the process.

The amount of thought and planning that went into the projects was so staggering that it left me speechless. I was in awe of the human ingenuity and cooperation represented in the work that these people were accomplishing. Likewise, when I view the complexity of the universe's design, which far surpasses the complexity of what I witnessed that day, I stand in awe of the mind that brought it to be.

The fact that there is disorder and ugliness in the universe does not shake my conviction about the existence of a creator, simply because the ugliness is quite obviously secondary to the beauty. Our apples have spots; our spots don't have apples. People develop diseases; diseases don't develop people. The world accumulates pollution; pollution doesn't accumulate new worlds. The way I see it, if the world were truly as chaotic and random as some scientists claim, most of the natural world around us would fail to resonate with us. Most of our environment would look like the set of a *Mad Max* movie – dry and dead and colorless. The instances of beauty and the opportunities for pleasure would be few and far between. They would be the exception and not the rule. But that is not our experience.

Furthermore, as humans we have this inclination to add to the beauty and pleasure around us. We design and wear fashionable clothes and construct magnificent buildings. We landscape our front yards, decorate our homes and grow gardens in our backyards. [4.2] We play games and build amusement parks. Even the aerial views of our cities can be turned into pieces of artwork worthy of hanging on our walls.[4.3] Apparently, the same impetus for beauty and pleasure that exists in the natural world lives in our DNA as well.

The Bible, the book that forms the basis for my Christian faith, has always suggested exactly what I feel to be true in my heart – that there is a God who created the world to be a good and beautiful place. Later on we'll discuss some reasons for the ugliness that does exist in our world, but for now, let's agree that the world is predominantly a good place. We don't spend billions of dollars looking for other blue planets like ours because of how hostile the conditions are here. Nor do we consider suicide a normal reaction to life's difficulties.

Anyone who agrees that life is good must either concede that it was designed to be that way or that its resonance with us is the grandest of coincidences. The compatibility between us and our planet is a significant consideration. Imagine, if you will, tongues with 10,000 receptors in a world with nothing to taste, or where everything tastes the same. Strangely enough, every tree, plant, herb and seed in our world has its own unique taste. The same compatibility can be seen as it relates to our other four senses – all of the colors, sounds, smells and textures. It's hard to deny that our ability to enjoy beauty and pleasure was intended, that some force greater than us made our world to be explored and experienced.

Prominent atheists have been known make reference to the worms and parasites that sometimes wreak havoc on the human body, asking how a God so intent on beauty and pleasure could possibly allow something so ugly and unpleasant. But it doesn't take a great philosophical mind to understand that we can only label the worms and parasites as awful in juxtaposition to all of the beauty and pleasure that we enjoy on a regular basis. Minor aberrations don't negate the obvious overarching design.

On one occasion while driving with some college friends, my 1987 Volkswagen Fox had a terrible malfunction while crossing the Tappan Zee Bridge in New York. Apparently, the rear left wheel well had weakened over time, and upon hitting a pothole on the bridge, the entire strut broke free from the wheel well and drove down into my tire, instantly puncturing it and throwing my car into a swerve. I managed to maintain control of the vehicle, but my heart stopped for a few seconds when I finally got out of the car and saw what had happened. The malfunction was a shock to me only because I had enjoyed the engineering of the vehicle for so long. Obviously, I understood that all things in life break down. I didn't lose all faith in car manufacturers, or begin to wonder if the vehicle I thought was created by Volkswagen came together by some other means.

The beauty and pleasure that fills our world is so powerful that anyone who tries to suggest a non-intelligent source for it is bound to look absurd. In his book, *The God Delusion*, Richard Dawkins allocates an infinitesimal page and a half to the colossal discussion of beauty as an argument for God's existence. And in that page and a half, he makes absolutely no mention to the beauty of the natural world. None. But then again, what would he say? Any argument would be as absurd as that of the parasite, a creature that, by the way, is a marvel of engineering in its own right.

What if we experience beauty and pleasure because there is a God who embodies those things? What if he really did make us compatible for the enjoyment of beauty and pleasure? Wouldn't that say something about his love for us? Ten million shades of color. Ten thousand taste receptors. What if we watch sunsets and paint pictures and write music and grow gardens because we've somehow been made in God's likeness, and when we do those things something inside our spirit resonates with the eternal Spirit and brings a strange sense of peace and satisfaction?

Problems to chew on.

Chapter 5

LOVE IS THE CENTRAL THEME OF THE UNIVERSE

I believe that imagination is stronger than knowledge – myth is more potent than history – dreams are more powerful than facts – hope always triumphs over experience – laughter is the cure for grief – love is stronger than death.

–Robert Fulghum, (Author of *All I Really Need to Know I Learned in Kindergarten*)

Love—is anterior to Life—
Posterior—to Death—
Initial of Creation, and
The Exponent of Earth—

–Emily Dickenson

There is only one happiness in life, to love and be loved.

–George Sand (pseudonym of Amantine Aurore Lucile Dupin, Baronne Dudevant, French novelist, feminist)

The Beatles were before my time, but their music continues to inform the spirit of the day. Can you think of any one band that has been more successful in influencing their generation? Some bands have had staying power, but none have left a mark as deep as the Fab Four.

ALL YOU NEED IS LOVE

On June 25, 1967, the Beatles first performed *All You Need Is Love* on the BBC's *Our World* – the first-ever global television link. The song was heard by some 350 million people in 26 countries around the world. (That's incredible considering it was 45+ years ago; think about those numbers.) Apparently, the band was asked to write and perform a song that could be easily understood by viewers of all nationalities. I think they succeeded.

> *All you need is love.*
> *All you need is love.*
> *All you need is love, love.*
> *Love is all you need.*

The song was an instant worldwide hit.

Even today when I visit my francophone father-in-law in Québec, he is able to sing most of the English lyrics to this, and many other, Beatles tunes. Come to think of it, I suppose most of the English my father-in-law knows comes from the Beatles or Bob Dylan. (Pretty amazing, considering Dylan's enunciation.) There could be a lesson here for those aspiring to speak a new language: Mumble a lot. [5.1]

I find it rather revealing that in 1967 it took the Beatles to bring to light the fact that love is the central theme of the universe. One would think that here in North America, a land built upon and at that time still very conversant in the Bible, this central fact would have already been obvious. But apparently it wasn't.

From everything I can glean about the 1960's, love was the central issue of the times. In general, the older generation in North America still paid lip service to the Bible, the Ten Commandments, and Jesus. But the faith of this older generation failed to capture the imagination of the new generation. The emerging generation cast off the pervading, heartless legalism of religion in favor of free love, and believed that peace could be achieved through non-violent means. (Thankfully for the hippies, weed counted as a "non-violent means"!) Had the younger generation been taught the truth about Jesus and the heart of his message, the Hippie Movement may never have taken place. Eventually, the Jesus Movement did rise up out of the Hippie Movement, but in many ways it was the old legalism of their parents wrapped in a new "organic" package.

Incidentally, my father-in-law was a part of both of these movements, coming to faith in Jesus along with a group of radical, very "organic" Christians. The group that led him to faith, eager to follow the Bible verbatim, threw out all of their photographs, thinking that they were obeying the commandment not to have any "graven images." They also took the Lord's Prayer to an extreme, citing "give us this day our daily bread" as a reason to never have more food in store than the current day required. Obviously, it was pretty radical. I love talking with him about his experience, because I think a lot of young people today could relate to the authenticity and simplicity of his generation.

The hippies eventually grew up and tempered their ways, but the spirit of that generation remains strong today. The reason is, they were right about the main thing. Love *is* all you need. Love *is* the main thing. It is the central theme of the universe. Anyone who took the time to really think that through back in the 60's and 70's believes it to this day, because whenever truth is encountered, it can never be denied. It captivates both sides of the brain, making logical sense while at the same time *feeling* right – a supremely powerful combination.

What a shame that it took the Beatles to bring this to light. With one song they drove home this truth better than hundreds of thousands of preachers and Sunday school teachers had done in an entire generation. I have no right to castigate that generation of believers any more than my own, but I can't help but wonder if the outcome would have been different had the churches and Christians been better exemplifying the love of Jesus in front of that generation.

Regardless of how a professed Christian chooses to live, they can't deny that love is all you need, because God *is* love.[5.2] The Bible describes love, not so much as a feeling, but as a deliberate choice to act unselfishly. It is a determination to see the good in others and to do them good. While mankind doesn't have a lot of tangible examples of this on a broad or sustained scale, whenever we see it happening it resonates inside us (in our right brain, to be precise) and we know that love is the answer. It's the feeling that we catch wind of at Christmastime when for a moment everyone – within a certain scope, anyway – is at harmony with their neighbor. It's the spirit that the Coca-Cola company managed to tap into with its 1971 commercial, *I'd Like to Teach the World to Sing*.[5.3] (Coke continues to lead the way when it comes to advertising that depicts cross-cultural peace and love. Haven't you noticed?)

WOULD THE REAL JESUS PLEASE STAND UP?

According to the Bible, all true love finds its source in God.[5.4] When we live in harmony with God we cannot help but live in love.[5.5] Because God *is* love, his nature constantly compels him to act benevolently toward his creation. This was the impetus behind the defining event of history – God's choice to become a human being and sacrifice himself on behalf of mankind.

I love being a Christian when it comes to discussing the central theme of the universe, because no one can deny that love is the main thing. And true Christianity has always been all about love – God's love demonstrated through Jesus and through those who have come to understand and embrace Jesus' message. Unfortunately, the demeanor of so many who call themselves Christians has discouraged people from embracing God's love as the Bible describes it. Jesus says that his true followers will be known by their love[5,6] and yet many Christians today, especially high-profile ones, are known instead for their bigotry, arrogance and judgmental spirit.

Whenever my unbelieving friends point this out to me I humbly acknowledge the accuracy of their observation, but I also challenge them to distinguish true Christianity as Jesus described it from the cultural Christianity adhered to by so many in North America today. Nothing about true Christianity requires a person to become an arrogant and judgmental bigot. Those of us who try to adhere to the heart of Jesus' message may be annoyed by the bad press brought on us by those who wear the Christian label, but we have no reason to therefore abandon the truth Jesus taught. I kind of wonder if those who reject Jesus on that basis are simply looking for an excuse to do their own thing.

People may not believe in the deity of Jesus Christ, but they can't deny the ideals that Jesus lived and died for. Even the most entrenched adherents to other faiths openly admire the passion of Jesus – his mission to love the unlovable. I know lots of people who can't stand Christians, but I don't know anyone who hates Jesus. What's not to like? The guy is totally genial and gentle while at the same time passionate and thoroughly dedicated to his cause – a crusade of love. He even dissed the heartless religious leaders of his day for their hypocrisy. You have to like that! It's hard not to

> *I know lots of people who can't stand Christians, but I don't know anyone who hates Jesus. What's not to like?*

appreciate someone who voluntarily dies for other people, even if you happen to think he's a nut bar.

JESUS' KIND OF LOVE MAKES CHRISTIAN FAITH UNIQUE

I also love being a Christian because this focus on selfless love separates it from every other world religion. It distinguishes itself from new-age, inward-focused religions by putting the focus on others above introspection and self-improvement. It distinguishes itself from other authoritarian faiths by asserting that life is not a desperate scramble to reach God by following a list of rules. Instead, it asserts that life is a response of love toward God who loved us despite our inability to keep the rules.

> *This is love: not that we loved God, but that he loved us and sent his Son as an atoning sacrifice for our sins* (1 John 4:10).

> *And he died for all, that those who live should no longer live for themselves but for him who died for them and was raised again* (2 Corinthians 5:15).

This difference may not appear significant at first glace, but the implications are huge. It's the difference between a child earning his parents' love and "keep" in his family versus receiving unconditional love. The first is bondage, guilt and manipulation; the second is grace and freedom.

I'd be burying my head in the sand not to acknowledge that everyone who claims to be Christian doesn't live a life in response to God's love. It saddens and embarrasses me to say that *most* Christians I know don't live this way – including me oftentimes. Christian or not, it's in our human nature to resort to choosing rules over relationship when it comes to religion. That's because following rules satiates our pride, allowing us to believe that our own goodness is what makes us acceptable to God.

In my heart of hearts I know that following Jesus out of love for him is more powerful and noble than following a list of rules. I know that the first is a pure motivation, while the second is corrupted by my own pride. The latter is devotion to myself masked with pseudo-devotion for God. The soul that follows God out of anything but love lives in fear of eventual condemnation, because it knows that its motivation has not been pure. But a life lived out of pure love toward God is free and fearless.

God is love, and all who live in love live in God, and God lives in them. And as we live in God, our love grows more perfect. So we will not be afraid on the day of judgment, but we can face him with confidence because we live like Jesus here in this world.

Such love has no fear, because perfect love expels all fear. If we are afraid, it is for fear of punishment, and this shows that we have not fully experienced his perfect love (1 John 4:16-18, New Living Translation).

Jesus taught that the reason why love is the main thing in our world is because it has always been the main thing in God's universe. Jesus claimed to have enjoyed unhindered intimacy with the Father prior to his time on earth. In other words, love always existed among the three Persons of the Trinity: the Father, the Son and the Holy Spirit. The point of this life, according to Jesus, is to discover God's love during this lifetime and commit to an eternal relationship with him so that this love will continue on in eternity. Jesus was very clear about this in his last recorded prayer in John 17.[5-7]

In many faiths, love is viewed as important and necessary, but only in true Christianity is it the theme of life prior to the creation of the world, the storyline of world history, and the end goal for life in eternity. It's relationship through and through. Man, I like that.

Heaven is not a cessation of existence. Nor is it a hedonistic frat party for the people who missed out on the most fun here on earth. Nor is it some sort of an impersonal resonance with all that is good. Heaven is enjoying God and others like I enjoy sitting on the couch on a lazy Sunday afternoon next to my wife with my child wrapped in my arms. No inhibitions. No inner anxiety. Just peace and love.

Unlike the Hippie Movement, heaven's peace and love will be uncorrupted by the innate human selfishness that causes love to become lust, relaxation to become laziness, and enjoyment to become hedonism. Heaven will not be a reaction, but a response – a response of love to a God who loved us first.

GOD... LOVES... YOU

In North America, the words "God loves you" can be seen regularly on church signs, t-shirts and bumper stickers. The phrase has become so trite that no one really stops to consider the full power of the meaning rendered by the combination of those three small words. But whenever I stop and chew on them, I feel a tangible sense of hope and peace awaken inside me. God...loves...*me*. There is a God who is the ruler of everything, and he loves *me*.

I don't really need to care what other people think about me. God loves me and I am deeply convinced that love is the core of life itself. Every action lived disconnected from the love of God is an exercise in futility. A life spent in pursuit of personal happiness is a wasted life. People who chase success and fame while disregarding relationships destroy themselves and the people to whom they owe love. But a life spent channeling the love that flows from God to the people around us is a life full of purpose and richness and fulfillment. We can't deny it.

Love is the main point of the universe. Jesus said so,[5,8] and although I struggle to make love the center of my life, it makes me want to be his follower.

At the end of the day I want to be known as a person who loved people like Jesus did. I want to be someone who gauged the use of his time by this single criterion: *Is this action helping me love God and people to the greatest degree?* I fail miserably at this goal, but it is the divine ideal that I hope will always guide me.

Chapter 6

IT SHOULD BE ABOUT A PERSON, NOT A RELIGIOUS SYSTEM

> *Fundamentally, our Lord's message was Himself. He did not come merely to preach a Gospel; He himself is that Gospel. He did not come merely to give bread; He said, "I am the bread." He did not come merely to shed light; He said, "I am the light." He did not come merely to show the door; He said, "I am the door." He did not come merely to name a shepherd; He said, "I am the shepherd." He did not come merely to point the way; He said, "I am the way, the truth, and the life."*
>
> – J. Sidlow Baxter, Australian
> pastor and theologian

If the universe hinges on the concept of love, then it follows that belief should be all about a *person* – someone who can exemplify what love is and who can be loved in return. On this point Christianity differs from every other known "religion." I put religion in quotation marks because in truth, Christianity is not even about religion. Religion has well been described as *man's attempt to reach God*; in other words, religion is about humans doing a variety of actions or rituals in an attempt to please God. The message of the Bible is precisely the opposite.

THE THESIS OF THE BIBLE

One of my favorite classes in high school was Honors English. Our teacher, Mr. Penny, was one of those teachers that you either loved or hated. He spent most of our class time in long, heady rants that sometimes actually touched on the subject we were supposed to be discussing that day. Some would say he seemed more like an actor than a teacher – an actor with a very captive audience. Personally, I looked forward to every class.

Besides making us learn over 100 different uses for the comma, Mr. Penny was fastidious about getting us to learn proper essay form. [6.1] It was common for him to give a student a 2 out of 10 on their first try at an essay, but he would always allow us to rewrite in order to get a better mark.

Many of the great works of literature we studied led into very spiritual discussions, and perhaps this is why I had a certain affinity for Mr. Penny's class. As a young person I had already come to see every deep issue of the human heart in light of what the Bible says about the human condition. Despite Mr. Penny's appreciation of me as a student, at times I could sense his frustration with my tendency to boil down every piece of literature to sin, conscience, forgiveness, and so on.

In all my days as a student I had a silent wish that someday, somewhere a teacher or professor would ask their students to write a thorough essay on the Bible, treating it like any other piece of literature, boiling down its contents to a clear thesis. I say this because I am fully confident that even students of average scholasticism would arrive at the same conclusion about the Bible: From Genesis to Revelation, the Bible is not at all about *religion*, but about God's plan to redeem mankind, to restore mankind's *relationship* with himself.

TOUCHABLE GOD

The Apostle John was unquestionably right-brained. He valued the experiential. Likely the youngest among Jesus' disciples, he was part of Jesus' inner circle along with his older brother, James. In his gospel, he refers to himself as the "disciple whom Jesus loved," drawing special attention to the relationship that he shared with Christ. A quick reading of both his gospel and his epistles reveals that he was fascinated with Christ's divinity, but even more specifically with the way that God chose to take an experiential approach with mankind and to make himself accessible to our five senses.

> *The Word became flesh and made his dwelling among us. We have seen his glory, the glory of the one and only Son, who came from the Father, full of grace and truth* (John 1:14).

> *That which was from the beginning, which we have heard, which we have seen with our eyes, which we have looked at and our hands have touched—this we proclaim concerning the Word of life* (1 John 1:1).

The term "Word" was not one that John came up with. Hundreds of years prior, Greek philosopher Heraclitus from Ephesus started developing some pretty complex philosophies. He wrestled with the meaning of the universe as it goes through constant change. (You are likely familiar with his meme that no man ever steps in the same river twice.) Heraclitus was the first philosopher to postulate what philosophers call a "unity of opposites" – the dualistic notion that every entity in the universe is somehow balanced by its opposite entity, and that in this way the universe constantly changes and yet remains the same. It was Heraclitus who declared that "all entities come to be in accordance with this Logos" ("word", "reason", or "account").

The stoic philosophers that came after Heraclitus picked up the term Logos and identified it with "the divine animating principle pervading the

Universe." In other words, the Logos became the undefined label for the center of all meaning and purpose and wisdom and reason – the scheme behind all rhyme and reason in the universe.

By the time John wrote his gospel, the concept of the Logos was well developed and commonly understood, and John, upon witnessing Jesus firsthand, had the epiphany that this Logos, that the philosophers were convinced underpinned the universe, was indeed Jesus of Nazareth. He was the one who made sense of everything – both the constant change of life and its immutability. And the thing that blew John away in all of this was the fact that the Logos was a flesh-and-blood human being – a person that he had heard with his own ears, seen with his own eyes and touched with his own hands.

Today's right-brained spiritual sojourner should be equally dumbfounded by what John discovered. That is, that God was not content to allow himself to be understood in rites and rituals and rules. The Logos was God's eternal plan who was in the beginning with God and who was God (John 1:1). The eternal plan was that God would, at just the right time in history, become completely accessible to our five senses. He could be observed, not merely in pen and ink or in age-old stories, but in warm-blooded, living and breathing human flesh.

I don't know how that makes you feel, but after decades of following Jesus I am still moved by this idea. See, I'm not looking for someone to *tell* me what to do. I've had more than enough authority figures in my life who were happy to tell me what I ought to do with my life; I want someone who is willing to *show* me what to do with my life. In Christ I have found someone who was willing to live by what he taught. I think people are fed up with mere rules. As the old adage goes: Rules without relationship equals rebellion. When Jesus, God in human flesh, finished teaching about loving your enemies and turning the other cheek and trusting the Father he was put to the ultimate test. He himself had to love his enemies and turn the cheek and trust the Father with his very life. He was falsely accused and brutally tortured for doing nothing wrong. He entrusted his case with the Father, who in turn, raised Jesus up from the grave and gave him a name that is above every other name (Philippians 2:9). Jesus' own disciples were so moved by this touchable version of God that they were willing to lose their own lives as well in order to be true to him. Their hearts were captured, not be religion, but by a person.

OUT OF CONTROL

As essay-writing students came to the conclusion that the Bible was all about a personal relationship and not religion, they would also discover that God's plan to redeem the world was also centered on the person of Jesus Christ, and that humanity's redemption was not in fact based upon one's own efforts to reach God, but upon a willingness to personally accept the free gift of Christ's love as displayed on the cross. This is an amazing conclusion!

For every person who has ever been frustrated by the evils of organized religion, this is like food for the starving. Being right with God, according to the Bible, is not about keeping a list of rules, nor does God's plan allow for selfish human beings to broker God's grace to their advantage. It is totally free and offered to every human being individually! God's plan for mankind is embodied, not in a list of rules, but in a person – a person who has demonstrated his love for each one of us to the point of spilling his blood and who now waits for us to respond to his offer of love.

> *God's plan for mankind is embodied, not in a list of rules, but in a person...*

As Bill Hybels, Senior Pastor at Willow Creek Community Church in South Barrington, Illinois, said at a conference I attended in August, 2006, the entire Bible is designed to bring the reader to ask one simple question: *Who am I depending on to atone for my faults?* Will I trust in my own good works? (They can never satisfy God's requirement of holiness.) Or will I accept Jesus' sacrificial atonement that was made for me on the cross?

No one can earn God's favor. We just have to accept it as a gift. Those who claim that salvation by faith alone is "too easy" have never learned just how humbling it is to admit that they have nothing good to offer God, that they are fully dependent on his grace and mercy. In our pride we try to earn God's favor, but Jesus said the only work God requires is faith,[6.2] and that those who will enter God's kingdom will be humble, meek and poor in spirit.[6.3]

The world's religions have always competed for people's allegiance. They always will, because we humans love to construct things and then get other people to submit to our constructions. We are control freaks. When God decided to come to this earth as a human being, he dealt a death blow to every organized religion of all time. This is not to say that organized religion is all bad. The goals of organized religion are often good or contain some good. But God has shown us that his real desire is to have a personal relationship with every human being independent of any human authority or religious structure. The offering of this relationship was embodied in Jesus Christ's atoning work on our behalf, and it's not about control. It's about us growing to know and love God. Any submission to him that we choose to make flows out of the love and relationship that we already share.

Jesus said it best:

Now this is eternal life: that they know you, the only true God, and Jesus Christ, whom you have sent (John 17:3).

It has nothing to do with religion; it's all about relationship. How can a message like this not resonate with people?

Chapter 7

THE MESSAGE OF THE BIBLE IS INCLUSIVE

He is the atoning sacrifice for our sins, and not only for ours but also for the sins of the whole world.

–The Apostle John (1 John 2:2)

As a pastor, I am constantly meeting people on the fringes of faith, and I can say with confidence that one of the greatest barriers that people feel when approaching the Christian faith is the notion that Christianity is an exclusive, western religion. Living in Toronto – one of the most cosmopolitan cities of the world – only highlights the existence of this perception. In a pluralistic city such as mine, people of all faiths shy away from pronouncing the exclusivity of their faith, even though every one of us considers ours to be the right way – an impossibility we all tacitly acknowledge.[7.1]

When we remember that the Bible doesn't present a religious system, but a *person*, our minds become freed up from the trappings of religion and can begin to tackle this subject fairly. After all, which religious system has a perfect track record when it comes to its treatment of non-adherents to their faith? None, to be precise. Religion is man's attempt at something, and we humans mess everything up.

AN EXCLUSIVE CLUB?

You may be surprised to know that he Bible doesn't contain the word "Christianity." It contains the word "Christian," an appellation created by non-religious people for a disciple of Jesus Christ.[7.2] "Christianity" is the systematization or institutionalization of Christian belief. And in this sense, I have to agree that Christianity as a whole has earned its reputation as an exclusive, largely western religion. But that is not the essence of the movement Jesus started.

True Christianity is about a person. It is about a baby, fully divine and fully human, born at God's appointed time and place so that he might grow up and die on behalf of all humanity. True Christianity is the Gospel, meaning the "good news," that Jesus Christ was God's solution for a planet that had fallen into sin and was helpless to rescue itself. Jesus himself claimed to be that solution, and did in fact state that he was the only way to God.[7.3] The question is: Is his statement truly exclusive?

When you approach the question from the perspective of "Jesus as the founder of Christianity," it can be easy to construe his remarks as exclusive. For example:

Jesus answered, "I am the way and the truth and the life. No one comes to the Father except through me" (John 14:6).

His followers understood the exclusivity that Jesus taught and carried it forward:

"Salvation is found in no one else, for there is no other name under heaven given to mankind by which we must be saved" (Acts 4:12).

There is no shortage of verses to demonstrate the exclusivity of Jesus' message. But when we consider that Jesus' statements about salvation transcended all religions, including the one he was born into, it is no longer fair to call him exclusive. According to Jesus, salvation is dependent upon the belief that he is indeed God's solution, the means for forgiveness. This salvation is distinct from religious dogma or practice. Furthermore, it has been offered to the entire world.[7.4] People of all faiths and backgrounds have been invited to share in this belief and receive eternal life.

> ...when we consider that Jesus' statements about salvation transcended all religions, including the one he was born into, it is no longer fair to call him exclusive.

There is no denying that many terrible things have been done in the name of Christianity, the religious movement. Nor is there is any doubt that many "Christian" groups today who proselytize are more interested in gaining adherents than passing along the love of a person. But the heart of true Christianity, the defining aspect of it, is the personal acceptance of Jesus as God's love gift for the world.[7.5]

Haven't you noticed that Jesus didn't make religion the point? In fact, the only people he had serious problems with were the religious leaders who were merely interested in perpetuating their power and control over others by enforcing religious rules and regulations. When we see people come to Jesus in the gospels, we see him loving them, helping them, and challenging them to acknowledge his divinity and place their faith in him. He did not avoid any demographic in his ministry. He went to men and women, rich and poor, healthy and sick, religious and irreligious. He went to Jew and Gentile alike. He told us that God's love for the whole world was the reason he must die,[7.6] and at the end of his time on earth he commanded his followers to go into all the world with this message of hope to people of all nations. (The Greek word used for "nations" actually means ethnic groups, not countries.)

Shortly after Jesus' time on earth we see one of Jesus' followers, the Apostle Paul, freshly embarked on his missionary journeys, actually commending people for trying to worship God in the only way they knew how.[7.7] He not only took the time to share the good news of Jesus with them, but emphasized God's justice and mercy toward people who had no previous knowledge of the true God and Jesus Christ. In fact, Paul's life mission was to take the good news to Gentiles (meaning "nations" of the world), which he did vigorously until he was martyred. While some faiths kill in order to spread their cause, true Christians have died, and continue to die today, in their attempt to share the good news of Jesus with people around the world.

People in "non-Christian" countries may feel that Christianity is exclusive. In their understanding of the word they may be right. You may have met Christians here in North America who are very exclusive. No surprises here. But I'll say it again – the essence of true Christianity in no way rejects people on the basis of race or religious background.

There is, however, one way in which true Christianity is clearly exclusive, and that is on a personal level. Jesus tells me that unless I believe he is who he said he was, I will surely die in my sins.[7.8] The same is true for every person, regardless of ethnicity or religious background. Again, if you see Jesus' statements in the context of an organized religion pitting itself against the doctrines of other religions, this seems like intense religious posturing. But examining Jesus' life reveals his message to be anything but: Jesus is as inclusive as truth will allow.

UTTERLY INCLUSIVE

It is of great comfort to me to know that Jesus is not just for westerners. When I talk with people of different backgrounds, I do not bristle at the knowledge that they have a differing religion. I respect anyone who tries to live for higher ideals. As I discuss matters of faith with people of differing faiths, I'm more than happy to share my point of view to those who want to hear it. The way I see it, many great teachers and moralists are deserving of much respect. But there was one man who came to us claiming to be God. One man who performed numerous miracles to prove himself to be God. One man who came back to life from death. One man who reduced the salvation question to one exclusive but personal, non-religious question: *Do you believe that I am God's solution?*

I do. And I'm comforted to know that there is nothing impeding anyone, anywhere, who wants to make the same decision. The inclusivity of the Christian message makes me proud to be a follower of Jesus.

Chapter 8

FAITH PUTS THE SMACKDOWN ON LOGIC

The kind of intelligence a genius has is a different sort of intelligence. The thinking of a genius does not proceed logically. It leaps with great ellipses. It pulls knowledge from God knows where.

—Dorothy Thompson (American journalist)

*You're packing a suitcase for a place none of us has been
A place that has to be believed to be seen*

—U2, *Walk On*

Ever since the advent of the scientific age, faith and its adherents have been taking a hit. Religious narratives and beliefs have been steadily replaced with scientific explanations, and adherents to those religious beliefs have been increasingly marginalized. I could share hundreds of stories over the past 200 years in an attempt to prove this statement, but I'd prefer to take a different route. Since the point of this book is to elevate the experiential, permit me to give you a little background about myself. I sincerely hope I don't come across as a pretentious tool; I just want you to grasp my experience with faith and logic.

LOGIC VS. FAITH

I always did well at school. In high school my circle of friends included some of my school's greatest brainiacs. I'm working hard here to avoid using the word "geek." I never considered myself one, but many people probably did. Although I knew I violated every rule of fashion (not an easy feat in the 80's), the way I figured it, because I played competitive sports I couldn't really be called a geek. But I was also in two different school bands and had an average in the high 90's, so I probably was a geek. If my friends were geeks, then I'd have to say I prefer the company of geeks, because they were great.

In Grade 11, one interchange with my history professor marked me for life. I will never forget it. Mr. Derrick was an eccentric old teacher who looked like he had personally witnessed everything he ever taught us about the early Greek and Roman civilizations. His hair was an ancient blonde color, highlighted yellow by the smoke from his pipe. His face was tanned and leathery like that of a fisherman, with squinty eyes that flickered with excitement whenever he taught. His voice, bold and British, enchanted his students to the degree that he rarely had to deal with discipline issues like the other teachers did. And if he wasn't distinguished enough already, his one leg had been injured in World War II, so he limped between the classroom and the staff lounge with the help of a cane. The man was a living icon, and I loved his classes, as did most everyone.

One day as class was being dismissed the discussion turned to the topic of post-secondary studies. We were getting ever closer to graduation and Mr. Derrick seemed to have a genuine interest in what each of us intended to do with our future. After hearing a few other students' plans, the gentle yet intimidating professor leaned back on his chair and stared me down.

"So, Sawatsky, what are you going to study when you graduate?"

It was a question I was wrestling with more every day, knowing that I soon had to decide. I was eligible for some sizable scholarships, depending on where I chose to study.

"I was thinking of studying theology," I responded, purposefully using a word ending in "-ology" in hopes that he might be impressed. Not quite. The words that followed went through my head in slow motion.

"Theology! Whatever do you want to waste your life on that for?"

To be honest, I don't remember how I responded. I'm sure I turned red and sputtered something.

Most of the teachers at Bridgewater High School knew I was a Christian, so Mr. Derrick probably wasn't as shocked as I initially thought. (My law teacher once asked me, without prior warning, to explain to the rest of my class what it meant to "consummate" a marriage. In a flush of red I succinctly supplied the definition. My classmates were all confounded as to how I knew, but the teacher was confident that a young Christian would have covered the topic. He glowed with satisfaction at his wager.) In any case, Mr. Derrick's pointed question gave me some insight into how some of my educators probably viewed my faith. Pursuing a career in theology was a *waste of my life*. [8.1]

By the age of sixteen I was effectively taught that faith was inferior to logic. Theology was not to be ranked with legitimate (logical) pursuits like math, chemistry, or even history. Faith had no place in the realm of respectable study or vocation.

The same belief was aptly expressed in biology class, a class I took knowing it would boost my overall average. An easy stint in comparison to chemistry, many of the less ambitious students found their way into the class, which boasted a class average of less than 60%. On more than one occasion I gently challenged the evolutionary theory being taught, and the teacher graciously accepted that I would only phrase answers on my exams in the form, "Someone who believed in evolution would state that…" I've shared in another chapter how I was taught things as fact that were contradicted by science within 5 years of graduating from high school.

As a young person I watched how matters of faith were constantly pushed outside the circle of public debate. In politics, people of faith were mocked and labeled as narrow-minded.[8.2] In music, people of faith were all painted with the same sinister brush and in entertainment the Christian values that our society was founded upon were trampled on or systematically untaught.[8.3] (I'm convinced that the advent of cable TV and in-home movies in the 80's had more impact on North American values than anything else to that point in our history. It was watching a fairly hedonistic movie at a school-organized function that I was first exposed to promiscuity and nudity. I had never experienced something that so offended and so excited me at the same time!) It could have been worse, I figured; at least my teachers weren't showing Playboy videos for sex education like at my brother's school.

Suffice it to say, from a young age I had a sense that I was in a battle – that I was swimming against the current of popular culture. And to be honest, it was somewhat confusing to me given the positive experience I had had with faith to that point in my young life. I couldn't understand why people were so intent on denigrating traditional values and beliefs that were so self-evidently good.

Through all of my experiences at school, I learned that if I was going to be a person of faith, I'd have to get used standing on my own. I dug in deep. Again, at the risk of sounding like a pompous schmuck, I finished top of my class in Grade 12 (narrowly beating out one of my brainiac friends). As I stood to give the valedictory address at graduation, the emcee announced that I would be going to Bible school and in my lackluster speech I thanked God for helping me every day of my life. It was a defining moment for me. I really liked a lot of my teachers, including Mr. Derrick, but I no longer worried about what they thought of me or my faith.

This openness about my faith was not merely a display of teenage cockiness; I just had a high regard for things of faith. I had grown up in a pastor's home where I had been taught to think logically and even to question matters of faith, but the things I had learned about God, Jesus and the Bible made so much sense to me. By Grade 7, not only was I more conversant in the Bible than many first-year Bible college students, I had had the opportunity to examine the lives of hundreds of people that came into contact with faith. My place as the pastor's kid gave me a unique vantage point to evaluate whether or not faith actually worked in people's lives. I saw the ones who really lived what the Bible taught as compared to those who merely wanted to appear as if they did. I didn't miss a trick.

My findings were astounding. I discovered that faith really did work – as consistently as science. It made people's relationships better, it made families stronger, and it made children more grounded, self-confident and successful. It gave people the strength they had searched for all their lives to overcome destructive habits and lifestyles, and it provided people with a caring network of friends. It gave people a sense of purpose about life and confidence about the future in this life and beyond. By way of contrast, I had never seen logic give people such power. Logic made people feel smart, but faith made people truly wise.

Anything I learned post-secondarily about the historicity of the Bible or the origins of life were merely decorations on a cake that was already baked. Because of my early experiences and observations, I knew I would always be a person of faith. To me, true faith and true science were the same – divine truth. Some would say that it's dangerous to lock in too many conclusions about faith at a young age. That's a fair statement, and I would respond by noting that my specific views on many issues have certainly evolved over the years and continue to evolve. But I still see a lot of advantages in establishing ideals at a young age before the realities of life push us toward compromise.

There have been many times as an older person, influenced by the ways of the world, that I have been enchanted by and even experimented with hedonism or materialism. But in my heart I know that these lifestyles cannot bring ultimate satisfaction because they are not founded upon God's laws. As an adult I have continued to compare the ways of faith with popular opinion, and so far I remain firm in my confidence in Christian ideals. My line of thinking may not appeal to the more left-brained reader, but it is backed up by years of observation and experience.

WHAT LOGIC EXPLAINS

What stock we place in human logic! Yet it doesn't give hope. Who cares if I can go to the moon if I can't change my own attitude? Logic doesn't explain so many things that need explaining in life. Take God, for instance. We all know that he must exist, but because we can't experience him with our senses, we must either embrace him by faith or not at all. The entire spiritual dimension that scientists are growing to acknowledge more and more is almost as impregnable to logic. Most people now agree that there are forces at play in our world that we can't prove with modern science.

Take, for instance, the existence of love. Can love be explained logically? As Albert Einstein asked, "How on earth are you ever going to explain in terms of chemistry and physics so important a biological phenomenon as first love?"

Other aspects of spirituality defy logic as well. Forgiveness is a great example. How spiritual, emotional and even physical health is restored through forgiveness is still a mystery. Or where a person finds the courage to try one more time, to give that one last effort in spite of terrible odds, is mysterious and fascinating – the stuff of great stories that we immortalize in books and movies. Even the very purpose behind life itself is inexplicable through logic alone. The best explanation that science has offered over the past century is that we're all the result of a big accident.

> *As Albert Einstein asked, "How on earth are you ever going to explain in terms of chemistry and physics so important a biological phenomenon as first love?"*

The current trend in science is to explain everything of a spiritual nature by the flow of hormones or chemicals through our bloodstream. "Forgiveness" is merely that which triggers the release of good hormones through the body, resulting in positive emotional health. It seems a pretty crude explanation to me. It depreciates matters of the spirit by labeling them as simple functions of physics and chemistry. Sadly (in my opinion) a growing number of people are choosing to view the reality of human experience in such a light.

It's not until we get to the subject of death that logic finally takes second place to faith for most people. This happens because we innately believe, or want to believe, that the spirit somehow lives on apart from the body. We have a hard time accepting that someone's true being – spirit, mind and emotion – can simply cease to exist, and science has no answers to offer when we get to this point. Having been by the side of a number of people at death, I can attest that witnessing the departure of the spirit and soul from the human body is indeed a bizarre experience, one that leaves you seriously contemplating what you've been taught about ultimate reality.

I said that science had nothing to offer in regard to what lies beyond this life. Not entirely true. We now have scientific data collected from near-death experiences that confirm that the mind does continue to function even after all bodily function (including any trace of brainwaves) ceases. I actually did a series at my church once called *Afterlife* that drew on information from a number of books I had read on NDE's[8.4] (I annoyed some traditionally-minded members of the congregation by wading into this extrabiblical subject. Some Christians are wary of science and feel the need to keep it separate from biblical teaching. I disagree wholeheartedly.) Anyway, the idea that the mind continues to function after death is certainly not logic as we've been taught it. It raises the very important question: Are we predominantly physical beings who merely have spiritual experiences, or are we predominantly spiritual beings who are having a physical experience we call "life?"

What if God has merely attached a physical aspect to our fundamentally spiritual existence? What if the impulses that we can monitor in the brain are merely a light show triggered by the spiritual activity to which they are connected? And what if when we die the mind simply disconnects from the body and puts and end to the light show? In other words, the body is merely the glove; the spirit is the hand. I see no reason why this could not be true; in fact, it rings more true to me than the naturalist's explanation. Stories of scientifically controlled experiments and NDE's are interesting, but my inclinations here are predominantly right-brained. They are not based principally on logic.

LOGIC HAS LIMITS

We use logic to form arguments, but logic doesn't solve arguments. It doesn't seem to bring peace out of war. Generations of great men and women attempted to put an end to racism and inequality, but then a guy named Martin Luther King, Jr. challenged his fellow sufferers to take a leap of faith called non-violent resistance. Many of his African-American brothers and sisters hated him for his vision, but eventually they started to try it and saw that it worked. Eventually they won the status they sought and deserved. Where logic failed, faith came up with a solution.

> *We use logic to form arguments, but logic doesn't solve arguments.*

Logic doesn't make me give a rat's arse about someone in need. Helen Keller agreed: "Science may have found a cure for most evils; but it has found no remedy for the worst of them all – the apathy of human beings." The growing gap between rich and poor the world over is just one more reminder that logic alone is not our solution. I can reason all day long as to why I should do something good, but my desire to execute remains weak in comparison to my selfish impulses. And instead of being useful in curbing my weaknesses, I find that logic only feeds my arrogance.[8.5]

Logic doesn't seem to make anyone happier. In fact, calculating realists tend to be among the most dour people that I am personally familiar with. Most faith-filled people I know live on a higher plane of enjoyment and suffer from less stress. Scientific studies show that faith really does relieve stress and foster health.[8.6] (But will the scientists who did the studies take the leap to act on their own findings? Deep thoughts.)

Logic has brought us technological advances that have made our lives easier. It has even eased our pain and increased our "enjoyment." But it hasn't brought anyone freedom or peace. It hasn't made anyone a better person – more forgiving or intrinsically honest.

Faith has accomplished all of these and more.

FAITH FACTOR

Make no mistake about it, I've always valued logic. God has given us brains that can evaluate natural laws and build truth upon truth. I admire logical people, and I consider myself to be one. I enjoy good debate and am appalled at Christians who cannot defend their beliefs with confidence. I am insulted to the core by unbelievers who assume that I am illogical simply because I am part of a faith community. I love logic. When logic is used to discover new technologies or mitigate the suffering of human beings, it is a wonderful thing. But logic has its limitations. The nature of logic is that is can only build upon what humans already know. But faith can project us to places we have never been. Consider the many scientific discoveries (based upon logic) that have required a leap of faith to go to the next level. [8.7]

There will always be a dynamic to faith that surpasses logic. Imagine for a second that there arrived a day when mankind could answer life's physical problems without faith: through science we discovered how to arrest the aging process, how to avoid illness, and how to live forever. In your opinion, would we then be happy? Would *you* be happy? (Stop! Don't read any further until you think about it for a minute.)

[Insert Final Jeopardy music here. Okay, good...]

I have a sneaking suspicion that even if our race could figure out how to live forever, we'd still be like well-cared for orphans trying to find their father. In other words, the question of our origin would still aggravate us to the core. Furthermore, we'd still be no further ahead in our attempts to love and respect one another. We'd still have no peace. And although we could live forever, we'd get bored with life and begin to feel the need to recreate our existence periodically in order to inject some mystery and intrigue into the universe. Naturalists could argue that this is what mankind has already done – created the concept of God so as to enchant ourselves, thus rendering our existence more interesting. It's possible. But my gut says that God has always existed and that we need him for all the reasons I just described.

I prefer to believe that all of life finds its source in a God who is by nature so infinite and complex and creative, that mankind will never be content until he lives in personal unity with him. I believe in a God for whom we were intentionally made. For the life of me I cannot picture humanity being happy until it discovers God (as he is traditionally defined) and taps into his eternity. It is a belief that is rooted mostly in my right brain, the part of the brain that embraces faith.

Faith is powerful! Faith is the ability to foresee a payoff for an activity and to pursue it even though it cannot be guaranteed. From what I've witnessed in my life, it can often be of more practical value than logic.

- I've seen people with no hope or energy left for their marriage trust a marriage counselor, following her directions until their lifeless marriage was resuscitated.
- I've seen people drop decades of pain and anger in an instant.
- I've seen couples and individuals embark on a new life of love, forgiveness and maturity while the rest of their extended family continued on a road of bitterness and self-destruction.
- I've seen desperate parents act contrary to conventional wisdom and experience breakthroughs with their children.
- I've seen people whose lives were filled with abuse and chaos miraculously gain control of their lives by giving up the control to God or a "higher power."

- I've seen a father forgive the man who sexually abused his daughter, even encouraging him and praying for him to become a better person.
- I've read stories of people who forgave their child's murderer and, incredibly, even became the offender's friend.
- I've seen people trade in the security of their wealth for a richness of life that comes from helping others.

These are the miracles of God. They are neither logical nor natural; rather, they are supernatural. They cannot be fully explained with conventional science, and yet they happen consistently. By faith, a poor dying man can have more joy than a healthy and wealthy young prince. As mysterious as it is, faith consistently renders amazing results. Logic, on the other hand, is fully predictable. It can inspire, but only to a point.

Logic walks; faith flies. It exists on a higher plane and works in ways logic never will.

In a society that tends to downplay the value of faith in favor of reason, I suspect that many people never take the time to consider the extent of faith's power. Those who are just discovering its value will certainly struggle to apply their right brain to life's challenges. But I'm convinced that those who try will discover more peace, energy and joy – not to mention resolution to some of their greatest personal obstacles.

Chapter 9

I LIKE BEING A PERSON OF FAITH

Skepticism is the beginning of faith.

–Oscar Wilde

It's faith in something and enthusiasm for something that makes a life worth living.

–Oliver Wendell Holmes
(physician, poet, writer, humorist
and Harvard professor)

Have you ever noticed that people like to poke fun at accountants? Between TV, movies, and the cartoons in the daily newspapers, most of us have developed a pretty comical stereotype of accountants. What's up with that? I have good friends who are accountants and they are great people like everyone else. My church would be sunk without the work of a few dedicated accountants over the years – people with whom I've become good friends. Without them, I would have surely spent the organization into the ground by now. Unlike the nerdy, control-freak stereotypes we've grown to embrace, the accountants I know are personable, good communicators, and enjoy a broad range of interests. (And I don't think any of them wear pocket protectors.)

Maybe the humor we enjoy at accountants' expense really has less to do with their mannerisms and more with the resentment we feel for the control they exercise over the rest of us. Let's be honest – we all hate to be controlled, especially when it comes to spending money! But we need the good, left-brained stability that accountants provide. Having lived my professional life on the right-brained side of the equation, it has always been my job to convince the accountants to *loosen* the purse strings. I'm quick to remind my board that fiscal responsibility alone won't make the organization successful. Innovation and experimentation are essential. Control must be balanced with creativity. The simple truth is that, when investors look for great companies, good bookkeeping skills do not top the list of reasons why they choose to invest.

I may be predominantly right-brained, but I'll admit it – I've got some control freak in me too. The older I've become, the more I loathe that aspect of my personality. Maybe I draw attention to accountants to distract people from my own need to control my environment. The more I've thought about it, I've recognized that when I try to control something or someone, I am making a bold statement: I am declaring that my faith extends no further than myself. My assumption that my control over something will render the best possible result is not only incredibly arrogant, but it is also short-sighted and confining. What dweebs we are when we think like that! And what a pathetically boring way to live – no room for experimentation, for trial and error, for discovery. No room to take risks, or to express my confidence in someone by trusting them for something.

FAITH IS RISK

Faith is risk, and oddly enough, as much as I've always had control-freak tendencies, I've always loved risk to an even greater degree. Maybe I'm a walking oxymoron. Or maybe God gave me a strength to compensate for a weakness. All I know is that when I play golf, if there's the remotest possibility of saving a stroke by shooting over trees, I'm all over it. My friends laugh at me. The few times in my life when I've decided to "lay up," I've only ended up doing worse, so I persist as a helpless risk-taker. In golf, as in life, I've noticed that the worse the odds are, the better I seem to like it. To my mind, ten failed attempts are well worth the glory of the one try that works.

When my friends and I were kids and it was taking too long to pick teams for a game of street hockey, I'd offer to take on everyone myself. Not that I thought I had a realistic chance to win; I just loved the thought that the possibility was there. As a teenager, I drove all over the Maritimes in old, unreliable cars. I don't remember how many times I needed to call someone to come and rescue me. (Dad usually got the call. Somehow he seemed to enjoy the adventure of traveling for hours to rescue one of us boys when our car died. It actually made for some great memories. I'm sure my brothers and I got our risk-taking side from Dad; he raced stock cars when he was a young man and was even at the track when I was born. Mom wasn't too impressed about that, but I think it's pretty funny.) When I play poker, the risk-taker in me wants to bluff on every hand. The only problem is, it doesn't take experienced players very long to spot the undisciplined risk-taker. And I never buy extended warranties. That's a tax for dummies, as far as I'm concerned. I'm always willing to take a chance if it can mean saving a buck. The last person I want to be is the sucker who paid more than he had to.

Somehow taking risks seems macho to me. (I hope that doesn't mean I have some underlying masculine insecurities. That's all I need.) No, risk-taking *is* macho. You can't deny it. Think about every movie hero you can remember – James Bond, Indiana Jones, Jason Bourne. These guys are macho because they throw caution to the wind, and men and women alike adore them for it.

It's funny, isn't it, that although risk and faith are essentially the same thing, people of faith are nearly always looked upon as weak and insecure, while people who take risks are considered adventurous, even macho. They're the same thing! We make heroes out of businesspeople who fail miserably over and over only to finally hit pay dirt. But isn't that faith? Why then are people deemed dimwits for holding onto a belief in something that extends beyond this life? Shouldn't that classify them as even more admirable, more willing to take risks, more heroic?

I think of people of faith in the same vein as people who take risks. I think they're heroic. The times when I act the most out of faith (or risk) are the times I'm most pleased with myself as well. As a kid I would hear stories of great people of faith who took amazing risks in order to share God's love with other people. These stories inspired me. I would love to be that kind of a person too.

> *It's funny, isn't it, that although risk and faith are essentially the same thing, people of faith are nearly always looked upon as weak and insecure, while people who take risks are considered adventurous, even macho.*

Jesus was a hero. He gave everything he had, even his very life, in faith that the Father would reward his obedience. Although we don't know to what degree his divine nature protected his heroism, we know he felt the risk as he cried out on the cross: "My God, my God, why have you forsaken me?"[9.1]

I guess we'd all like to be heroes in one way or another. I'm of the conviction that many if not most heroes go uncelebrated on earth. After all, isn't it even more heroic to go unnoticed, such as the soldier who dies heroically in battle and whose body is never identified, or the mother who sacrifices everything to raise her child alone in obscurity? With this in mind, even if my faith never gets celebrated, I can live with that. There's still a lot more I like about being a person of faith.

Being a person of faith is more fun, more optimistic. I like living with the presupposition that something is guiding the process of my life. I like living with my box wide open – open to the possibility that someone higher and greater than me might have something special in store for me today. That I could potentially interact with another human being today for the shortest moment in a divinely appointed encounter with eternal implications. That's cool.

> *I like living with my box wide open – open to the possibility that someone higher and greater than me might have something special in store for me today.*

THE BUTTERFLY EFFECT

I've never seen this dynamic played out better than in the movie *The Butterfly Effect*. (Yes, Ashton Kutcher is in it, but the overall story is enthralling.) The story is based upon the scientific concept by the same name, coined in the 1960's by American mathematician and meteorologist Edward Lorenz, who suggested that the slightest movement of a butterfly's wing in one part of the world could set off a chain of events that could eventually result in a tornado on the other side of the globe.

The Butterfly Effect (also known as Chaos Theory), concisely posited, states that despite a controlled environment, tiny variations in the initial conditions of a system can and do result in huge variations over the long term. The movie is intriguing in showing how one moment early on in someone's life could result in huge differences later on. A tennis ball falling on one side of a net rather than the other… a phone call answered or not… a thought acted upon or not. You can undoubtedly identify similar minute yet critical moments in your own life and waste hours thinking about the "what ifs."

I had one such moment when I was playing AAA Midget hockey. It was our team's first year in the league and we finished the regular season at the bottom of the standings. We were scheduled to play against the Cape Breton Colonels, the top team, in the first round of the playoffs. We had a new coach the first night of a best-of-three series, and I was slated to start in net. We had lost games to Cape Breton by scores too embarrassing to mention in this book (seriously – not even in the endnotes), so we were all pretty nervous. We had heard that pro hockey scouts would be present in the stands that night, so we were determined to put on the best showing we could muster.

After a long, hard-fought battle, we somehow managed to beat the Colonels 2-1. I'm still not sure how it happened. I faced over 50 shots in the victory; it was the game of my life. After the game, as we hooted and grunted in the dressing room, we were informed that the scouts never made it to the rink. We were not at all impressed. What if.[9.2]

Chaos theory deduces that life, when boiled down to these infinitesimally brief but critical moments, is ultimately random, or chaotic. (Think about how many athletes' careers could have ended up completely different had the ball on one play in one key game taken a different bounce.) As I walked away from *The Butterfly Effect* I thought about how limited a control freak like myself is in comparison to this dynamic. Let's face it, we all know that dumb luck[9.3] accounts for way more in this life than we'd like to admit. Wise people have wrestled with this frustration for ages. As the Ecclesiast wrote 3000 years ago:

> *I have observed something else in this world of ours. The fastest runner doesn't always win the race, and the strongest warrior doesn't always win the battle. The wise are often poor, and the skillful are not necessarily wealthy. And those who are educated don't always lead successful lives. It is all decided by chance, by being at the right place at the right time* (Ecclesiastes 9:11, New Living Translation).

The implications of this theory are very unsettling. Does chaos really reign in the universe? As a Bible-believing creationist, I believe that God created the world to be orderly and "good." Everything was made with a purpose and works in harmony with the things around it. But my Bible also tells me about the fall of mankind and the curse that was placed upon the world that resulted in weeds, sweat and pain. Could it be at the moment of the fall that the cosmos – created to be orderly – was plunged into chaos? That seems to be what the narrative is saying. If so, are we really trapped in a world ruled by mere chance as opposed to a purposeful God?

In a world where things like timing and chance seem to work automatically alongside of natural laws, I believe that God can and does overrule the natural scheme of things – sometimes in bold, obvious ways, but most often in subtle, almost undetectable ones. But upon what basis does he choose to do so?

A PATH THROUGH THE CHAOS

Months ago, as I read my Bible in reflection of this Chaos Theory, I realized something very interesting. As I did a quick read-through of New Testament passages dealing with concepts like fate and purpose, I noticed that in the Bible, only people of faith have ever been given reason for optimism in regard to the chaos that seems to reign in the cosmos. In the New Testament, the Apostle Paul makes it clear that God is working behind the scenes in the Christian's life:

> *In him we were also chosen, having been predestined according to the plan of him who works out everything in conformity with the purpose of his will* (Ephesians 1:11).

Somehow, despite the apparent chaos, God manages to work out *everything* in keeping with his desires, particularly the life path of believers. Again in Romans 8 Paul says:

> *And we know that in all things God works for the good of those who love him, who have been called according to his purpose* (Romans 8:28).

While the average person may indeed be dependent on nothing more than good timing and dumb luck, I take a lot of comfort in the thought that for me, God is working through the chaos of the world to achieve his desired purposes in my life. I may still resist these purposes and fail to achieve everything God desires of me, but I need not live in constant fear of not getting lucky or "missing my one shot."

I live in a random world, but I am not destined to be a victim of circumstance. Nor do I have to live with the blind optimism of a humanist who convinces himself that he can achieve absolutely anything if he only tries hard enough. (I'm a firm believer that hard work improves your chances of success, but let's get real.) God has a plan for my life. He created me with specific purposes, and he wants to guide me to a desired end, one that fulfills his plan as I live out my purposes.

I'm a person of faith. Like Paul, I am confident that God, who began a good work in me, "will continue his work until it is finally finished on that day when Christ Jesus comes back again" (Philippians 1:6). When people align themselves with God through faith, they provide a channel for God's order and purpose to interject themselves into the world's chaos. Not only does that life take on a purposeful shape, but it also has the opportunity to be used by God to bring beauty and order to the lives of others. Chaos Theory doesn't get the final word in the life of the believer.

THE REBEL WITHIN

Finally, I'd have to say that I like being a person of faith because it makes me a bit of a rebel. At least it feels that way. That may not be a great reason, but I'm just being honest. How boring it would have been to be a person of faith in the early 1800's in North America, what with all the Pilgrims and Puritans walking around. Today, in post-Christian North

America, I kind of like being in the minority when it comes to faith. I enjoy the challenge. I like being different. I think it must be wretched to have to find a natural explanation for everything that happens in the world or to simply drift in the tide of popular opinion like so many do. Living your life like a politically correct echo. Everything between the lines. Everything predictable. That's just my perspective.

I am aware that being a person of faith may brand me, in some people's minds, as a religious nut or a fellow of all of the evils of religion. I've tried in this book to clarify that I am not religious at all. I do not follow lists of rules. Nor is my time taken up in the observance of sacred rituals. I am as appalled as anyone over the atrocities done in the name of religion, and there are many. I am simply a person who believes in God and who embraces the biblical description of him over all others. The clearest description given of him came in the person of Jesus, who asked us to love others as we love ourselves.

Contrary to what people like Christopher Hitchens might say, my faith does not lead me to seek power in this life, nor do I feel threatened as I coexist with people of differing faiths or perspectives.[9.4] The truth is, I celebrate the right that each person is given to do or be whatever they choose.

People all over the world choose to be a variety of things – from police officers to insurance brokers to tattoo artists. In the same way, some people choose a life of faith while others don't. Most of us are mature enough to understand that we have to live with the consequences of all of our decisions.

Simply stated, I find myself inclined to believe – to believe in a personal God, a purposeful creation, in the fall and redemption of mankind, and in Jesus: God's solution to humanity's problem. Furthermore, I like the implications of faith on my life. It is not contrary to reason, but like the 16th century explorer William Adams said, "Faith is a continuation of reason."

I just like being a person of faith, and personally, I think that's a very good reason for believing.

Chapter 10

GRACE - THE BEST THING IN LIFE IS FREE

Stop and stare
You start to wonder why you're here not there
And you'd give anything to get what's fair
But fair ain't what you really need

–One Republic, *Stop and Stare*

Rain is grace; rain is the sky condescending to the earth; without rain, there would be no life.

–John Updike

Rural Nova Scotia where I grew up is probably pretty much like rural anywhere in North America. There was only one secondary highway that ran through Pleasantville. (How's that name for idyllic?) In the middle of the village was a sand-sealed little side road upon which stood a small, white Baptist church. It was the center of the community, and I guess you could say that the pastor was kind of like the village pope.

Every Sunday, all activity stopped and just about everyone (except for a few well-known reprobates) gathered inside the little church. Everyone dressed up. We sang hymns from hymnals (even though everyone had them memorized) and after Sunday school in the dank church basement (where my brothers and I first ate paste) we would listen to the pastor preach. (I'm a pastor today, but in fairness to pastors I grew up under, I really only "talk" in comparison.)

Before I say what I'm going to say, let me inform you that some of my fondest memories go back to that church and to other similar churches in which I grew up. People there really were devout and did good for other people.

THE UNWRITTEN LIST

But something wasn't quite right. As I grew older I noticed that some of the rules that we lived by didn't match up very neatly with what I read from the Bible. We read stories about how Jesus criticized the Pharisees for piling rule upon rule, and then we did the same thing. There were rules for drinking, rules for dancing, rules for what to wear and when, and rules for what you could do on Sunday. There were rules for what words you could say, what games you could play, and what holidays were okay. There were more rules than I can recall. All unwritten.

Over time, I began to realize that every church I entered had an unwritten list of rules on the wall. The only way that you could learn the rules was by joining the church and then inadvertently breaking the rules, one by one, over time. When a newbie broke a rule, everyone silently "tsk tsk'd" and "harrumph"ed. Heads turned and then shook in disbelief. The rule breaker was then made to feel very uncomfortable until their actions began to conform to the unwritten standards of the entire group.

I found it funny that every church I knew of had its own list. Each church would claim that their list came straight from the Bible, and yet no two lists were exactly alike. Go figure. In one church, all forms of dancing were wrong. In some, square dancing might be okay. Alcohol was just about always wrong, unless you went into a mainline church like a United Church, where it seemed to be okay. Using playing cards was okay in some churches but not others. The lists went on and on. As you might guess, it was normally the pastor who determined the list in each church. [10.1]

Today I lead an orientation class at my church about every 6 weeks. Newcomers to the church – some longtime believers, others checking out the church for the first time, gather and eat lunch as I share with them the vision and values we hold. At some point in the class I always share a story very similar to what I just shared with you. And then I look every newcomer straight in the eyes and tell them, "We don't have an unwritten list of rules in our church." Smiles begin to form on people's faces when I say that sentence; I can see the relief on their faces.

Sad but true, many Christians have been raised to believe that everything in the world can be divided into either black or white. Every action can be catalogued as either right or wrong, regardless of the context. Having been brought up to think this way, I can't tell you how many months and years I wrestled with this bizarre line of thinking before finally being able to see it objectively. From the time I was a kid I had a sense that the "everything-is-black-or-white" philosophy was bogus; it's not even consistent with clear scriptural passages. The book of Ecclesiastes (chapter 3) says there is "a time for *everything*, and a season for *every* activity under heaven". There is a time to kill. There is time for war, and a time to hate as well. But what's even worse for starched Christians, there's even a time to *dance*! Heaven help us all. [10.2]

I have identified a number of reasons for this black-and-white mentality. First, there's the ever-present desire to control that creeps into every religious system. Plain old laziness is another reason. After all, it's easier to control someone with exterior controls than through relationships and the heart, which takes much more time and effort. And then there are always people with ignorant zeal; they just believe a certain thing is what's right and will die to defend the status quo.

Of course, all of these Christians will say their desire is simply to properly distinguish good from evil so as to encourage the good and discourage the evil. I don't suggest that this is entirely false. But the deeper truth is that black-and-white Christians oversimplify life with their (extremely left-brained) approach. Life is full of gray areas, and deciding what is right and wrong in the real world is hard, emotionally taxing work. It means involving the heart and not just the head in decision-making. It requires examining the context in each situation and getting clarity from God before acting.

See how much simpler it is to enforce a list of rules?

NIFTY SHADES OF GRAY

As a pastor I can appreciate how much easier it would be to simply tell everyone that drinking alcohol, for example, was always wrong. This position saves the pastor's conscience from ever having to worry that he allowed someone to fall into alcoholism. Moreover, it saves the pastor from having to teach people how to discern for themselves in what context drinking alcohol might be okay or not. That's a lot of work. It's risky. It's messy. It's very draining.

For the sake of example, let me illustrate how the drinking of alcohol has many shades of gray, and how even the Bible backs this up. First, we have the color black: Ephesians 5:18 says not to get drunk with wine. That's crossing the line. I agree with legalists on this point. My next question for legalists, however, would be a very subtle shade of gray. For example, "Would you give alcohol to a dying person in order to mitigate their suffering?" A firm legalist will answer an emphatic "no" to this question, despite the fact that Proverbs 31:6 says, "Let beer be for those who are perishing, wine for those who are in anguish!" (Isn't it a tad strange that pretty much all legalists would approve of giving *morphine* to a dying person but not alcohol?)

I could go further and ask if it would be okay to drink alcohol in moderation to relax or to celebrate. Again, a legalist will definitely say no, and yet Jesus himself attended a wedding where wine was flowing and even *made* wine when the host of the wedding ran out. (The Greek word for "wine" in that passage is the same as we see in Ephesians 5:18, where we're told not to get drunk.) The Psalms even say that God, in blessing mankind, has given him "wine that gladdens human hearts" (Psalm 104:15).

Now, I'll be the first to admit that the Bible gives numerous warnings about the dangers of alcohol consumption. I wouldn't be a good pastor if I didn't know these risks and share them with my congregation. But lots of good and legitimate things in life have risks associated with them, including buying houses and driving cars. (Hey, being born is a risk!) Not only do legalists who live only in black and white miss out on the opportunity to teach people how to discern for themselves, but my observation is that they also make their own positions a subject of pride. It's really too bad.

SHADES OF GRACE

I've taken quite of bit of space here to highlight the general failure of the Christian church to appreciate something that is actually at the heart of true Christianity. I'm talking, of course, about *grace*. The Christian church is not alone in its inattention to the concept of grace; religious systems the world over have missed it. But Jesus was all about grace – a concept that is not only right-brained but powerfully resonant.

Grace is undeserved favor. It is giving people more good than they deserve. It is one of the most promulgated ideals of the New Testament, and the very essence of Jesus' sacrifice on the cross – God himself laying down his life on behalf of sinful human beings who don't deserve it. As recipients of God's grace, I believe with every ounce of my being that we who claim to follow Jesus should, very literally, embody this value.

The New Testament word for *grace* is the word from whence we get our modern word "charity." It's a no-strings-attached type of action. To be the recipient of grace is a powerfully heartwarming experience. Grace is when the guy at the ice cream shop winks and gives you an extra scoop, at no extra cost. Grace is a mother taking on a part-time job before Christmas and wearing herself out just for the momentary joy of seeing her children's eyes light up at their gifts on Christmas morning. Grace is a father offering his 16-year old his car keys, even when he knows the risks involved.

Grace is God creating a world full of things that can be enjoyed, and grace is giving the freedom along with it for people to go overboard in the use of those things, whether we're talking about food, alcohol, sex, music, dancing, money, sports, shopping, fashion or about a billion other things.

Grace is truly amazing.

> *Grace is God creating a world full of things that can be enjoyed, and grace is giving the freedom along with it for people to go overboard in the use of those things, whether we're talking about food, alcohol, sex, music, dancing, money, sports, shopping, fashion or about a billion other things.*

Grace is also a very winsome quality. It is precisely why people so admired Jesus as he strolled the Judean countryside. As his own disciple declared with amazement, he was "full of grace and truth." [10.3] I so would have liked to have met Jesus and seen how he interacted with people.

When I think about all the reasons why I believe in Jesus, grace is at the top of my list. There have been many great religious leaders throughout history, but only Jesus introduced this concept of pure, simple grace to mankind. Various prophets of other religions gave us a glimpse of God's character, but they focused mostly on his sternness and his justice.

God seems so angry in most faiths. I think the majority of us assume that he wakes up with a scowl on his face every morning. I like to tell my parishioners that if God did wake up every morning, his first thoughts about every one of us would be warm, positive thoughts – thoughts like I have for my 22-month old son. [10.4] His first inclinations toward us are to bless us and to give us every good thing he can provide us.

Grace means that the pressure is off. It means that I don't have to spend my life trying to earn God's favor in hopes that he will accept me on the other side. Grace was God traveling through a human birth canal and into an animal's feeding trough. It was him subjecting himself to sinful mankind and our abuse. It was his willingness to be mocked, scorned, misunderstood and brutally murdered so as to provide us with salvation.

Grace is often translated "gift" in the New Testament, and that's exactly what it is. Try to earn it and you've insulted the giver. As the Apostle Paul told the early Christians in Asia Minor: "For it is by grace you have been saved, through faith—and this is not from yourselves, it is the gift of God—" (Ephesians 2:8).

Thank God for grace. Not only did I need it to be reunited to God; I need it every day of my life. Although I am God's child, I am still plagued by a sinful nature that regularly wins out in my decision-making.

The older I have grown, the more I have become aware of my own depravity. I am very clear on the fact that I am fully capable of doing the most wicked things imaginable. When I counsel people who are caught in addictive and destructive behaviors, I sympathize, knowing that if I had walked in their shoes I would probably be in a worse state than they are. Yet every day I wake up with the knowledge that I am still forgiven and loved as a child of God.

I am fuelled by grace. It is God's grace that motivates me to live a life of love and sacrifice. It is God's grace that makes me strive to temper my passions before they turn into destructive vices. I do not live by an invisible list of rules; I live out of love and gratitude in an invisible relationship.

The world at large does not understand grace, only striving and earning and retribution. People in various religions tell me that grace is insufficient – that God cannot possibly offer salvation to mankind on the basis of grace alone; there must be a list of rules to keep.

But the essence of true Christianity is that God is big enough and secure enough and loving enough to offer me and the rest of humanity the free gift of salvation by grace alone. At the root of true Christianity is God's knowledge that only when salvation is freely offered is mankind truly motivated to love him in return and obey him wholeheartedly.

That just makes so much sense to me.

Chapter 11

HUMILITY IS GREATER THAN INTELLECT

It must be humbling to suck on so many different levels.

–Sheldon, *The Big Bang Theory*

I used to rule the world
Seas would rise when I gave the word
Now in the morning I sleep alone
Sweep the streets I used to own

–Coldplay, *Viva la Vida*

On September 3, 2006, I came home from church, grabbed a sandwich, and then made myself comfortable on the couch. I had some serious business to attend to.

I've never been an avid tennis fan, but I wondered who could possibly not want to watch Andre Agassi and cheer him on to a third-round victory at the US Open? After all, he had already announced that this would be the very last tournament of his 21-year career. No matter how it ended, it was going to be epic. The pain-ridden veteran managed to advance through the first two rounds, receiving anti-inflammatory injections between matches to fight his searing lower back pain. Everyone watching hoped this would *not* be his last match.

His third-round match-up saw him face Benjamin Becker of Germany (no relation to Boris). Everyone at Arthur Ashe Stadium was pulling for Agassi. (I'm sure even Benjamin's mom was. Heck, hasn't everyone's mom had a crush on Agassi?) Despite his pain, Andre must have drawn energy from the sold-out crowd that was literally willing his shots to stay in-bounds. But eventually the hard-serving Becker proved too much for Andre, who was unable to survive the fourth set. Becker won the match 7-5, 6-7 (4), 6-4, 7-5. When Becker won the match point, a hush fell over the crowd, as if an immense bubble had just been popped. The players met at the net, Becker obviously humbled to have dealt the final blow to Agassi's career.

What happened at that moment was something I will never forget. Agassi walked off the court and sat down, overwhelmed with emotion. I can only imagine the swirl of thought and sensation that clouded the mind of this 36-year old man as he exited the court for the last time. As the over 23,000 fans at Arthur Ashe Stadium rose to their feet and applauded, the once brash "image is everything" kid was humbled to the core.[11.1]

Agassi wept, at times uncontrollably. He pulled his towel over his head and buried his face in his hands. His eyes were bloodshot with tears and at moments even his breathing was labored. When he regained his composure enough to speak, he took the microphone from CBS's Mary Joe Fernandez and addressed the crowd in what would become an instant quote for the ages.

> "The scoreboard said I lost today, but what the scoreboard doesn't say is what it is I have found. And over the last 21 years, I have found loyalty.

You have pulled for me on court and also in life. I've found inspiration. You have willed me to succeed sometimes even in my lowest moments. And I've found generosity. You have given me your shoulders to stand on to reach for my dreams, dreams I could never have reached without you. Over the last 21 years, I have found you and I will take you and the memory of you with me for the rest of my life. Thank you."

HUMBLING EXPERIENCES

Schooling

The world is a proud place. It's a place where we're taught to claim everything for ourselves and to never take a back seat to anyone. Here in the West we long for our 10 minutes of fame, and we spend our lives in a quest for significance. Even our greatest acts of charity are often just a backdoor effort to gain the applause of our peers.

Ever since I was a kid, people around me considered me a humble person – people other than my immediate family, that is. They knew better. Because I was polite and well-mannered, many of my peers and teachers made the assumption that I was truly humble.

I did try to follow the Proverbs in terms of not promoting myself. The Proverbs say to let another person's mouth do the bragging if there is any to be done. So that's what I did; I strived to excel at a whole bunch of things in order to gain praise – music, hockey, church activities, scholastics – you name it. I managed to garner a steady stream of praise from all of them. I graduated at the top of my class, excelled in music and played competitive hockey at the highest level as a 17-year old.

I left high school convinced that the world was my oyster. But since that time, my life has been one series of humblings after another.

It began in Bible college, where as a cocky 18 year-old, I thought I had the world by the tail. As I mentioned in an earlier chapter, I entered college with more Bible knowledge than the typical student – so much so that I found the majority of my classes frustratingly dull. I entertained myself by drawing pictures of the professors during class and taking creative license on my assignments. Unfortunately, not all of my teachers shared my sense of humor. One teacher thought I was particularly flippant on a paper I wrote in my freshman year and as a result gave me an F. He certainly knew which of my buttons to press.

F's were simply something I couldn't handle, but I still wasn't ready to become the compliant student people seemed to want me to be. I lived with an edge. I had run-ins with most of my professors. On one occasion I was publicly chewed out in front of my entire class by the president of the school. On another occasion I left home on spring break ahead of time – something no one dared do at a strict school like ours. When I returned after break I was "campused" – placed under house arrest – for two full weeks. Except for classes and meals, I was confined to the privacy (and extreme boredom) of my dorm room. Until the day I left the school I continued in this pattern of passive-aggressive behavior.

From that small school in New Brunswick I moved on to Washington, D.C., to finish up my post-secondary education. In 1994 I completed my Masters of Divinity from Capital Bible Seminary, again finishing at the top of my class. Despite my ups and downs through college, I figured I still "had it".

Québec

During my time in Washington I married Sarah Fugère, a French-Canadian girl I had met in New Brunswick. Upon completion of seminary my wife's church in Cap-de-la-Madeleine, Québec, offered me a job. I was excited by the idea of launching into the real world of church ministry, with one exception – I didn't speak French. (My wife didn't speak English either when we met, but we spoke the language of love!) The first time I met her parents they emphatically told me that they were not going to learn English; it would be *me* who would have to learn French. I managed to decipher what they were saying and forced a smile.

My first assignment upon arriving at the church was to be a counselor for 10-year-old boys at a summer camp named "Camp joie de vivre" (Camp Joy of Living). Only I wasn't feeling the joy. The very first boy I met was excited to meet me, and spoke to me in French at 100 km/h. "*Je ne comprends pas,*" I repeated three times, until he finally blurted in frustration – "*Ah, toi tu ne comprends* rien!" (You don't understand *anything!*) It was the first sentence he said that I was able to make out, and I felt like a doofus.

The ensuing months were excruciating for a perfectionist like myself. Putting my errors on display for everyone to see was almost more than I could bear, but you just can't learn a language without trial and error. One time while I was teaching the teen Sunday school class I explained to the teens how the prophet Daniel ate the lions in the lions' den. Wrong verb.[11.2] Whenever someone would point out my errors in public it felt like a knife slicing into my pride.

Thanks in large part to the patient coaching of my parents-in-law, by the end of two years I was speaking up front every Sunday. I even got to develop and teach a New Testament Greek class in French, a challenging but fun experience. It was also in Québec that I was driven to question numerous theological positions I had previously held. I grew to understand that Chrstianity in Québec didn't carry all of the same baggage as it did in English culture, and it was more than humbling to begin to admit that many of the positions I held so firmly were actually cultural trappings of Christianity as opposed to pure Christian belief. [11.3]

Toronto

After three years in Québec I was invited, through an amazing series of events, to attempt a church plant in Toronto. It was an easy but emotional decision to make. Along with my wife and two friends from seminary (one of whom was also married) we moved to the city of Mississauga, a massive suburb just west of Toronto. We knew absolutely no one, but we were fearless and began to meet people and brought a small group of Christians together.

The church began very well. After about a year in the city, we had gathered a core of 13 adults, and on September 13, 1998, we launched the church. Having extensively advertised and promoted the church's grand opening in the community, we had almost 150 people show up at our first service. Everyone else who was involved in the church plant was amazed, but to be honest, although happy with the result, I just figured it was par for the course. Everything else I had been involved in before had succeeded, so why would this be any different?

I made bold growth projections and shared them with the congregation. Sarah and I had our second child and as the church grew, I had more and more demands on my time. The intensity of the job grew quickly, but just gradually enough that I didn't notice how stressed out I was becoming. The heart palpitations that I had struggled with as a teen came back; I was constantly on edge. Whenever I stopped working I was like a crack addict in withdrawal – fidgety and unable to focus.

On February 5, 2000, I hit a wall that would leave me permanently changed. I was driving back to the office with my family after having already had early morning meetings. As I approached a major intersection close to the church office, I began to lose my vision – I was blacking out. "I'm losing it!" I told my wife. "I'm going to pass out!"

I managed to pull over into a parking lot before my head flopped back on my headrest and I fell unconscious. Sarah freaked out. The kids thought I was playing a joke, but Sarah quickly figured out that nothing funny was happening. She got out of the car and began throwing snow in my face, screaming at me and slapping my cheeks. Over a full minute later I regained consciousness and Sarah told me what happened, the fear still written on her face.

She had me get into the passenger's seat and drove me straight to the hospital where, after an EKG, I was told that I probably hyperventilated. "Are you under a lot of stress, Mr. Sawatsky?" I guess I was.

Church ministry is brutal. Just prior to my fainting episode a key family in our church (and our single largest financial supporter) informed me that they were leaving to go to another local church. It crushed me, and at the time I sensed that they weren't being forthright in their reasons for leaving. In my mind I went over and over what I could have done differently to keep them. Then another ministry leader left the church and took a number of young adults with her to a newly organized church just down the street.

My schedule was beyond packed. I was doing a lot of counseling and having meetings almost every night of the week. I had no mentor to guide me, to warn me that the path that I was on was going to bring me harm. I needed extra help, but the church was nowhere close to being in the financial position to bring on more staff. I began to get depressed. I hid it well on Sundays, but people who were close to me could see that my spirit was drying up. I cried a lot in private. My hobbies and interests went from being simply ignored to becoming virtually nonexistent.

The next few years were the darkest of my life. The church's growth plateaued and I began to feel trapped; I was maintaining a ministry from which I derived no enjoyment or fulfillment,[11.4] but I had put all of my success eggs in this basket, so there was no backing out. I found myself looking for excitement in other areas, some of which were not healthy. Temptations that had never even crossed my radar screen as a younger man now accosted me at every turn.

To make matters worse, the new church that had started down the street grew quickly and surpassed mine. Yes, we're all on the same team, but that's little consolation to a competitive person like me. If you're familiar with the *Strengthfinders* personality assessment, my top "strength" is *competition*. What a joke! The characteristic that was supposed to be my greatest asset was becoming my greatest nemesis, perpetually throwing me into bouts of depression. I became panicky and ineffective, barely managing to maintain my weekly responsibilities. To this day only a few members of my congregation know just how dark the world had become for me.

To be honest, I can't tell you what eventually pulled me out of that rut. Someone must have been praying somewhere. Although things have improved in more recent years, I still don't think I've fully recovered. Maybe I never will. I wish sometimes that I was as knowledgeable and confident as I was some 15 years ago, but it seems the older I get, the more questions I have and the more I have to face my own humanness.

I will never reach the level of an Andre Agassi in my field of work; I'm not even sure what that would be. But I think I have learned some of the same lessons. I've learned that I'm not bigger than the game; the game is bigger than me. I hope that someday I can be as competitive and yet as classy as Agassi was on September 3, 2006.

HUMBLED BUT MORE HEALTHY

In the past 10 years God has begun an amazing transformation in me. It is far from finished, but it is well underway. Apart from God's help and grace, I am unable to be the disciplined person I have always considered myself to be. I am unable to overcome my sinful attitudes and my negativity without him.

I have had some success in facing life's little challenges on my own, but when real challenges have come along, I have found myself weak and often fearful.

In a word, I have been humbled. And yet, I know in my heart that I am in a better place than I was 10 or 20 years ago. My usability to God has increased as I have learned that I cannot lean on my own intellect and abilities. I have newfound grace for the fellow-strugglers in my church, and am a lot more empathetic to their weaknesses.

The Proverbs say that humility comes before honor, and that gives me hope. It is also the kind of wisdom that reinforces my faith. As much as I have resisted (and continue to resist) the painful process of being humbled, I know it is necessary. Regardless of who originally penned this proverb, I know without a doubt that this is divine wisdom. My greatest confirmation of this is how God himself acted when he took on human form.

OUR HUMBLE HERO

Jesus was a humble hero. History records no one equal to him in his humility. Not only was he God Almighty, stooping to be born in an animal's feeding trough; he also lived a life completely detached from materialism, hedonism or the pursuit of glory.[11.5] The gospels record that he voluntarily put his divine rights and abilities aside in order to fully experience our humanity, and that he, at every moment, submitted to the Father's will. This submission ultimately extended to the horror of crucifixion.

Submission is divine. It is hated in our world because it does not find its origins in our world. The person who lays down their rights in blind faith that a better outcome will result demonstrates their belief in something beyond this world.

> **Submission is divine. It is hated in our world because it does not find its origins in our world.**

People who have followed Jesus' example have been history's greatest figures of inspiration – people like Mother Teresa and Mahatma Gandhi. I read their stories and I become overwhelmed with a desire to be more like them. Very few people inspire us the same way. I'm sure these icons of self-sacrifice wrestled with pride as well, but somehow they forced themselves to live differently than the culture that surrounded them.

Today's "elite" may do a lot of good things, but I suspect that many of them are still holding onto wrong motives. I hope I'm not being judgmental in this regard. I just know my own heart, and I can't help but think how much harder it would be to maintain a humble posture with the encumbrances of wealth, fame or power.

The mantra of the day is to "look out for Number One." It's taught in our children's TV shows and continues all the way through university. It's a subtle lie that our ultimate happiness is to be found in selfish pursuit. Even the American constitution names the "pursuit of happiness" as an ultimate goal. If the world's best wisdom urges me to lose myself in the crowds of people clambering over one another in an attempt to stand at the top of the pile, then I think I need to look elsewhere for wisdom.

Arrogant people turn me off. Perhaps I see my own dark side in them and I'm repulsed. I hold an equal disgust for arrogance on the part of believers and unbelievers. How people who claim to know anything about God can be so condescending toward people who disagree with them is unfathomable to me. I'm also appalled by the conceited fervor with which many atheists today attack people of faith.

In my opinion, whether one is a person of faith or not, humility is appealing, and ought to be part of any value system. The fact that Jesus was the poster child for humility may not play into most people's faith decisions, but for me it's huge. Every religious leader claims to know the truth; Jesus knew something more, and I feel myself drawn to it.

Chapter 12

I LIKE DOING "GOOD" MORE THAN DOING "WRONG"

Claire likes to say, "You can be part of the problem, or part of the solution." But I happen to believe you can be both.

−Phil Dunphy, *Modern Family*

When I do good, I feel good; when I do bad, I feel bad. That's my religion.

−Abraham Lincoln

There are two approaches to take in every pursuit of wisdom. The first is the left-brained approach. It is factual in nature. It is the approach most of us begin with as we learn what is right and wrong. From our earliest days, our parents and guardians attach words like "good" and "bad" to our actions in an attempt to encourage what they understand to be "good." As a whole, the system is neat and tidy, and initially effective.

As we get older, however, the clear lines that our authority figures drew for us begin to blur. We begin to recognize that context plays a role in many decisions, and this reality complicates the decision-making process. By the time we complete our education and enter adulthood, many of us come full circle and begin to question the very legitimacy of the objective labels of "right" and "wrong."

As I mention in the introduction to this book, over the past few decades, a spirit of relativism has settled over North America as we've gravitated away from "authoritative" sources of truth toward more "experiential" ones. The media has added fuel to the relativity question by bringing numerous moral quandaries to light – parents euthanizing their handicapped children, the use of recreational drugs, questioning the validity of war, and so on.

The rapid rise of relativism has sent shock waves through the Christian community, which struggles to get the message out that truth is not relative and does not vacillate with ever-changing public opinion. I also see this danger of relativism. Philosophically, some things simply *have* to always be right and others wrong, or morality is nothing more than a surface-level trend. A growing number of people, I suppose, would view morality as such.

Despite my hesitations, I recognize that relativists are predominantly right-brained. (So they can't be all bad!) They use arguments based on experience to defend their positions. And while many Christians have come to see the use of experience in defining morality as *anathema*, I have to say that I wish more Christians would recognize the importance of the right brain in establishing their moral positions.

The way I see it, as much as there is danger in establishing morality solely based upon feelings, so is there danger in not engaging the right brain. There are times when I sit down to apply my black-and-white rules to situations and I realize that something simply doesn't feel right. In such situations my right brain is throwing up red flags to warn me that something is amiss. I guess what I'm suggesting, in a nutshell, is that morality is as much an art as it is a science.

I think this is true because when it comes to right and wrong, there is a serious danger of making a "correct" decision with the wrong spirit, or with the wrong motives. When Saddam Hussein was hanged on December 30, 2006, not many people were terribly upset that he died – not even people who oppose the death penalty. But many people were upset by the way in which he was executed. Some argued that his trial was unfair. Even more were appalled by the words of the executioners who carried out the proceedings.

I think it all comes back to the "grace and truth" balance. To lack grace in administering truth is to miss something of the truth, a lesson that Jesus taught clearly.

MORAL INTUITION

Being a theist, I see life as given and directed by a purposeful creator. Annexed to this belief is the idea that this creator has named some things as being right and others as wrong. This is the exact representation of life articulated by the Old Testament. In an ultimate sense, this negates the possibility of relativism.

I appreciate that atheists will never share this exact perspective, but I also wonder just how far they would be willing to pursue relativism. I, for one, am convinced that some moral questions require no divine interpretation. Murder – to kill someone without just cause – is always wrong. Killing is not always wrong, but murder is. I believe that even the most irreligious person in the most remote part of the world knows this when they spill another person's blood in a moment of passion. I am convinced of it. If this is true, then a morality higher than the codified and enforced rules of humans exists in our universe. Stealing is another example of an innate moral absolute. We all know instinctively that to take something that does not belong to us is wrong.

Upon deeper reflection, moral intuition is seen to be very deep within us, coming alive when we stomp on ants for nothing more than sadistic pleasure or when we crush a perfectly good apple just for the sake of destruction.

Now, I'm aware that moral relativists have well-conceived arguments to poke holes in this concept of moral absolutism. And you don't need to have your brain washed by a university professor to realize it. Just watch *24* and see Jack Bauer kill someone for the country's greater good. It'll leave you scratching your head (and scrambling to watch the next episode!). More and more of today's popular TV shows wrestle with such questions – *The Walking Dead, Breaking Bad, Homeland,* and dozens of other shows have done the same in recent years. Even those of us who have spent long hours forming our responses to tough moral questions still get stumped on some of the scenarios presented in these programs. We can even start confusing antiheroes for heroes.

But exceptions do not negate rules. Even relativists know that. Even relativists have to cringe to imagine a world in which values like honesty, kindness, self-control and respect are discarded like the latest trend. And it is at this point of admission that my right-brained argument for morality comes into focus.

I am a believer because I see the innate laws of morality in the world. Just as ignoring the law of gravity results in certain negative consequences, so does ignoring this higher moral law. Lives lived in dishonesty, selfishness and reckless self-indulgence inevitably self-destruct.

Granted, some of my unbelieving friends would see these innate moral laws as no different from any other laws in the universe. Just like the laws of gravity or thermodynamics, they were just part of the package that the Big Bang delivered, and should not be seen in any other light. Others would say that these laws are a product of continuing evolution, and that our minds – and societies in turn – may eventually completely redefine our morality.

I cannot deny this as a possibility, but it does not resonate within me. I much prefer to see the innate laws of morality as evidence of personality behind the creative force of the universe[12.1] – that the one who designed life as it exists possesses qualities of morality that find their DNA in me as well.

This means that I like to do good because when I do so, I am living in harmony with the one who made life. In other words, I have been formed in God's image, meaning I like to do good because God likes to do good.[12.2] I find it somehow comforting to think of morality in this way.

Just as I have certain interests and abilities that reflect those of my physical parents, so also I have been formed in the moral image of the One who parented the universe. By the same token, when I violate God's moral laws I experience a sense of guilt, of impropriety – a sensation that saps my confidence and postures me for an expectation of retribution. (I realize that this sensation can only come about if one believes in a personal and moral God.)

> *Just as I have certain interests and abilities that reflect those of my physical parents, so also I have been formed in the moral image of the One who parented the universe.*

Every Master of Divinity grad learns in their theology studies that God's laws have been revealed in two ways – *generally* and *specifically*. General revelation refers to how God has revealed himself in nature, through his creation. Specific revelation refers to the times and places when God describes himself, his thinking, and his laws to mankind in clear and specific ways (such as in giving the Ten Commandments or performing some miracle.) Obviously, the weight of evidence is very different between general and specific revelation, and the Bible has some key passages that deal with how God judges people differently based on the quantity and quality of revelation they have received.[12,3] (This is a concept that even many Christians do not understand.)

Without specific revelation, a person has no clear way of knowing what God thinks, particularly on certain moral issues. It is for this reason that specific revelation (which is intrinsically left-brained) will always be important for those who desire to live moral lives. But our right brains also add important, experiential confirmation to the left-brained, moral decisions we make.

THE ULTIMATE BENEFIT OF DOING GOOD

I like doing good things. Even though my selfish self tends to control the "time of possession" statistic in my life (to use a little football analogy), whenever my better self takes control and gets me to act unselfishly, I always feel a rush of real life go through me.

I love helping and encouraging people. As much as I tell people I don't like counseling, I have to admit that every time I come away from helping someone I have a deep sense of joy and accomplishment.

I love seeing people in my church become motivated to help other people. On one occasion during a church-wide challenge I called "Learn to Love," one of the small groups in our church spontaneously reached out to a woman who they heard of through one of the group members. She was in financial distress. Her phone and gas had been cut off. She and her daughter could only take cold showers and they had no more food in the cupboard, despite the woman's working two jobs.

Then one day this group of people showed up at her workplace with a whole van full of food. She was so moved that she came to church and began to get involved. Another woman in our church found her a better job, and the teens in the church befriended her daughter. The way this group responded was amazing, but they had learned to have this focus as a result of helping one of their own members through a rough bout of breast cancer just months earlier.

As I listened to the group members share their stories through these events, I could see a glow about them. They loved to do good things for others. Like so many throughout history, they discovered in a new way that doing good brings true enjoyment.

In the evolutionary model of survival of the fittest, life should be like a season of *Survivor*, where every act of kindness is suspect – an insincere gesture offered with covert selfish intentions. I suppose many people today live with this perspective, but I find that most depressing. Some of my fondest memories are of times when people helped me who had no hidden agenda of repayment. In those moments, I felt an energizing wave of hope and joy, a deeper connection with humanity. It was undeniably good, and seemed to tap into deeper truths that have been built into the universe.

I feel the same inner warmth when I make a good choice, when I work on something of value, or when I invest in relationships. This innate morality is so strong within us that contestants in a game like *Survivor* get frustrated when people play by the game's clearly stated "survival-of-the-fittest" rules: to *outwit, outplay, outlast*. Even in a game that is all about double-crossing and dishonesty, our penchant is to live morally and to expect others to do the same.

Atheists will always argue that they too like to do good, and that they do as much or more good in the world as many Christians. I don't deny that atheists can and do act morally, and may even outshine many Christians.

Having been made in God's image and inhabiting his universe, we are all apt to embody these desires to some degree, regardless of where we're from or what we believe. But the Bible states that God's Spirit indwells true believers, thus giving them special motivation for doing good.

Furthermore, faithful believers live in constant remembrance of their own need of God's benevolence. I love and forgive people because I have been loved and have been forgiven by God. People may receive love and forgiveness from other people, but that love and forgiveness is always limited. Only God's infinite and unconditional love and forgiveness can give us an unlimited motivation to live good lives.

Whether or not we acknowledge God's part in morality doesn't change the fact that we sense a certain moral obligation to something beyond human authority. Suppose that an atheist violates a law in the universe and no human knows about it. Say he shoots a squirrel for the mere pleasure of killing it. To whom does the atheist go to purge his conscience? I guess he could confess his fault to the general population if he understood the squirrel as having belonged to everyone. (People would no doubt look at him funny.) My point again is simply to highlight the very natural notion that personality is somehow connected to the heart of the physical universe. And as long as this notion rings true, I will always feel good when I do good. The atheist still has no satisfying explanation for the source of this impulse.

I don't mean to pick on atheists. Most are solid, deep-thinking people who are wrestling with the concept of belief just as I am. Most of them live respectable lives, do good to others, and admit to the existence of morality. Very few people deny the existence of objective right and wrong entirely. Those who would try to do so must focus on the exceptions in an attempt to convince themselves that their moral choices have no real consequences.

But they'll have a hard time convincing me of that. My gut tells me otherwise.

Chapter 13

ALTERNATIVE PHILOSOPHIES DON'T RING TRUE

When the philosopher's argument becomes tedious, complicated, and opaque, it is usually a sign that he is attempting to prove as true to the intellect what is plainly false to common sense.

–EDWARD ABBEY, AMERICAN AUTHOR

I swallowed all of your ideas. I'm going to digest them and see what comes out the other end.

–MICHAEL SCOTT, *THE OFFICE*

You may never have acknowledged it before, but you too are a person of faith.

Yes, you.

Every day you choose to place your trust in a variety of things – your friends, your spouse, your car, your employment. Every time you sit down in a chair you are exercising faith. (The combination of certain backsides with certain chairs creates a variety of risk levels.)

Beyond these very simple illustrations, I will say with confidence that you exercise faith in many deeper ways as well. Say you're a person who lives every day to amass more wealth or possessions, thus demonstrating faith in *matter*. You could rightly be called a *materialist*. If you're someone who denies any intrinsic purpose for life or the universe but still find yourself creating meaning for life in various activities, such as having a family or donating your time to a worthy cause, you could rightly be called an *existentialist*. (These and other popular worldview perspectives will be clarified by any basic philosophy class. I would encourage everyone to try one of these. The clarity it renders can be life-changing.)

While most North Americans are not trained or inclined to verbalize their specific beliefs, we hold intrinsic beliefs in every area of life – our origins, our purpose, what is right and wrong, the existence and nature of God, what brings true happiness, and so on. Those who try to deny a devotion to any form of faith betray their own claim by their everyday actions.

Everything we do is based on belief – conscious or subconscious. Everyone believes in something.

So far I've presented twelve different right-brained reasons for Christian faith. They are meaningful to me, but may not be that impressive to you. Before you discard them altogether, I'd ask you to consider them in light of some of the most popular philosophies our society embraces today. I've included ten of the most popular ones here. In reading, you may come to realize that you have faith in some of these philosophies yourself.

In my opinion, many of today's popular philosophies are – to put it in the most simple terms – just lame. Even without taking the time to scrutinize all of their flaws and inconsistencies, they simply do not resonate. I can honestly say that one of the things that has convinced me of my Christian faith more than any other is seeing just how shaky much of our society's "wisdom" is. It doesn't ring true.

Not all of the beliefs I will discuss in the following pages are accepted as truth in the entire world, but most of them are touted in the most "developed" countries. As I see it, each one is a demonstration of stubborn human determination to live free from the divine laws that exist in the universe; each one is confirmation of the Bible's primary truth: that we all need to be rescued from ourselves.

Let me share a few of my favorites.

NEO-DARWINIAN EVOLUTION

All matter originates and exists only by virtue of a force... We must assume behind this force the existence of a conscious and intelligent Mind. This Mind is the matrix of all matter.

—Max Planck, German theoretical physicist
who originated quantum theory

Before you toss this book in disgust at my blatant ignorance, just hear me out. It would be unproductive for me to harangue the general population over their appetite for Neo-Darwinian evolution. After all, if you're 40 years old or younger and a product of public school education, you've been taught the theory of evolution as fact, or at least as the best option, since your earliest days in elementary school.

Unlike some Christians, I don't believe that every bit of science related to evolutionary theory is bogus. I believe scientists have brilliant minds and work as much as possible within the framework of known laws, guided by the scientific method. I assume the vast majority are well-intentioned people. I even believe in microevolution.[13.1] The problem, as I see it, is in line with Steven Levitt's criticism of typical economists in his bestseller *Freakonomics* – that is, that people are famous for asking the wrong questions. Scientists and economists alike can do years of flawless research and study, but if this study is built upon the wrong original premise, it is essentially of no value.

Go back to your Grade 6 science class. In science, you'll remember, we learned that in order to discover truth we must follow a clear and consistent process known as the "scientific method." With the objective of arriving at a scientific certainty (or law), we begin with a hypothesis and then test it repeatedly, using our five senses. If the results of the testing back up the hypothesis, then the hypothesis moves to the next phase of being called a "theory." Eventually, after years of scrutiny and testing, if a theory proves to be correct 100% of the time, it becomes a scientific law – no longer questioned, but accepted as fact and used as the basis for further scientific discovery. Attempting to base new research on unproven laws is risky, as everything built on top of those laws risks tumbling down if the original premise ever proves incorrect, even just in part.

Caution, as it relates to wholehearted devotion to the *theory* of evolution, is warranted when we consider the scientific method. Like any other theory, evolution begins with a hypothesis. The basic premise of popular evolutionary theory is that the world began with a Big Bang, a terrific explosion that resulted from the combination of certain gases. The eventual result was the development of simple life forms that over time evolved into life as we now know it. This process took billions of years and continues to progress.

In normal scientific testing, the way to test a hypothesis is to try to prove it wrong. In other words, the normal process is to conduct repeated experiments, pushing the theory in question to the limit in order to prove that it is impervious to criticism. But for some reason, this has not been the general approach of the scientific community in regard to the Big Bang theory or to Darwinism. Instead, turning the scientific method on its head, the scientific community has worked tirelessly to prove evolution *right*, even when clear supporting evidence has been hard to find.

To scientifically test the Big Bang would require creating numerous explosions using various gases and combinations of matter in an attempt to replicate something like what scientists have theorized gave birth to the universe. This line of testing has been going in in various forms since the 1960's, but has yet to produce any clear evidence for the Big Bang theory. Most recently, scientists have been excited by the advances in understanding subatomic particles like the Higgs boson (a.k.a. "God particle"), which could explain how mass came into existence in the universe. But even this would be a small piece in the infinite puzzle of how an explosion resulted in a world anything like the one we know. Furthermore, even if we discover that mass came into existence in this way, it in no way would rule out the possibility that God caused it to happen, any more than our modern understanding of atoms negates God's part in the universe.

Moving beyond the Big Bang into the inception of life, much repeated testing *has* been done in the attempt to bring life from non-life, but the results have been disappointing to say the least.[13.2]

The same overly optimistic approach has been used in relation to Darwin's theories – researchers have attempted only to prove natural selection and the transmutation of species rather than test and see if these theories hold up. Despite an abundance of information that contradicts the theories, secular science plows on in an attempt to construct a plausible framework for the development of life.

My point here is simply this. If scientists are determined to prove a certain hypothesis, even if only because a more palatable option is not apparent, true science has been violated. For example, to this day most people who have been educated in our universities would be stunned to know how very miniscule the fossil support is for intermediary life forms (missing links). Darwin himself admitted that the fossil support that ought to exist if his theory were true simply didn't exist:

> *Geology assuredly does not reveal any such finely-graduated organic chain; and this, perhaps, is the most obvious and serious objection which can be urged against the theory.* (Origin of the Species)

What little evidence exists is held together only by the sheer determination of the scientific community to support the predisposition that life did not develop in the way the Bible describes. Yet the overwhelming evidence continues to be that organisms have always reproduced after their own kind.

Think about it. Because the vast majority of universities today teach evolution, the vast majority of our scientists leave university and apply their knowledge to pursuit of researching and developing this evolutionary theory. To be honest, I'm not even sure why they waste their time; they seem determined to believe it regardless of what they turn up. Aren't they as guilty of blind faith as much as the "ignorant" Christian community they complain about?

And what is the ultimate goal of all this study anyway? What will filling in the blanks on the evolutionary chart do for mankind? Is all this work being done simply to disprove the accuracy of the Bible or other creationist teaching? I suppose some starry-eyed idealists might say we could eventually chart the future of mankind. Forgive my pessimism, but can't even solve problems we have in front of us, let alone try to impact life a million years down the road.

It is here that one has to admit that evolutionary theory is as much about faith as any Christian doctrine. To not admit as much is intellectually dishonest. It is undeniable that evolutionary doctrine is driven by people who reject the notion of God. The only truly worthwhile motivation in pursuing this theory that I could possibly see would be, (a) to discover our true origins (which, if impersonal and unintended, seems rather irrelevant) or (b) to forecast the direction of humanity in the evolutionary process. In other words, the theory is valuable only to people who are determined to see mankind as the controlling agent in history – namely, humanists. (It seems arrogant to me, as I'll discuss later, but I can see how humanists would perceive this pursuit as being noble.) Even if we could eventually forecast and control the future of the human race and the entire universe, this theory still leaves us at a loss when it comes to our origins.

Even the most convinced evolutionists know there is a fundamental problem with life coming from non-life; intelligence from non-intelligence; purpose and order from disorder; personality from impersonality. Contrary to popular opinion, it is *very good science* to conclude that life emerging from non-life is unlikely to impossible based on the fact that we

> *Even the most convinced evolutionists know there is a fundamental problem with life coming from non-life; intelligence from non-intelligence; purpose and order from disorder; personality from impersonality. Contrary to popular opinion, it is very good science to conclude that life emerging from non-life is unlikely to impossible based on the fact that we have never once in recorded history witnessed such a thing happen.*

have never once in recorded history witnessed such a thing happen. It is a more scientific conclusion than what evolutionists propose because the observation (upon which all science rests) is more concrete, more objectively verifiable.

If evolutionists' ultimate agenda is dissuading the masses of the existence of God, they might be well-served to start listening to UFO stories and developing more plausible hypotheses on how life got seeded on our planet. The bottom line is that the concept of life coming from non-life is terribly hard to swallow, and while many people may say they're cool with it, in their right-brain they know it makes no sense. When you stop and consider things in this way, don't atheists and evolutionists start to seem as lame in their beliefs as they make theists out to be?

With what I know about science, I think it's fair to ask the question: If virtually no one is looking for evidence to prove creationism, then why would anyone expect scientists to find any? They might stumble across proof every day, but because they aren't looking for it, it will go unnoticed. In fact, with the determination of scientists being so strong to disprove creationism or any other intelligent design theory, it may well go *suppressed*.

Not too long ago I watched the new movie by Ben Stein (Google *Ben Stein's Millions* and *Ferris Beuller's Day Off*). In his documentary film, *Expelled*, he demonstrates the extent to which anything contradicting Neo-Darwinian theory is being suppressed. Many people who see this form of intellectual pursuit as being free-minded and generous would be stunned to learn how supporters of this theory bully their rivals and stomp on freedom of expression. It's too bad that most people will never take the time to watch the movie. (I was the only person on the entire theatre when I watched it. Doesn't anyone have an open mind anymore?... Anyone?...Anyone?) If you are interested in this matter at all, you really ought to check out the film. Stein raises some excellent questions and conducts some intriguing interviews, including one with Richard Dawkins.

I have done a fair bit of research into creationist and intelligent design findings and theories, and while there are certainly obstacles to overcome, I have found many of the ideas presented by men like Ken Ham and Hugh Ross to be very intriguing and worthy of deeper research. Sure, I know these men disagree on many points and that they are both heavily criticized by the general scientific community, but upon what basis are they criticized? For proposing theories? For contradicting popular opinion? How dare they propose something different from other scientists! Their critics sound a lot like the people who criticized Darwin for thinking outside the box over a century ago.

The Bible attests that the world and its creatures were created by a purposeful creator, that living things have always reproduced after their kind, and that humans all have a common ancestry. It also seems to suggest that the earth is a fairly young planet; just how young is up for debate. All of these statements seem pretty believable to me. The Bible also attests to a worldwide flood as recent as 4500 years ago, a belief that, strangely enough, has been passed down through cultures all over the world, with over 200 existing flood legends to support the notion.[13.3] Not only do scientists ignore God in favor of evolutionary theories, they all but ignore historical accounts that could provide great insight into the history of our planet.

In all honesty, I believe that evolution is more about religion and philosophy than it is about science. I have looked at many of the left-brained arguments for and against evolution, but the real decision to embrace it lies with the right brain.

People today trumpet evolution like a modern Messiah. To be an evolutionist is to be part of an elite community, one supported by higher education and the media, and everyone who wants to be seen as intellectual feels compelled to embrace the theory. But if evolution is such a wonderful scientific discovery, name one thing that it has brought us. Real science is practical. It leads to discoveries that make life easier or heal sickness. Can you name one thing that evolution has given us? (I hear about lots of things that it "could" do for us.) I have great admiration for the fields of physics and biology and chemistry and genetics and botany and so on because they result in real differences for mankind. The best evolution can seemingly do is disprove God and motivate humans to be their own savior.

> *Real science is practical. It leads to discoveries that make life easier or heal sickness. Can you name one thing that evolution has given us?*

Atheists point to theistic religions and cite all of the trouble they have caused in the world. (We'll examine the accuracy of this statement a bit later.) Meanwhile, atheists ignore the huge amount of good that theists do every day, all over the world, motivated by higher ideals of faith and moral virtue. I'm not saying there isn't an argument to be made on both sides of the origins question (as you can quickly witness by visiting any number of blogs on the subject); I'm just tired of naturalists, humanists and evolutionists treating theists like they're morons. Their insistence upon our ignorance goes a long way in demonstrating their own.

The evolutionary theory is not only fraught with scientific roadblocks; it's also fraught with philosophical ones. I've already made mention of life from non-life, intelligence from non-intelligence. Psychologists also agree that true happiness in life is found through dedication to a worthy cause, not through self-gratification. This runs contrary to Darwin's concept of survival of the fittest, which measures success by self-preservation.

Ultimately, every evolutionist has to admit that morality is an illusion, or at best an ever-morphing meme, disconnected from any superseding intent. And that's simply not what we observe in society as a whole.

Richard Dawkins, in his bestseller *The God Delusion*, laments the lack of success his fellow atheists have had in promoting their beliefs: "Unlike evangelical Christians, who wield even greater political power, atheists and agnostics are not organized and therefore exert almost zero influence."[13.4] What is Dawkins whining about? He firmly believes that random chance processes, devoid of personal intelligence or will, gave rise to everything beautiful we see in the universe. Is he unwilling to trust the same process to take mankind to the next stages of evolution? *Do you believe in evolution or not, Mr. Dawkins?* Dawkins goes as far as including an appendix full of "friendly addresses, for individuals needing support in escaping from religion."[13.5] Strange how affectionate he is of mind, will and purposeful organization in the real world.

Dawkins uses the argument of irreducible complexity (often used by theists to prove God's existence) against the argument for God, saying that God is far too complex to not have been created by or from something greater. Obviously the argument that God is irreducibly complex is the atheist's very reason for disbelief and the theist's very reason for belief. This is and always will be the crux of the argument: it's two sides of the same coin; a pervasively irreconcilable difference in perspective.

For me, when it comes to understanding where mankind has come from and where we are headed, I like to get philosophical; I ask the question of ultimate resolve: "Is there a point in history at which everything is resolved, a point at which everything begins or ends or reaches perfect stasis?" I believe in ultimate resolve. As a theist, I see God as a philosophical necessity for achieving ultimate resolve.

If evolutionists believe natural selection is leading somewhere specific, then they too have to admit to belief in ultimate resolve. I would venture to guess that most optimistic evolutionists do believe that the universe has ultimate resolve, probably in the form of blissful stasis sometime in the future. (Humanists – evolutionists' "cousins" – certainly possess such optimism.)

The way I see it, existence necessitates ultimate resolve (at some point). It only seems consistent with everything we see in life: people are born and people die, things are made and things are destroyed, nations rise and nations fall. Evolutionary progress (or regress) necessitates ultimate resolve at some point as well; after all, the words *evolution* and *progress* both assume positive advancements toward a goal. The very laws of thermodynamics necessitate ultimate resolve – either energy finds its source in an ultimate entity or the universe continues to decelerate toward nothingness.

I believe that the energy and creative mind for all that exists finds its source in the Alpha and Omega, who will one day bring us back to a state of perfect stasis. Regardless of your take on the evolution-creation debate, philosophically, you cannot ignore this question: Where, ultimately, is humanity headed? Will the world's problems eventually be resolved, and if so, by whom?

As I read the work of atheists like Richard Dawkins, I can't help but ask why he feels so threatened. Evolution is taught in every major university in America. It is taught as fact to our children on TV and in the schools. Our museums are filled with evolutionary doctrine. In regard to the origins of the universe, it is by far the most socially acceptable belief in the western world. So why does that fact that a portion of the population (a very silent portion here in Canada) holds on to creationism or intelligent design so annoy people like Dawkins? Do we really pose so great a threat? Does Dawkins really see us as the bane of society, the roadblock to Utopia? Are we really that annoying for holding a different position?

Have you read *The God Delusion*? Everything I was ever taught in college about respectful debate is lost on Mr. Dawkins. He's downright offensive. As a pastor I am comfortable with passionate debate and I'm pretty quick to forgive people who overstep the line now and again because I often need their forgiveness as well. But I can't help but think that Dawkins' caustic approach turns more people off of his crusade than it enlists. Ultimately, if the theory of evolution is so good, he shouldn't have to work so hard to get people to believe it. The sad truth is, people just aren't convinced. The theory isn't that good. I would say that it's full of holes, except there are really more holes than fabric.

Dawkins would surely contest that science is self-correcting, unlike absolutists' religious doctrines. But I say, you'll be correcting forever if your science is being done on the wrong foundation. Furthermore, I don't have the time to wait for science to get it right. (How long would you sit and wait for a mechanic to fix your car if he was working on the wrong vehicle?) I want some answers now; I have places to go.

At the end of the day, the debate over the origins of the universe and life in general is as much about faith as it is fact, as much about philosophy as it is science, and as much about the right brain as it is about the left brain. Evolutionists look at the dearth of information and lose faith in God. I look at the dearth of information and make a leap toward God. (Actually, I think the dearth exists for this very purpose.)

I think there's plenty of room for people to be believers and still wrestle over these questions. And when you think about it, regardless of whether or not evolution is true, it still doesn't eliminate the God question.

I know I still have lots of questions. I'm sure you do too. Until we know everything for sure, let's agree to disagree – passionately, but respectfully.

SEXUAL LIBERTARIANISM

A number of years ago now, I picked up my then 11-year old daughter from school. On the way out the front door I noticed a poster for an upcoming

Valentine's dance. I was intrigued to see that the dance was a *Much Music* video dance. (*Much Music* is the Canadian version of MTV, and they can be hired to put on elaborate video dances complete with high-tech sound and lighting.)

Only a week earlier I was speaking on sexuality at church, and I presented the tweens and teens of the church with a challenge: read through the lyrics I had typed up to twenty or so of the most popular pop songs of the previous year, and write out 3 things from each song that could be harmful for your mind. The assignment was not complete until their parents had read the lyrics along with the teens' observations. If returned to me within 30 days, each young person would receive $20. (To my delight, many of the young people took me up on my offer and reported having eye-opening experiences – paying attention to the lyrics they were ingesting for the first time. The money I paid out was well worth the investment. Years later they still talk about the assignment.)

The fact that I had just tendered this assignment really was unrelated to my daughter's scheduled dance. I listen to pop music frequently and keep in touch with what's hot. There are many good songs that I enjoy, but obviously, there are many that I wouldn't want to listen to regularly, let alone my young and impressionable daughter. She also had read the lyrics I handed out and knew, along with me, what type of videos would be shown at the dance.

On the day of the dance I decided to pay the principal a visit. He didn't hesitate to welcome me into his office and hear what I had to say, and for a few minutes I simply shared some of my concerns. The dance had already started and, to be honest, I wasn't sure what my daughter had decided – I had given her the option of checking out the dance if she desired, trusting her to act on her own convictions. (I learned later that she opted out and sat with a friend in a vacant classroom.)

Before picking up my daughter and going home, I asked if it might be possible to see the playlist for the dance. The obliging principal left for a few minutes and then reemerged into the office with three pages of songs in hand. I quickly scanned the list and was not at all surprised to see most of the same songs I had given to the teens at church, many of them very explicit lyrically, to say nothing of the videos that would accompany them. (At the time I remember seeing artists like Nelly Furtado, Pink, and the Pussycat Dolls on the list.) "Have you actually watched any of these videos?" I asked. He shook his head. "You may want to do that sometime. I think you may be sending a mixed message to your students."

The students, of course, have common standards in our middle schools, such as no profanity on t-shirts, no belly tops, etc. Such things might have a negative impact on students. Meanwhile, artists like Iggy Azalea and Nicki Minaj are afforded the privilege of giving our young girls their first sexual education – like how to entice men to lust and how to use sex to gain an advantage over people. (Don't get me started on what they're teaching the boys!) As I left the school I knew that I needed to vent a little.

When I got home I headed straight to my computer and whipped off an e-mail that I sent to the local newspaper. I didn't mention the fact that I was a pastor or even a Christian; to me, this seemed like something every parent should be concerned about, regardless of religious conviction. I was surprised to receive a response back within the hour from the editor, who said she agreed with me. She promised to publish the article.

A week and half passed before the article appeared. Besides reworking the title to include the word "smut" (which wasn't in my title) the editor printed my article exactly as I sent it. In my previous city the local newspaper was merely a container for a weighty wad of retail flyers, so I didn't expect to create much buzz, but when I arrived at the hockey arena the next day for my son's game I quickly learned different. Apparently everyone in my neighborhood reads the paper, and within minutes half a dozen hockey parents came up to me and said, "I read your article!" (Most of the parents already know I'm a pastor, but seem to have forgiven me for it by now.)

Everyone was polite, but I'm sure a few of the parents thought my article was over the top. As I mingled with more of the parents, however, I began to see that many of them were genuinely pleased that I had written the piece. (I deal with people a lot, so I have a pretty good sense of when people are being genuine.) One dad attested to turning off a video he had rented not too long ago for his kid's birthday party. Another mom wrote me an e-mail after the game thanking me for the article.

Sex is one of those areas that highlights the inconsistency of humanist philosophy. People who take any sort of a stand against sexual immorality (whatever that is!) are, by today's standards hopelessly uptight, unadventurous, and backward. We are jittery nerds who deserve to be ridiculed and laughed at. That's the message that TV and the media consistently broadcast, and people believe it – that is, until it comes to the boundaries they set for their own children. Then, dweebs like me aren't so bad. Sure, on rare occasions parents dive headfirst into helping their children cast off sexual restraint, but most love their kids enough to want to protect them from the many dangers connected to sex.

The Bible is very consistent on the boundaries that it sets for sexual practice and relationships. God designed sex to be enjoyed by a man and a woman inside a committed, marital relationship. In fact, one of the books of the Bible, the Song of Solomon, is an ancient love poem so steamy that age restrictions have traditionally been placed upon Jews who read it. The book is a passionate and erotic celebration of love. (Granted, the metaphors used don't always translate well to the modern reader, but a little imagination goes a long way.)

Some people are surprised to learn how positive the Bible is about sex, having only ever been told that the Bible condemns it at every turn. For people like myself who have grown up believing that God is loving and therefore likes to treat his creation to good things, it is no surprise at all. And while my humanness drives me to crave all the same off-limits sexual pleasure as anyone else, my conviction of God's love motivates me to live within the boundaries that he sets for sex in the Bible.

Consider the sex-related harm that grows as our society continues to abandon committed married relationships: There's the obvious increased risk of STD's, which can cause everything from constant discomfort and shame to terminal HIV/AIDS. There is the ever-present risk of unwanted pregnancy, which then often leads to the physical and emotional scars of abortion or the greatly increased odds of single parenthood and the emotional and financial strain that goes along with it. Of course, there is the emotional pain that always accompanies the breakup of people who have been sexually active together, whether inside or outside of marriage. Then there is the undermining of true intimacy, as people are taught that sex exists in a vacuum where there are no moral consequences. And finally, and perhaps most devastatingly, there's the exploitation and repression of women.[13.6] (It doesn't take a lot of observation to discover how powerful the pull is on women to measure up and be noticed. Because of this pervasive culture of exploitation, girls as young as 9 or 10 are already trapped in image obsession.)

Over and above these ills are the problems of sexual deviance, child pornography and exploitation, and even sexual violence. Some people have correctly argued that not all pornography leads to sexual violence, but the causal relationship between the two is undeniable. Show me a pedophile or a rapist who has never fallen headlong into porn and I'll promptly rethink my position.

The crazy thing about all of this is that we are more than capable of changing things. We have the ability to curb the sexual permissiveness of our day; we simply refuse to do it. We have a variety of educational

UNAPOLOGETIX

systems at our disposal. Either we all secretly enjoy the sexual permissiveness we've come to know or we just don't have the stomach to try to corral a horse that has long left the barn. Maybe it's a combination of both.

We continue to allow companies to peddle sexually suggestive dolls to our little girls; we continue to ingest sexually overt movies and television, even shows that glorify promiscuity and unfaithfulness. (Just try renting a comedy today that is not filled with extreme sexual lewdness.) We continue to listen to sexually charged music and watch almost pornographic music videos. Most parents are completely oblivious to the explicit lyrics that their kids are ingesting on a daily basis.

It's not like the kids are working hard to hide anything like they did a generation ago. They don't need to. Explicit sexuality has gone mainstream to the point that nobody even blinks an eye. It is commonplace to hear songs like *Whistle* by Flo Rida playing on the loudspeaker at the mall or in the warm-up of my 10-year old son's hockey game. Check out the lyics:

> *Can you blow my whistle baby, whistle baby*
> *Let me know*
> *Girl I'm gonna show you how to do it*
> *And we start real slow*
> *You just put your lips together*
> *And you come real close*
> *Can you blow my whistle baby, whistle baby*
> *Here we go*

That's right. It's a song about giving a blowjob. Parents who stop long enough to listen to what is being said may be shocked, but this is tame compared to what young people have been listening to for years in the privacy of their ever-inserted earbuds. Iggy Azalea was already singing about her genitalia back in 2011. Ask your kids about it and they'll shrug and say that practically all of today's artists use sexually explicit language. Canada's own Drake released his newest album in 2015 entitled *If You're Reading This It's Too Late*. Every song on the album has been tagged as explicit. Seventeen out of seventeen. Maybe Drake's right – if you're reading this it *is* already too late!

Understand that I'm not suggesting that it's never acceptable for adults to listen to lyrics of a sexual nature; if the music is being used to draw committed partners closer to one another it could be very healthy. I'm talking here about kids who have nothing to gain from becoming sexually stimulated at such a young age. Yet we continue not only to permit them listen to such music, we go so far as encouraging them to dance to it, complete with graphic videos. We won't allow them to wear belly tops or low-cut shirts in our schools, yet our same schools will corral them into a gym at 11 years old and expose them to singing strippers.

Is it any wonder our society has lost all stigma against strip clubs and the like? (In fact, we call them *gentlemen's* clubs. Was I the only one who was taught that gentlemen were something different?) At the risk of sounding like a not-so-old prude, where I grew up, men who ogled naked women were called *pigs*. Don't get me wrong – in my fallen nature I love ogling naked women too. I'm an oinker at heart. I just know that ogling anyone other than my wife would be less than noble; it would tear the fabric of my marriage, as well as set an incredibly poor example for my children. No one hopes that their daughter will become a stripper, myself included. So why would I make a habit of ogling someone else's daughter?

How, you may ask, does all of this discussion on sexuality somehow contribute to my faith? Well, our society's response to sexuality confirms what the Bible has said all along: that we humans value our own pleasure above everything else. Although our hearts and minds know that our desires are evil, we are helplessly controlled by the flesh.

Those who live according to the flesh have their minds set on what the flesh desires; but those who live in accordance with the Spirit have their minds set on what the Spirit desires. The mind governed by the flesh is death, but the mind governed by the Spirit is life and peace. The mind governed by the flesh is hostile to God; it does not submit to God's law, nor can it do so. Those who are in the realm of the flesh cannot please God (Romans 8:5-8).

Our culture of sexuality shows just how depraved we really are, to sacrifice our own physical and mental health and even the well-being of our own children for the sake of our temporary pleasure. Every morning radio hosts across the continent tee-hee to the newest sexual stupidities while they and their own children are being destroyed by them. (One popular radio station here in Toronto has been known to do a morning snippet called "Bad Boyfriend Poker" where contestants try to one-up their opponents with stories that take sexual shamelessness to a new low.)

If the entertainment industry would at least be honest about sexuality. It continues to peddle a consequence-free illusion of sex. No guilt over engaging in illicit behavior. No emotional turmoil over one-night stands. No STD's. Virgins enjoying intercourse without a hitch on their first try. No harm in short-circuiting true intimacy. No sexual addiction. (In fact, porn is a regular punch line on sitcoms.) And even though Hollywood hypocritically promotes "safe sex," when was the last time a movie even alluded to new sexual partners making use of a condom? It's pretty rare.

Sure, people of faith are hypocritical too. The percentage of Christian men who are addicted to porn is no less than the percentage of non-Christian men who suffer the same scourge. The results of sexual deviance and damage are as prevalent in the church pew as they are in the grocery store or the movie theater. Many times those who are the most outspoken about the problems of non-Biblical sexual activity are the ones who have the biggest personal problems with it. Witness the number of high-profile failures by pastors in megachurches over the last 20 years.

Our failures start early. Every year thousands of Christian teens across North America promise to remain chaste until marriage, often failing within months. But I do applaud the fact that they even dare to try swimming against the current; they certainly aren't getting a whole lot of support. School-board leaders are afraid to even teach abstinence, even though for centuries it was taught and largely adhered to (and continues to be adhered to in many countries of the world). Deferring sexual activity until marriage is far from impossible to achieve, as spoken by one who fought hard to reserve sex for marriage and somehow succeeded. (Oink, oink.)

Whether people succeed at maintaining Biblical sexual boundaries or not, my hat goes off to everyone who isn't simply following the herd when it comes to today's sexual attitudes. I believe they will reap great rewards for it.

Can I share what I really think about sex? I believe that sex is one of God's greatest gifts. It leaves me in awe of him, of his creativity, and of his love. It is powerful, dangerous, exciting and fun. If nothing else in the world could convince a person of God, surely a good, guilt-free orgasm could.[13.7]

> *If nothing else in the world could convince a person of God, surely a good, guilt-free orgasm could.*

I also believe that the forces that wage war against the human soul are passionate in their attempt to ruin this gift. As the world teaches people to engage in sex outside of God's loving parameters, sex loses its luster. In many cases it becomes a source of guilt, hurt, emotional turmoil and resentment. Some use it as a weapon, even destroying people's lives with it. Instead of praising God for this most awesome invention, we are often left hurt and confused by it.

I'll be the first to admit that Christians are sometimes ridiculously cautious about sex – even more cautious than the Bible typically depicts or even prescribes. For some reason, it has become the church's biggest pet sin, and I do not share the paranoia that Christians in general hold in regard to it. But by the same token, today's society is undeniably over-the-top in its sexual permissiveness. It doesn't sit right with me.

THE PURSUIT OF HAPPINESS

Before we examine this most American of statements, let me first say that I have many friends from the U.S., lived there for a number of years, completed my schooling there, vacation there every year, and am now the Executive Director of a fellowship of churches from the United States. If I didn't feel called to where I am in Toronto, I'd move to Southern California in a heartbeat and promptly learn how to surf. So for me to feel I have the right to complain about America in any way must make me a real jerk to Americans who are reading this. Touché. More than anything I just like to joust with people, and I've found no collective group any better for satiating this fixation of mine.

One thing I really like about Americans is that they stay true to their beliefs. Is there any other nation in the history of the world that was founded and continues to run in keeping with such clearly thought-out ideals? While I believe that American ideals like democracy and capitalism have their limitations, American determination to stay unified around these and other beliefs has made the United States the most prosperous nation on earth.

One ideal that has shaped the American landscape is the "pursuit of happiness." Enshrined in the Constitution, this ideal is the heart of the American dream. If you've studied any American history at all, you know that the founding fathers included these words to protect the freedom of everyday people from the intrusion of other selfish people, especially people in government, who might impinge on the freedom of citizens to enjoy certain basic pleasures in life.

I'm doubtful that the founding fathers ever imagined that these words would become a mantra for a generation of people who have made life all about self-indulgence – an endless clawing and grasping to get more, to be better positioned, to have a leg up on one's neighbour. (I'm trying to picture Thomas Jefferson watching *My Super Sweet 16*.) Many Canadians, and people from nations around the world, sneer at Americans, all the while trying to imitate them. This idea of the pursuit of happiness is a prime example of why these countries mirror American culture. The American dream has become the dream of the entire first world, the same strata of the world that is supposed to be so "enlightened."

The determination of people everywhere to secure their own happiness is a huge confirmation of the truth of the Bible and it reinforces my belief in God. Why? Because it confirms that our hearts are tainted with selfishness. So selfish are we, in fact, that when we do give a tiny bit of what we have to charities or third-world causes, we generally do so with the primary motivation of making *ourselves* feel better. Charities today know this too well, and sadly, most have succumbed to fundraising efforts that play into people's innate selfishness. Most funds raised today for charities are raised through lotteries that present the donors with an opportunity to win something in return for their "generosity." As a pragmatist, I can appreciate the expediency of this approach, but I can't help feeling sad about it somewhere inside. Isn't generosity its own reward?

> **The determination of people everywhere to secure their own happiness is a huge confirmation of the truth of the Bible and it reinforces my belief in God.**

Abraham Maslow was a leading American psychologist of the 20th Century. The son of Jewish immigrants from Russia, Maslow became most recognized for his examination and analysis of the human *Hierarchy of Needs*. According to Maslow, people had five levels of needs, starting from basic, essential needs and moving up the pyramid to "self- actualization" – Maslow's term for every human's instinctive need to make the most of their abilities and to strive to be the best person they can be.

In his extensive study, Maslow identified numerous factors that played into a person becoming "self-actualized" (*ergo*, fulfilled). His findings are uncannily consistent with the teachings of Jesus and other great moralists:

> "The only happy people I know are the ones who are working well at something they consider important. Also, I have pointed out in my lecture and in my previous writings that this was universal truth for all my self-actualizing subjects…expressed in their devotion to, dedication to, and identification with some great and important job. This was true for every single case."[13.8]

Jesus also clarified that true happiness was not found in trying to please oneself. He described happiness as more of a by-product, something that people happen across only after they have given of themselves to a greater cause, such as showing love or generosity to others. Happiness is not achieved through self-absorption; in fact, self-absorption ultimately leads only to misery. As songwriter Sarah McLachlan says, "Happiness is like a cloud: if you stare at it long enough, it evaporates."

Despite Maslow's research and the undeniable truth that resonates from it, our world still resists it: we are intent on selfishly pursuing happiness as opposed to letting it come to us after we give of ourselves. We neglect relationships as we work harder and harder to buy bigger homes and fancier cars. We stash away money so we can maximize our retirement, but keep enough on hand to visit resorts with names like *Hedonism*. The greatest voices in our day sing the same old song: *If it feels good, do it. If it makes you happy. As long as it doesn't hurt anybody.* This philosophy is bogus, and we all know it.

> *Not so with you. Instead, whoever wants to become great among you must be your servant, and whoever wants to be first must be slave of all.* (Mark 10:43-44).

> *Then Jesus said to his disciples, "Whoever wants to be my disciple must deny themselves and take up their cross and follow me. For whoever wants to save their life will lose it, but whoever loses their life for me will find it. What good will it be for someone to gain the whole world, yet forfeit their soul? Or what can anyone give in exchange for their soul?"* (Matthew 16:24-26).

The words of our culture are tempting, but the words of Jesus are penetrating. Not all truth that resonates within us plays in a major key. Some truth is very sorrowful, because within it is the realization that we must change our minds and our actions.

Down deep we all know that there is much more to life than finding pleasure for ourselves. I firmly believe that God loves and wants his people to be happy and to enjoy the life he gives to us, but not as an ultimate pursuit. *Goodness* is meant to be pursued, even when it costs a disproportionate amount.

Our hearts leap at stories of great sacrifice. We hear of people laying down their very lives for the love of others and a dormant fault line in our soul shifts, sending shock waves to the surface. In those moments we are challenged to be something greater than we are, and we are terrified by the prospects of what we could be. Without anyone ever telling us, we know that true happiness is found within such sacrifice.

Couples who fight to keep their marriages alive find true joy. The mother who loses her freedom in order to raise a disabled child discovers true joy. The businessman who sacrifices lucrative promotions in order to be available for his family discovers true joy. The person who withstands abuse and criticism to fight for what is right knows true joy.

Blessed are those who mourn, for they will be comforted (Matthew 5:4).

Very truly I tell you, unless a kernel of wheat falls to the ground and dies, it remains only a single seed. But if it dies, it produces many seeds (John 12:24).

Many people embrace Jesus for the eternal life he offers. Others follow him for his morality. While I embrace him for both of these, I am happy to say that I largely embrace Jesus because he clearly knew and taught about what brings true happiness. I want to be happy. I may not always like what Jesus taught about true happiness; I may not like what it takes, or find the courage to act upon the truth Jesus taught. But in the times when I find that courage, I know in my gut that Jesus was exactly right.

MATERIALISM

I love Restoration Hardware.

I'll never forget the first time I happened across one of their stores in Alexandria, Virginia. I didn't know stores like that existed outside of my dreams. I've always had a fascination for old furniture and architecture – the stuff from the 50's, when a leather armchair was actually made from leather and when a dresser was made from solid hardwood.

That first day I walked into the store was a surreal experience. One of my dreams has always been to have a gentleman's study, complete with towering bookcases, hardwood floors and classic lamps. I've fantasized about having an enormous desk and a deep leather armchair in one corner where I can put my feet up and read a good book. Restoration Hardware had everything I had ever pictured and more, right down to the authentic hardware knobs and fixtures, which I've learned were the company's initial bailiwick.

When we moved into our current home in 2005, I was excited that we had set aside a ground-level room, albeit a small one, on the front of the house to be my office. Despite its small size it had a 13-foot ceiling, enormous windows and floors made of rich Brazilian cherry. I soon got a friend to help me (OK, I helped him) build in a bookcase that stretched up to the ceiling. I even found a retro schoolhouse pendant light to hang from the center of the room. (It looks *sweet*.) They had one in the Restoration Hardware catalog, but to be honest, I can never afford anything from Restoration Hardware; I just look there for ideas. I was elated to find an exact replica at half the price somewhere else. (Although, come to think of it, I did buy the paint from Restoration Hardware.: Silver Sage. Very cool.)

I was making pretty good progress on my dream office until I ran out of money. I was at the part of the dream where I put in the desk and the armchair. Only problem is, this part of the dream is a little pricier, so I'm making do with an old IKEA table and a Poang chair. Yes, it's painful. The worst thing is, there's no real target date in sight at which I think I'll be able to procure these items. I guess I would say my dream has stalled.

I think I'm old enough to realize that I'll always have unfinished dreams like this one. You know how it works. You obsess over that one thing you want until the day you finally get it. You no sooner get it and your mind – without any effort of your own – immediately latches on to some new thing that you now "need." It's an endless cycle.

As humans we've always been drawn to desire material things. We're material girls (and guys), living in a material world. The challenge is that the Bible states that we are predominantly spiritual beings, and that the greatest reality of all is spiritual. This is a difficult pill to swallow for everyone.

Our society's attitudes toward materialism are much like our attitudes toward sexuality. Although we see the vanity of these selfish pursuits, we just can't bring ourselves to renounce our obsessions. We know that true happiness is not to be found in satisfying our cravings, but we continue to suspend our disbelief long enough to buy the next thing on our list. Indeed, materialism is a treadmill that consumes our time, energy and finances so that these resources are no longer available for nobler purposes.

> **We know that true happiness is not to be found in satisfying our cravings, but we continue to suspend our disbelief long enough to buy the next thing on our list.**

Unlike some religions, biblical Christianity does not go to the other extreme of asceticism. While Jesus was known to have no home or possessions of his own, the heart of his teaching on materialism was not that we renounce all earthly acquisitions,[13.9] but rather that we keep the most important things (i.e. his "kingdom") as our top priority.

> *So do not worry, saying, 'What shall we eat?' or 'What shall we drink?' or 'What shall we wear?' For the pagans run after all these things, and your heavenly Father knows that you need them. But seek first his kingdom and his righteousness, and all these things will be given to you as well* (Matthew 6:31-33).

Jesus knows there are many things to enjoy in life. One could argue that Jesus was only referring to our basic needs when he said "all these things will be given to you as well," but just previous to these words he reminded his audience that even Solomon wasn't dressed like one of the lilies of the field that God had formed. Acknowledging the extravagance God built into his creation, Jesus wasn't against beauty or luxury. In fact, many incredibly wealthy people in the Bible were said to be friends of God.

The Apostle Paul understood this as well. At one point in his ministry he challenged a young pastor named Timothy to help people gain the proper perspective on material wealth:

> *Command those who are rich in this present world not to be arrogant nor to put their hope in wealth, which is so uncertain, but to put their hope in God, who richly provides us with everything for our enjoyment* (1 Timothy 6:17).

God wants us to enjoy life, but he prefers that we find that enjoyment as we pursue the things that are important to him.

So far, I have used the word "materialism" in one specific sense: that of acquiring possessions. It is important to understand, however, that our present struggles with materialism stem from the greater philosophical definition of materialism – the theory that states that only physical matter is ultimately real and valuable. This line of thinking also suggests that all non-material entities, such as emotion and reason, are merely functions of the physical, and cease to exist outside of their material housings. With the rise of the scientific era, mankind's view of the world has become more and more *materialistic*, in this broader philosophical context.

I believe that this improper perspective on material things is to blame for our distorted view on happiness, as discussed earlier. Novelist John

Updike put it perfectly: "When we try in good faith to believe in materialism, in the exclusive reality of the physical, we are asking our selves to step aside; we are disavowing the very realm where we exist and where all things precious are kept – the realm of emotion and conscience, of memory and intention and sensation." (*Self-Consciousness: Memoirs*)

And yet, the material world is where we find ourselves. We really believe that the most important things in life are physical looks and possessions. We live for the moment because we have grown to believe, consciously nor otherwise, that life really does end with the death of the physical body or that whatever life might exist after death can't compete with the present.

Because life after death cannot be experienced with our physical senses, concepts such as heaven have largely lost their appeal. We're simply too distracted with the physical world to see beyond it. The paradox with materialism, however, is that we embrace it in an attempt to gain *happiness* for ourselves – and happiness is a *non-material* entity! This inconsistency draws attention back to the fact that our greatest needs and desires are not physical at all, and that we will be better off investigating non-material solutions for the enjoyment of life. It's not like we haven't been warned:

> *Then he said to them, "Watch out! Be on your guard against all kinds of greed; life does not consist in an abundance of possessions"* (Jesus, Luke 12:15).

While the Bible doesn't condemn our possession of material things, it consistently asserts that genuine enjoyment of life stems from things unrelated to the material world – love, friendship, forgiveness, sacrifice, and so on. In keeping with this unpopular philosophy, the Apostle John warned us not to become too attached to the world.

Do not love the world or anything in the world. If anyone loves the world, love for the Father is not in them. For everything in the world—the lust of the flesh, the lust of the eyes, and the pride of life—comes not from the Father but from the world. The world and its desires pass away, but whoever does the will of God lives forever (1 John 2:15-17).

The Bible's teaching turns materialism on its head. It is not the physical world that is most real and enduring, but rather, God's will and those who embrace the implementation of it.

As a physical, human being, I struggle with materialism as much as anyone. I like nice things. I like to look good. I go to the gym. I resent having to be seen driving a minivan. (Doesn't every guy?) I obsess over things I want and get all frustrated inside because I have to wait. It's just like the Apostle James states in James 4:1-2:

What causes fights and quarrels among you? Don't they come from your desires that battle within you? You desire but do not have, so you kill. You covet but you cannot get what you want, so you quarrel and fight. You do not have because you do not ask God.

As much as I struggle to align my life with the Bible's teaching, I acknowledge its truth, and it helps me temper my materialistic cravings in favor of nobler pursuits. When my church decides that it wants to raise money for a ministry center that will help families in our community with their marriages, parenting skills and financial management, I am willing to wait on buying a killer desk and armchair. In fact, I can do it with a smile on my face. And because of my non-material view of life – this conviction that life carries on beyond the physical – I can live in peace even if most of my material cravings never get satisfied.

This is a powerful way of thinking, and it makes me embrace Jesus and his teaching in favor of the materialistic messages of the world.[13.10]

HUMANS ARE BASICALLY GOOD

If you had grown up in the same circles as I did, you would have lost hope in this philosophical presupposition by age 5. In our earliest Sunday school classes we were taught about Adam & Eve, the fall of mankind, and the depravity of human beings. We knew that we were "steeped in sin" from birth. Some teachers went so far as to say that people are so depraved that we are *incapable* of doing good, save by the intervention of God himself.

The arguments used to defend this premise were convincing. For example, *you don't need to teach an infant to do wrong.* I have four kids of my own, and I have to admit, I never had to teach any of them to lie, take toys from their siblings, or fight. Jean-Jacques Rousseau insisted that people are born good and that society corrupts them, but those of us who raise children of our own see the corruption long before society gets a kick at the can.

Furthermore, stories like William Golding's *Lord of the Flies*, while fictional, convince us further that something more internal than society is responsible for the corruption of human beings.[13.11] As German actor Klaus Kinski once said, "One should judge a man mainly from his depravities. Virtues can be faked. Depravities are real." In light of this evidence, I am amazed at how many people today, parents included, hold onto the idea that people are innately good.

Persisting in their belief that humans are basically good, many parents have downplayed the necessity of boundaries. Some go so far as to say that a child left on her own will stand the best chance of becoming an upright and respectable adult. (After teaching many parenting classes over the years, I have discovered that most parents change their tune by Suzy's second birthday and start looking for help in setting boundaries.) All this being said, most people are still resistant to call mankind "depraved." On the contrary, we celebrate the good in people and even spend millions of dollars each year trying to rehabilitate the worst of our offenders, which I agree, seems like the right thing to do. North American society is confused over this issue.

Let me briefly share what the Bible says about this subject. You may be happy to learn that I am a little more positive than were some of my Sunday School teachers. While I agree that mankind has fallen into sin, I see sin as an illness. The Bible describes it as such: passed down from Adam and Eve, we are born with it coursing through our bloodstream, and we will inevitably pass it along to our children as well. This explains mankind's greatest evils right down to the unkind actions of our toddlers.

But according to the Bible, while sinfulness is our strongest nature, it is not our *first* nature. The book of Genesis says that we were created good: in fact, we were created in God's very image. While the fall of mankind corrupted the human race, I am happy to say that God recognized that the human race was not a lost cause. In fact, he demonstrated his belief that we were worth redeeming by sending Jesus to do just that. Instead of letting justice fall upon us, Jesus took our punishment and showed us how to give control of ourselves over to God – difficult as this may be. Jesus taught us how people could receive spiritual rebirth, the awakening of a new spiritual nature that would tap into the original goodness with which God made us. And while our sinful nature remains with us so long as we retain our physical bodies, our newly awakened divine nature gives us the strength to overcome our evil desires.

The biblical perspective on human goodness is something that makes me a believer. Its explanation makes perfect sense. It explains why people in general still have a capacity for good, even if their selfish desires most often get the better of them. It explains why people everywhere feel good when they do good. It explains why people who truly experience redemption in Christ find much greater success in overcoming their own selfishness.[13,12]

On the flip side, it also explains the necessity of laws and boundaries. (The giving of the Law to Moses was God's recognition of this necessity.) We needed very practical truth not only to understand ourselves better, but also to parent our children better, to create better rules for ourselves, and even to exercise grace toward those who may not seem to deserve it. With God providing the ultimate redemption we all need, it brings me comfort to know that even a man condemned to die who is living on death row can experience redemption if he reaches out to God for it.

The biblical perspective on man's goodness settles centuries of debate among some of the world's greatest philosophers. In a way, most of them were partly right, but the biblical explanation for why a person acts the way they do is by far the best I've seen. It resonates with me. Society's typical understanding that "man is basically good" – not so much.

ALL ROADS LEAD TO GOD

Growing up living in rural Nova Scotia, you had to learn to make your own fun. There just wasn't a lot to do. Our town was the biggest on the entire South Shore, and we still only had a population of about 7000. We did have a bowling alley under the IGA. And we had a roller rink in the early 80's, but that fad only lasted for a few years. I wasn't allowed to go to the arcade; rumor had it that it was the regional drug distribution center. I'm sure that idea was exaggerated.

Either way, my friends and I were a fairly creative bunch, and we had no trouble finding things to do. My buddies Paul and Craig had an AMC Eagle that we and the Boys drove just about everywhere. Best of all, their dad had a tab at a local gas station where Paul or Craig could fill up whenever the tank got low on fuel. Free gas – how sweet is that! We definitely didn't know how good we had it.

It's quite possible that we discovered every major and minor road on the South Shore throughout our teen years. We'd just drive with no destination, listening to Billy Joel, CCR, and the Traveling Wilburys. As we drove, we'd make meaningless conversation about anything and everything. Every once in a while someone would say something that would make us laugh out loud. These statements became keepers that we'd repeat on every subsequent trip. They never failed to make us laugh, and the stories behind them continually expanded like fishermen's tales.

On one trip someone made a very powerful observation. No matter where we went, or how long we drove, before the day was over we always seemed to drive through an intersection in Wileville where a private business named Ritchie Rentals was located.

"All roads lead to Ritchie Rentals," someone chimed. (It was probably Paul, the most creative of the Boys.)

"You're right," we agreed. "All roads *do* lead to Ritchie Rentals!"[13.13]

It was an epiphany. From then on, every trip crossed that intersection at some point, evoking a joyful chorus of the now-timeless proverb. We never bothered to consider the fact that Paul, who coined the phrase, was always driving the Eagle or that the intersection was located between Paul and Craig's house and the free gas station.

People like to use the "roads" analogy when discussing the pursuit of God. I guess the thinking is that a "road" is the equivalent of a defined path or a formalized religion that can lead people to God.

This analogy is probably a little silly to begin with for a number of reasons. First of all, just because there are roads doesn't mean they necessarily lead to any one location. (Except Ritchie Rentals, or course.) Secondly,

140

as the Boys and I proved many times, just because there are roads doesn't mean that the people traveling them are trying to get anywhere in particular. (Interesting, another famous proverb of ours was, "You can't get there from here." For some reason this seemed to be a famous South Shore expression that can't be fully appreciated without hearing it in a South Shore accent. I digress.) Finally, what if God doesn't even live on a road?

I'm amused that people will say all roads lead to God. I'm even more amused that some of the same people will adamantly deny the existence of God. Obviously, one can't have it both ways. People who try demonstrate pretty clearly that they are more interested in being free from God's authority than they are in actually pursuing him. That's disappointing to me.

Truth be told, the "all roads" argument really doesn't work in any other area of life. Let's try a few random examples.

- "Every combination of ingredients makes apple pie."
- "The answer to all equations is 3.125."
- "All books are about sex."

On the other hand, we may come up with other statements that seem to defend the "all roads" logic…

- "All combinations of pop in a soda fountain make swamp water."
- "All lines of longitude dissect the North Pole."

In fairness, the first set of questions serves as a better metaphor of the "all roads" argument. The second set of examples all contain a limited number of options that are far too restrictive to apply to the God question. There's a big difference between saying "all roads lead to God" and "the Transcanada Highway intersects Winnipeg."

For the sake of argument, suppose that all roads (defined as religious paths) did lead to God. Even these conditions couldn't assume that the traveler is moving in the right direction. What about people who act in ways that are completely contradictory to a defined "road"? For example, suppose someone in a Christian or Muslim community does everything that's opposed to what a devout Christian or Muslim is supposed to do. Would the path of this person be a legitimate road to God as well?

If all of these roads lead to God, what does that say about God? One must conclude that he is the easiest person in the universe to please. He has no preferences. He cannot be offended. And if he can't be offended, then he can't even be a person. And what if God *is* nothing more than a set of natural laws? Even then the "all roads" logic doesn't work. It would be like saying that all substances can be combined to activate photosynthesis, or that every chemical reaction produces carbon dioxide.

The "all roads" argument ultimately asks, "What must one do to please God?" The response that any religious action will do so simply cannot work. Even humanists, who would replace all religious dogma and control with a generic moral code, couldn't say that all activity (moral or immoral) is favorable or will lead to utopia.

Building on this question of what an "all roads" philosophy says about God, what does it say about the value of heaven if everyone can go there regardless of their actions? A club with no qualifications for membership is no club at all. The whole beauty of heaven is contained in the fact that certain activities will be left

> **A club with no qualifications for membership is no club at all. The whole beauty of heaven is contained in the fact that certain activities will be left outside of its gates.**

outside of its gates. I have even had congregants confide to me that if "so-and-so" will be in heaven someday, they have no interest in going. I don't think these people are ruling out the possibility of the redemption of their offender as much as they are affirming that heaven needs to be a place where certain things are permitted and certain things are restricted.

Then there are Universalists – people who believe that for whatever reason, everyone is okay in God's eyes. In Christian faith, some believe that because Jesus died on the cross to cover human sin, everyone is going to heaven. The Bible certainly teaches that God loves all mankind and that his death was on behalf of all mankind,[13.14] but numerous verses are clear in describing Jesus' sacrifice as a gift that must be received.

Yet to all who did receive him, to those who believed in his name, he gave the right to become children of God— (John 1:12)

According to the New Testament, the possibility is there for everyone to embrace God. Through Jesus, the invitation has been extended for everyone. But salvation is a gift that must be received or embraced.

While "all roads" enthusiasts often frown upon "restrictive" Christian dogma, the Bible's firm position on this matter wins my mind over to true Christian faith. I concur wholeheartedly that all of life's events provoke thoughts about God. I also believe that all of nature around us leads us toward faith in God.[13.15] But Jesus was very clear about there being only one path to God. And he didn't balk at stating that it was narrow and difficult to find.

Jesus answered, "I am the way and the truth and the life. No one comes to the Father except through me" (John 14:6).

Enter through the narrow gate. For wide is the gate and broad is the road that leads to destruction, and many enter through it. But small is the gate and narrow the road that leads to life, and only a few find it (Matthew 7:13-14).

That sort of contradicts the "all roads" argument, eh? I can empathize with the frustration that a non-Christian might experience in hearing that Jesus said this. But that doesn't change the fact that it makes perfect sense. You may not like the path Jesus described, but all roads simply *can't* lead to God. It's a bogus philosophy. Even though I ultimately disagree with non-Christian faiths, I have more respect for their adherents than I do for the "all roads" crowd. If you don't believe your faith is exclusively right, why adhere to it at all? Faith is about substance, not just flavor.

INDIVIDUALISM

A few of my closest friends growing up were Trekkies. With all of the things we had in common, this fascination was simply something I never got. Every Saturday afternoon when normal boys should have been playing ball hockey, these guys were holed up in their basement watching the adventures of the crew on the Starship Enterprise. (Sorry, boys, that was cold.) I was never taken with science fiction to begin with, but even if I was, I'm sure that the silliness of Captain Kirk and Spock in their tights running around in their plastic starship would have done me in.

My memory is admittedly horrific, so I'll concede that the storylines may have been better than I remember. I may have simply been distracted by the aesthetics. I say this because when the producers of Star Trek spent a little more money to make their movies for the big screen, I actually enjoyed them. (Let's keep this our little secret.)

To be honest, I was genuinely moved by one scene from Start Trek II: *The Wrath of Khan*. With a bit of surfing I discovered that it is considered one of the most memorable scenes of all time by Star Trek fans. I am referring, of course, to the death of Spock. The scene picks up when Spock, who has just saved the ship, is dying (and in fact must die in order for the others on the ship to survive). In an emotional final exchange with Captain Kirk, Spock revisits a truth shared earlier in the movie.

Kirk: Spock.

Spock: Ship... out of danger?

Kirk: Yes.

Spock: Don't grieve, Admiral. It is logical. The needs of the many outweigh...

Kirk: ...the needs of the few.

Spock: ...Or the one. I never took the Kobayashi Maru test until now. What do you think of my solution?

Kirk: Spock...

Spock: I have been and always shall be your friend.
[*Holds up his hand in the Vulcan salute*]

Spock: Live long and prosper.

"The needs of the many outweigh the needs of the few, or the one." [13,16] (Leonard Nimoy's authoritative tone still rings in my head.) In a messianic scene for the ages, Spock slumps and the impetuous Captain Kirk is suddenly alone in the universe without his invaluable alter-ego.

Funny I should make use of this illustration on individualism in a book dedicated to intuitive thinking. Spock is, of course, the epitome of *logic*, not intuition or emotion. (In fact, the entire history of Star Trek could be summarized as the interplay between logic and emotion, as personified by the ice-veined Spock and the passionate Captain

Kirk. In fact, the day my Trekkie friends informed me of this reality my perspective on the show improved greatly. I could suddenly relate to Captain Kirk. [13.17]

I love this scene because it contains undeniable truth – truth that resonates. The needs of the many do outweigh the needs of the few. In a society that champions individualism at every turn, it is a powerful and unexpected message.

Surely you've noticed how strongly group rights are being challenged in recent years in favor of the rights of the individual…

- The rights of a person to play on a sports team comprised of members of the opposite sex.
- The protection of a child in school from effective discipline versus making the entire class suffer because of one child's misbehaviour.
- The professional athlete who renounces any allegiance to teammates or city in order to hold out for a higher salary.
- The parent who files for divorce so that they may pursue the path they desire, while their children and extended family live with the devastation of a broken family, devoid of any say in the matter. [13.18]
- The rights of religious or special-interest groups to maintain their lifestyle, thus requiring the entire population to relinquish their traditions.

Some may see this as a political matter, but I don't. Liberals and conservatives alike have been guilty of disregarding the rights of larger groups, and many of the examples I've cited aren't political at all. Nowadays we are simply focused on the needs of the *one*. As Whitney Houston used to sing so many years ago, "Learning to love yourself is the greatest gift of all." Regardless of where the trend started, preference for the individual seems to be deeply entrenched in the mindset of North Americans.

Our first child, Maggy, was born in December of 1995 in Trois-Rivières, Québec. Upon assisting my ready-to-pop wife to the maternity ward, I couldn't help but notice the posters plastered all over the walls. The pictures were varied, but the slogan was the same on each print: *Le bébé avant tout*. (The baby before everything.) I hoped that the motto was conceived to help delinquent parents take responsibility for their children, but I suspect that the message went deeper. Child-centered parenting, in my opinion, has created a generation of children with unrealistic expectations. My heart goes out to them knowing they will shortly discover that the world does not revolve, and never has revolved, around them.

This society's penchant for the individual is just another confirmation for me that God's ways are better than ours. By no means do I think that any amount of individualism is evil; I just think that society's views are out of balance. God loves individuals, and cares for them deeply. But it is because of this love that he has given us larger groups that also deserve consideration and protection. Families, churches, communities, and even nations are all gifts from God.

As the old saying goes, my rights end where another person's rights begin. For every right we enjoy we have responsibilities. But today few people are willing to take responsibility for their actions. We are a culture of blamers, suing whomever we can for whatever we can. (Do you remember hearing about the Washington D.C. judge who, in May of 2007, sued a drycleaner for $65 million dollars over a pair of pants? When our judges sue like this, you know we're up the creek.)

If we were consistent across the board with our individualism, we would affirm individual responsibility as well, don't you think? The truth is that we are really proponents of selfishness more than individualism. This is what the Bible has said all along.

HUMANS AS THE MEASURE OF ALL THINGS

By now you must be clear on how I feel about humanism, so I won't spend a lot of time harping on this non-resonating philosophy. The statement that humans are the measure of all things is humanism in a nutshell. For anyone who hasn't done much research into humanism, I'd encourage you to read one of the Humanist Manifestoes, the first one dating back to 1933. Do a quick Google search you will find a thorough (though still evolving) statement of the humanist faith.

Humanism basically states that everything that mankind is ever to become in our universe is solely up to us. There is no God. Human problems are of human origin and can be solved by human means, and all human potential for forward progress exists solely in our physical, intellectual and emotional power.

Humanism fails at many points in my mind. First of all, it assumes that we are the most powerful entities in the universe. Yet we know that we were not the originators of the universe or even our planet Earth, so how can we be so sure that we're in control of it?

Many humanists are also evolutionists, who generally confess that the more powerful memes of natural selection and survival of the fittest are truly in control of the universe. In other words, in the grand scheme of things, humans might be the most in control at this very brief point in the timeline of history, but who's to say whether humans, dinosaurs, bacteria, or some new mutated life form will ultimately become the savior of our planet? I find humanists to be presumptuous in their belief that our particular strand of hominids will save the universe. (I wonder if we'd be willing to step aside if another species threatened to surpass us in its evolutionary development?)

If humanists were seeing some real progress on the part of humanity in solving the world's ills, their philosophy would be easier to embrace. Yet century after century passes and we still wrestle with all of the same injustice and inequity. Wars rage on. Selfishness and strife intensify. Hunger and poverty continue to ravage parts of the world, and governments continue to oppress people. What's more, lessons we were supposed to have learned generations ago need to be relearned by emerging generations. Like our own children, these new generations seem doomed to have to learn by trial and error. Humanism is a hopeless scenario, and some humanists are courageous enough to admit it. They simply resort to the claim that human ways and means are the best option we have right now for the betterment of the world.

> *Humanism is a hopeless scenario, and some humanists are courageous enough to admit it.*

I am not so hopeless. I do have great admiration for the human race and for the potential that is latent within humankind. I have seen humans work together to do amazing things to improve life for our fellow beings. For instance, I just recently watched an interview with former President Jimmy Carter and his wife, Rosalynn, who described how the guinea-worm that once ravaged millions of people across the globe has now been all-but eliminated. I was amazed and inspired at how people cooperated together to spare millions from this horrific parasite. So yes, I believe humans can, and do, do good for other humans.

As a theist I believe that God gave humankind the responsibility of stewarding the Earth and made us with the ability to successfully carry out this task. But I am also a believer in the Bible's description of the fall of mankind that has left us intrinsically selfish. Humanism has no satisfying explanation or solution for this obvious dilemma, whereas the Bible proposes that humans can be changed from the inside out through a spiritual transformation that occurs when one embraces Jesus Christ by faith. Jimmy Carter and I concur on this point.

If the Bible is right, mankind will one day arrive at a place where we convince ourselves that we have succeeded at bringing peace to the entire planet. But the peace will be superficial and short-lived. It will take Jesus himself, the very "Prince of Peace," to bring sustained goodwill and serenity to the world. This may seem like some pie-in-the-sky idea to some, but it in light of the human condition as we know it, it resonates with me more than any solution I've ever heard humanists propose.

My greatest conviction of these realities comes from the personal realization of peace I have found through Jesus. I've tried the product and I know it works; Jesus *can* give people peace. This peace is based on voluntary submission to God through love, and until people around the world experience this transformation, I just don't see things dramatically changing.

Humans are not the originators of history, nor are we ultimately in control of it. Every year the sun loses a bit more of its power, and energy within our universe is lost to entropy. The Bible teaches that the earth is wearing out like a piece of clothing, and we see the signs of it all around us. [13.19] To believe we are in control of history is both arrogant and delusional. Our ability to affect history is limited, especially considering our fallen state. When humankind fell, we lit a conflagration too big for us to control. We need to be rescued. We need redemption – personally and globally.

I certainly do not condemn humans for trying to make the most of our existence on planet Earth; I want to work alongside humanists to bring health and happiness to every human being. I believe this was part of Jesus' vision of bringing God's Kingdom to earth. But humanism, despite its popularity, is seriously lacking as a philosophy. I'm not feeling it.

WE ARE ALL GOD

There are lame philosophies, and then there are mutant lame philosophies – combinations of lame philosophies that mutate into beliefs that are totally absurd. The "we are all God" philosophy is one such mutation. It pleases pantheists who believe God is in everything – that God is some sort of presence that is indivisible from the physical world. It pleases humanists (who deem that humans are the measure of all things) but who agree that the best we have to offer is a combination of our collective thought. It pleases naturalists because it removes from consideration the concept of a supernatural God.

The problem is that this theory is just downright absurd. We are not God. We obviously didn't create the world. Although we can now measure the weather with a certain degree of accuracy, we certainly have no control over it, let alone the seasons, or the rotation of the Earth, or the planets, or the stars. When a hurricane or a tsunami hits, we run for cover. One errant asteroid would blow us all away.

Man has proven his inability to solve his own problems. It seems to me that self-management would be something God could handle (if indeed we were God). Instead, we humans hurt and kill one another. (God doesn't hurt or kill himself.)

Man is also immoral. We lie, cheat and steal on a regular basis. This also clashes with every common notion of the divine.

I could go on, but I see no point, really. If your concept of God is someone who has no authority, no power over nature, no supernatural knowledge, and no real morality, then this philosophy's for you.

RELATIVISM

Relativism is a broad subject. For the purpose of this book I am referring mainly to what we call *truth relativism*, with a special emphasis on its impact on ethics. While relativism of this form was a hotter subject a decade ago, it still remains a popular philosophy that underlies a lot of people's thinking.

In a nutshell, relativism it is the philosophical position that all points of view are equally valid and that truth is simply relative to the individual. I can't help but think the popularization of relativism goes hand-in-hand with individualism, seeing as it places the individual at the center of every equation. That proposition throws some red flags up for me right away.

We've all heard the classic knock against relativism – that no one can state that everything is relative, because that statement in itself is an absolute (not relative). Because of the untenable nature of full-blown relativism, you'll be hard pressed to find many people who claim to be true relativists. But a soft version of relativism is popular in our society today, especially with right-brained thinkers in our postmodern era.

For people who balk at authority, relativism is a comfortable fit. It also has a certain panache, as it makes its adherents appear more intellectual and nuanced in their positions than people with black-and-white positions on topics like religion or politics. In many cases I've witnessed, relativists really have thought through a broader range of arguments than the average person and are more fun to debate.

Sad to say, many authority-loving Christians overlook just how important relative context is in the decision-making process. This is a genuine shame, and demonstrates just how deficient many Christians are in their understanding of their own faith. Numerous Bible passages demonstrate the need to evaluate context in deciding what is right and wrong. Jesus surprised many people with some of the judgment calls he made, such as healing people on the Sabbath. The Apostle Paul clearly states in Romans 14 that some issues are right or wrong depending on the individual's reason for doing what they do. And the ancient Ecclesiast said "there is a time for everything, and a season for every activity under heaven" (Ecclesiastes 3:1). In my earlier discussion on grace, I vocalized just how annoyed it makes me that many Christians aren't more nuanced in their beliefs.

At the same time, the existence of grey does not eliminate black and white. If you've played around with the histogram in Adobe Photoshop you know that a good photo has true blacks, true whites, and a full range of color (or grey) in between. Just as the existence of absolutes does not eliminate relatives, neither does the existence of relatives eliminate the absolutes. Certain actions are clearly right or wrong; certain philosophies are clearly true or untrue. And why would we expect it to be any different? Our world has many examples of natural absolutes, mathematical absolutes, factual and historical absolutes, as well as moral absolutes.

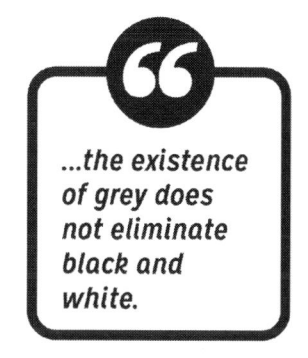

> ...the existence of grey does not eliminate black and white.

Telling enough, most of today's soft relativists will only ever argue about moral absolutes, an indication that they are more interested in casting off moral restraint than they are true adherents to an overarching philosophy. For example, I don't hear them arguing against the law of gravity, the value of pi, or the location of the pyramids. Those who try soon fall off into worthless disputes such as "everything is a dream," in which case we're all wasting our time to discuss anything at all. A few will go so far to defend their moral self-determination.

All of this discussion is intended simply to demonstrate that there is objective truth shared by everyone in the known universe, and that this truth must have a source. A common source, were it provable, could be equated to God.

As the cultures of the world continue to converge, I believe that the moral absolutes will become clearer, and will affirm the fundamental moral laws that from ancient times were said to have come from God. Mankind will no doubt repackage these moral absolutes and separate them from any divine authority, lest we be left accountable to anything or anyone greater than ourselves. I see this motivation as the real issue, which will long outlive the fad of relativism.

The truth is (and I state this absolutely), no one really wants to live in a truly relativistic world anyway. Either life would be perpetual frustration and chaos or nothing would matter whatsoever. Unless one lives in a cave, one must realize that one person's relative philosophy will inevitably clash against another person's relativism. This is hardly a recipe for a peaceful coexistence.

Once again, I like the Bible's treatment of epistemology. It provides answers for the material and spiritual, for truth and untruth, rules and exceptions. You may not agree with how the Bible defines reality, but I think you'll agree that total relativism is a problematic belief system. A lame philosophy, I say.

§

So there you have it.

There is no definitive list of anti-Christian philosophies. In fact, Christians may well disagree with some of my opinions here. My goal has simply been to highlight certain popular mentalities and make you consider what you really believe about some of life's fundamental questions.

The more I challenge people in this line of thinking, the more I discover just how few people have really landed the plane on some of their most basic beliefs. More people than you might guess are honest enough to admit that they have simply allowed the stream of popular opinion to carry them along.

I hope that won't be the case with you. Even if you don't arrive at my same conclusions about the Christian faith, I hope that you will at least examine your beliefs carefully, and then embrace philosophies that not only make logical sense, but resonate with you as well.

Chapter 14

THE ARGUMENTS AGAINST FAITH AREN'T AS STRONG AS YOU'VE BEEN TOLD

Squidward: "I have a theory, people talk loud when they wanna act smart, right?"
Plankton: "CORRECT!!"

–SpongeBob SquarePants, Season 2, Episode 14

"The Christian ideal has not been tried and found wanting; it has been found difficult and left untried."

–G. K. Chesterton

I don't think that most people are out to attack faith or people of faith. To be honest, I see the decline of faith to be inversely proportional to the rise of the scientific era and the popularity of materialistic philosophy. This isn't because science and faith are necessarily opposed; rather, it is because science is a concrete practice that appeals to physical beings much more than faith does. According to a fun book I recently read called *Made to Stick*, brothers Chip and Dan Heath demonstrate that concreteness is one of the six greatest reasons why ideas "stick." Let's face it, physical truth that can be experienced with the five senses is much easier to explain, test and transmit than spiritual truth. This doesn't make physical truth any more "true" than spiritual truth; it just makes it easier to latch on to.

Certainly there are some who, for whatever reason, detest faith and do their utmost to undermine it. But even most of these people, I believe, are well-intentioned. After all, if a person truly believes that the universe is merely physical, that life in it happened by chance and that man alone is responsible for humanity's destiny, I can completely understand why he or she would speak out against faith and do everything to discourage people from believing in God or practicing religion.

Intelligent people agree that for the world to arrive at a place of peace and harmony, we all must come to agree on certain ideas and concepts. Theists believe that everyone should come to agree on God, his nature and on what he has truly communicated to humankind. Atheists believe that physical observation and the scientific method are the only source of objective truth, and use these as their only authority for the collection of that truth. Both groups need to be kind to one another and recognize that their philosophies rest on entirely different foundations.

People have leveled, and continue to level, many criticisms at systems and people of faith. The frequency and intensity of these criticisms seems to have increased in recent years. (Maybe those in the opposing camp also feel that criticism has increased against *them*.) From my vantage point, I think that many people have become jaded at the political agendas and hypocrisy of the world religions and people of faith that they witness in the news. Some appear to be downright unjust, hateful and violent, so I can understand why people react so strongly.

The danger with reaction, however, is that it clouds clear judgment. Opinions become disproportionately formed and constructed solely on emotion, which even a right-brained person like myself has to admit is dangerous.

In this section I want to review a few of the popular criticisms brought against faith communities. Not all of them would apply to all faith groups, but the ones I have listed have been used against Christian faith, of which I am a part.

CREATIONISM IS LAUGHABLE

I've already taken some time to treat this subject, so I'll not go into too much detail here. Creationism has been under attack by atheists in our institutions of learning for many years now. It is no longer taught in most public schools, even at an elementary level, so whatever exposure people get to creationism will be from their place of worship or faith community.

Considering the fact that the majority of North Americans don't even attend church any more (many fewer here in Canada than south of the border), most people are never even given the opportunity to consider the theory in any detail. I'm quite sure that if I had grown up outside of the church, I too would instinctively treat the creation story as on par with Greek mythology or aboriginal folklore. *A deity speaks and light appears. More speaking and the sun and moon and stars appear.* (Wouldn't that be where the light came from?) *Woman is made from a chunk of man's rib.* (Sounds not only ludicrous, but sexist to boot.) *A talking snake. An apple (or some kind of fruit) is the reason for all of mankind's pain and suffering through all of history.*

To be honest, a significant number of Christians have abandoned a literal understanding of the creation story in the past few decades as well. Some assert that the seven "days" of creation are really time periods that are thousands or millions of years in duration. (An approach that simply doesn't work. [14.1]) Others have taken the entire account as allegory. Are they simply caving in to the pressure of their secular peers? Perhaps. My acceptance of the creation story is not so much based on my affection for the story itself as it is in factors unrelated to the details contained in Genesis.

First of all, Jesus made reference to the creation story. He talked about Adam and Eve as factual characters. [14.2] He affirmed God as the Creator. He never once sought to clarify or tidy up the creation story as it was given and subsequently transmitted from generation to generation. In short, from everything we can tell, Jesus was cool with it. As a follower of Christ, I am most of all interested in what Jesus thought and taught, so if Jesus saw no need to redact the creation story, I figure I'd better just as well leave it alone too. Jesus seemed much more concerned about loving God and loving people, and teaching others to do the same, than he was about debating the details of the creation account.

The second major reason why I continue to embrace creationism is that I haven't been presented with a more favorable alternative. The creation narrative, coupled with the subsequent fall and curse, make perfect sense to me. Despite the clarity of them in the biblical narrative, atheists rarely give the effects of the curse any consideration. [14.3] They cite biological flaws and aberrations as proof that God doesn't exist. Genesis is clear that God made everything "good," but that sin's entry into the world has resulted in all of the imperfections. This explanation resonates with me as I try to make sense of the world around me. It agrees with what I observe to be true.

On the other hand, the evolutionary model has utterly failed to inspire me. No one can explain the origin of the gases that combined to create the Big Bang, nor can they explain what circumstances would have caused them to come together. No one can explain how an explosion, unintended by some higher power or intelligence, could ever result in any order whatsoever, let alone the magnificent, infinitely intricate detail of our universe. The whole concept is intellectually insulting and artistically absurd.

The supposed progression of evolution is just as laughable. We can't create even the most basic beginnings of life under the most carefully orchestrated conditions in our laboratories, and yet people firmly believe that life not only arose from non-life, but that it also continued to evolve toward higher species – this in spite of the fact that virtually all mutations are negative to the development or existence of any species. (Consideration of this fact alone would mean that more time is not the *answer*, but rather the *demise* of the evolutionary theory, as I stated earlier.)

Scientists invent the geological column and then use it as the measuring stick for classifying fossils thereafter, a most circular and unscientific approach. They invent missing links (such as coelacanth) and draw up origins charts with all of the creativity of kindergarten children. (Just for fun, ask a preschooler to draw a fish, a human, and then something halfway between. Not much imagination required.)

I do believe in adaptation within a species, or microevolution. But this is something we can actually test and prove to be true, like on Gypsy moths. I have no problem whatsoever with that. This is real science.

I just can't help but think what good the world could experience if all of the scientists who work on the evolutionary theory would put their efforts to solving real matters of science. I will say the same thing of Christians who waste all their time playing mental gymnastics with creation theories and disregard the millions of people who need God's love and care. Every field of study, theology included, is an empty pursuit in and of itself. The way I see it, any study of God or his creation that does not result in more loving attitudes and actions toward others is a waste of time.

I wrote a portion of this book while at my parents-in-law in Cap-de-la-Madeleine, Québec. They have a modest split-level house outside of the town (in St-Louis-de-France). Their house backs onto a large woodlot and has towering maple trees over the backyard deck. In the morning the sun beams down as shadows of maple leaves dance on the wooden deck. The sound of a dozen different birds can be heard along with the shrill cry of the locusts, which announce the day's rising temperature. The humid ferns and moss emit a rich but pleasing odor from the forest floor, just yards away. A great place to write, to be sure.

As a creationist, every sight and sound and smell inspires me to love. I receive every one as a gift from a loving Creator and I'm presented with an immediate opportunity to open my heart up to him. This perspective fills me with a sense of thankfulness and purpose.

I often wonder what goes through the mind of evolutionists on such occasions. Do they feel blessed as I do, or are they just the beneficiaries of dumb luck? Does nature inspire feelings of love, or does it breed frustration at the thought that we will never evolve quickly enough to know anything different from life as we know it? Do evolutionists feel thankful, as I do? If not, my best speculation is that they must have an empty, hopeless feeling inside. Or maybe they just feel indifference.

I suppose it's the difference between finding a $50 bill blowing down the sidewalk versus finding one neatly folded and tucked under your pillow in the morning when you awake. If you had to choose which way you received your $50 bill, which would you choose? (I *so* like being a Creationist.)

My final reason for embracing Creationism is that it seems to make pretty good sense. Once you make the leap toward believing in God, you

> *I suppose it's the difference between finding a $50 bill blowing down the sidewalk versus finding one neatly folded and tucked under your pillow in the morning when you awake. If you had to choose which way you received your $50 bill, which would you choose?*

really don't get hung up on the details of the creation story. If God wanted there to be light prior to making the sun, then he must have had a reason for it. Maybe he simply wanted to establish that he was the natural center of creation and the real life source of our universe, not the sun or any star.

I know naturalists consider my approach to be a cop-out – a circumvention of scientific study and discovery. But their philosophy is simply futile. At some point before we die we all have to take a leap of faith – faith that the things we have chosen to believe in will continue to serve us after this life. I like my chances. I also like that I can get on with enjoying my life now that I have my question answered.

Evolutionists search deep in the earth for fragments of evidence for evolution. But to me, every leaf on every tree and every tiny bug screams purposeful design. I don't have to search for God; evidence of him is alive; it surrounds me and invades my senses continually.

Creationism is as good and palatable an origins theory as you will ever hear, and no one should feel ashamed to embrace it. I really don't have any more to say about that.

HELL

Of all the issues people raise against Christian faith, hell is close to the top of the list. As Homer Simpson once said, *I'm not a bad guy! I work hard, and I love my kids. So why should I spend half my Sunday hearing about how I'm going to hell?* The concept that God would condemn anyone to eternal, conscious punishment in a pit of fire for all eternity is just too much for many people to absorb or believe. As a result, many people believe that God is a cosmic ogre, vengeful beyond imagination. But in actual fact, most

...most people have never really studied what the Bible says about hell; they're going instead on what they've been told by others...

people have never really studied what the Bible says about hell; they're going instead on what they've been told by others, including religious leaders who desire to control their actions with this most dreaded doctrine.

The Bible clearly teaches that hell does exist, and that God made it. But that he made it for the devil and his angels.[14.4] This is not to say that no human beings will end up there. Jesus, even in all his graciousness, made it clear that hell is a possibility for any of us and that we need to guard our souls. In Luke 16, Jesus spoke of a rich man who was in hell. Some argue that he was speaking figuratively here, but usually Jesus clarified when he was using a parable. (He didn't in this case.) We know for sure from the book of Revelation that the devil, the beast, the false prophet and the devil's angels will be in hell. Those whose names are not written in the Book of Life will also be thrown into the lake of fire.[14.5]

These images of hell are obviously frightening, and have been used effectively by people throughout the ages to "encourage" people toward right living and faith. But the truth is that our understanding of hell is quite fuzzy. In the Old Testament, hell was *Sheol*, a place of darkness equated with the grave. In the New Testament, Jesus often used the word *Gehenna*, a word derived from a place called the Hinnom Gulch near Jerusalem, a burning garbage dump where the bodies of criminals were also burned. (Jesus was obviously referencing a place that was well known and that he knew would conjure up certain terrifying images and emotions.) The most common word for hell in the New Testament is *Hades*, the equivalent of Sheol in the Old Testament, which by that time had come to be understood to be a place of fire and torment like Gehenna. In Revelation, death and hell (Hades) are dumped into the lake of fire (the place where the devil and his cronies will ultimately find themselves).

The images used in Luke 16 (where Jesus speaks of a rich man and his servant Lazarus) are very powerful, as are the images seen elsewhere, especially the book of Revelation. But we still wrestle with many questions. For example, how could a human body survive literal fire forever without being consumed? Or how can a spiritual body be tormented by physical fire? Then there is Jesus' reference to a place of "outer darkness" that seems to relate to hell – but would a place of fire be dark? (Perhaps if the fire was invisible like the methanol fires resulting from stock car crashes.)

The Bible seems to indicate quite clearly that when our bodies are resurrected they will be fashioned to live eternally, whether in heaven or hell. The thought that God would prepare someone a body for the mere purpose of making it survive eternal torment is unsettling to me; honestly, I have more questions about that.

One thing that most Christians agree on is that hell will be a place of intense regret and deprivation from the goodness of God's presence. (If you believe that everything that is good emanates from God, that belief leaves you with one hellish vacuum.) For me, this is a better starting point for the discussion on hell. I've met many people who ignore God during this life in order to live a life of complete selfishness. They fight and claw and abuse other people in pursuit of their selfish ambitions to the point that their life spirals into a dark pit of self-absorption. Respected pastor and theologian Tim Keller suggests that hell may simply be a continuation of sorts of the path that we chose to follow here on earth. Says Keller, "Hell is the trajectory of a soul, living in self-absorbed, self-centered life, going on and on forever... hell is simply one's freely chosen identity apart from God on a trajectory into infinity." [14.6]

I mentioned in an earlier chapter that I've done a fair bit of research on near-death experiences (NDEs). As I said before, I don't put any factual stock into these stories, but have found them interesting to consider. Some of the accounts of those who claim to have witnessed the other side are very warm and positive, but some are quite the opposite.

In one story I remember reading, the person was taken to what he instantly recognized as being hell. In hell he saw many people, each being tormented by their inability to gain pleasure from the activities that so enamored them here on earth. The images were beyond disturbing. At one point in the Dickensian journey he recalls seeing a horde of people in a massive orgy, their naked bodies clawing at one another, completely tormented at their inability to gain a shred of pleasure from even the most perverse actions. As you can imagine, the NDE witness returned greatly troubled by what he saw. The story left me with chills as well. It graphically illustrates Keller's conception of a self-absorbed life following a specific trajectory into infinity.

Needless to say, the Bible leaves a fair bit of room for the imagination when it comes to hell. And it is significant to note that not all Christians see hell in the same way. Some Christians, particularly Catholics, see hell as having a precursor called "purgatory," a place of purging that gives individuals an opportunity for a second chance. While the biblical support for such a place is inferred at best, Christians of all different stripes agree that hell will include different degrees of punishment. Romans 2:12 asserts that people will be judged in accordance with the truth they were given: "All who sin apart from the law will also perish apart from the law, and all who sin under the law will be judged by the law." Some who accuse God of heartlessly casting into hell people who have never heard of him, may be surprised to learn about this passage in Romans. They may also be surprised by verses that talk about God's propensity for showing grace to people who live in ignorance.[14.7]

Nonetheless, God, in his grace and through his revealed Word, seemed to want to warn us as strongly as possible against this place called hell. I believe he used the most terrifying images that honesty would allow, because he really wanted to spare us from ultimately ending up in this horrific place.

Imagine that there is a busy street just next to your home. You want your child to have freedom to play outside, but you are terribly frightened of what might happen if she were to take your warnings even a little too lightly. A good parent might go into graphic detail of how terrible the result could be so that her daughter could vividly imagine what might happen to her should she venture beyond established boundaries. (Yes, I have used this very technique on all four of my own children.) That's how I see God and his warnings about hell. Out of love he is using the most frightening images honesty will allow to keep us away from danger. His motivation is not fear; rather, it is pure love.

For some reason, God has seen both the need for hell and the need for freedom in our universe. The truth is that no one wants to write off the possibility of heaven, and most people accept the concept of hell – for someone else. I mentioned in an earlier chapter that people want to know that certain people will *not* be in heaven. Most people also agree that there needs to be a place for those who utterly and absolutely reject what is right and good – people like Hitler who unrepentantly die after they commit the worst kinds of offenses. There are others who hate God so vehemently that they do not desire to be with God for eternity. For these folk, a place must also exist where this God of freedom allows their will to be done, a place from which God's infinite presence is in some way withdrawn.

If hell is a philosophical necessity, and I believe it is, we have to arrive at a place where we need to trust God and his ability to judge. The Bible presents God as a fair judge, an all-knowing being whose eyes and ears miss nothing that happens, and whose sense of justice is precisely accurate.

Furthermore, and most importantly, we have already discussed that the way to God is free. Jesus offered it to everyone. We must accept Christ's forgiveness so that we don't need to depend upon our own righteousness on that day when we stand before God. The more we learn about how infinitely good and holy God is and the more we learn about the lengths he took to sacrifice his Son, the more we are able to fathom the justice of a place like hell.

I empathize with the many people who have had the threat of hell used against them. [14.8] It's not that fear of hell should never be a legitimate motivation, but many Christians have distorted the gospel (what is supposed to be the "good news") of Jesus into bad news: *Turn or burn!* They have failed to recognize that God has always been about reconciliation, about restoring a relationship. I can't think of too many healthy relationships that are based predominantly on fear.

So hell is a philosophical necessity, but the message of God has always been one of love. I believe that Jesus intended for his followers to emphasize the good news that God loves them, not to quite literally scare the hell out of them. My hope is that this book will be a gracious encouragement for people to consider the good news of Jesus.

> *It's not that fear of hell should never be a legitimate motivation, but many Christians have distorted the gospel (what is supposed to be the "good news") of Jesus into bad news: Turn or burn!*

In my heart of hearts I hope that hell is less intense than it appears in the Bible. I hope that the Bible's images are more figurative and less literal. I hope that people who miss the mark will somehow be offered second chances. But I have no solid evidence of this and so I must act upon what God has revealed. I am not without questions when it comes to hell, but my right brain keeps reminding me that this is the same God who freely sacrificed his own Son in order to spare me from death, and I am reassured that I can trust him.

> *The Lord is not slow in keeping his promise, as some understand slowness. Instead he is patient with you, not wanting anyone to perish, but everyone to come to repentance* (2 Peter 3:9).

GOD IS BLOODTHIRSTY

No doubt about it, God has a reputation in the western world for being a bloodthirsty tyrant. A quick survey of the Old Testament will leave most people confused as to the character of God, someone they've otherwise understood to be loving and just.

Accounts of bloody animal sacrifice, war, and the annihilation of entire people groups are common in the Old Testament narrative. One website I recently visited actually gave a tally of the number of people the God of the Bible had killed. The total was 32,920,770. I had to admire the research this guy put into his site. I also acknowledge that some sort of explanation is called for. [14.9]

Let's begin with animal sacrifice. According to the Genesis account, God killed the first animal when he clothed Adam and Eve after their fall into sin. Apparently this began a pattern of animal sacrifice, as later we see Adam and Eve's own children bringing sacrifices to the Lord. When God accepted Abel's sacrifice and rejected Cain's, we learned that the two men were attempting to fulfill a requirement from God that involved a blood offering of some sort. The Law of Moses expands and clarifies this pattern, as God's people are required to present an annual offering to atone for their sins. And the New Testament presents Jesus as the final atoning sacrifice – the "Lamb of God who takes away the sins of the world."

The Bible reiterates the importance of blood sacrifice.

In fact, the law requires that nearly everything be cleansed with blood, and without the shedding of blood there is no forgiveness (Hebrews 9:22).

God required the sacrifice of an animal, as gruesome as it is, for the clear purpose of showing us that paying for our sin demands death. When a person committed to God's law killed an animal and saw its blood flow, it was a powerful reminder that they were the ones who deserved the fate of

167

the innocent animal. Jesus' innocent death on a hideous cross served as the ultimate fulfillment of this requirement, and animal sacrifices were no longer necessary after his death. Instead, we have been called to reflect on his death through acts like communion.

Just as a side note, animal sacrifice in the Old Testament was carried out with great respect, with the meat of the animal being eaten and the life of the animal always being appreciated. (I'm no expert in meat preparation, but I'm guessing that the professional purveyors of our fast food chains fall short of this level of respect.)

As for God's alleged bloodthirstiness depicted by the war and genocide recorded in the Bible, we North Americans must first admit that we are very far removed from the context of war. Growing up here in a land of peace, we are appalled by war in ways that other people in other parts of the world simply may not be. War has always been a stark global reality. Most people in most parts of the world agree that sacrifice is required to alleviate evil realities in the world, such as tyranny and the oppression of entire peoples. Many North Americans certainly agree with this, celebrating those who give of their time and talents to serve in the military, and honoring those who have made the ultimate sacrifice.

The Bible records very few of the wars that have been waged throughout history, but we do read that God, a number of times, decreed the destruction of one people by another. I think the bigger question we all want answered is this one: "How can God love people personally while at the same time allowing them to be destroyed in bigger events, as if they didn't matter at all?"

This was a question that went through many people's minds when a tsunami hit Sri Lanka and its neighboring countries on December 26, 2004. Here we all were, sipping eggnog and hanging out with our families by the Christmas tree, singing about God's peace and love while over on the other side of the world some 280,000 people were wiped off the map like ants. It takes a lot of faith to believe that God still does love those victims as individuals and cares about their plight when we're rounding the death totals to the nearest 10,000.

Whenever I'm confronted by this paradox, I recall equally confusing stories about the soldiers in WWI, who on Christmas Eve put down their guns, emerged from their trenches and met together on the battle line. They sang *Silent Night* and exchanged gifts. Our soldiers came to discover firsthand that most of the men they were fighting were not in agreement with their leaders. Desertion would have cost them their lives, so they opted to roll the dice and hope that they didn't die in battle. When the gunfire resumed the next day, many men on both sides were, of course, killed. As with these soldiers, at some point we as humans must resign ourselves to the fact that we are mere players on a much larger stage.

At various times in the Bible, God commanded and empowered his people to wipe out opposing forces – the Midianites, the Amalekites, and so on. He himself took action against the cities of Sodom and Gomorrah. When the children of Israel entered the Promised Land, God commanded them to destroy the enemy ruthlessly, leaving no one alive. God made it clear that he was giving this land to Israel because of the sin of the people who possessed it. This wicked society was so depraved that some sacrificed their own children in fire to the god Molech.[14.10] As a parent, I can't even begin to describe how unimaginably evil I think this is. Imagine how God must have felt.

Today, when people criticize God leading people to kill,[14.11] they often fail to examine the context. Many who levy these criticisms are already poisoned against God, and so they ignore any reasons that might be given for God's choices.[14.12] They also fail to appreciate that God is in control of human history and that when people or entire countries oppose his will, he reserves the right to execute judgment. There are many accounts in the Bible that detail times when God had his own people put to death for resisting his will.

Since the time of Jesus, we have lived in an age of grace, a time where God is demonstrating his gracious, patient side. But in the early days of recorded humanity, God showed us his power and justice.[14.13] Those who disobeyed God's law became enemies of God. The offenses for which God allowed nations to be wiped out were matters that didn't even require the special revelation of God's law. Their evil was obvious. In such massacres, innocent children often died along with the parents. But children have always had to live or die with their parents' bad choices; that's just part and parcel with the responsibility God has given us as parents. Knowing what I do about God and his appreciation for children, I hold great optimism for the eternal outlook of children who suffer as a result of their parents' (or other adults') bad choices.

One last comment about God's bloodthirstiness. It is only fair to note that God himself was not immune from bloodshed. The theme of the entire Bible is that our salvation required God to take on human form in order to shed his perfect blood on behalf of mankind.

> *And so Jesus also suffered outside the city gate to make the people holy through his own blood* (Hebrews 13:12).

Someday, if the Bible is correct, people from every tribe and nation of the world will recognize this fact and thank God for it.

> *And they sang a new song, saying: "You are worthy to take the scroll and to open its seals, because you were slain, and with your blood you*

> **One last comment about God's bloodthirstiness. It is only fair to note that God himself was not immune from bloodshed.**

purchased for God persons from every tribe and language and people and nation" (Revelation 5:9).

I certainly can't say that I have no more questions in regard to the destruction God has commanded and allowed at different times in history, but a little bit of context goes a long way in calming my angst.

ALL OTHER RELIGIONS ARE WRONG

We've already discussed the fact that all roads can't lead to God (or Ritchie Rentals, for that matter). I've also tried to demonstrate that Jesus was inclusive – that he invited everyone from all backgrounds to receive his gift of life. Yet there is no denying that his message is exclusive in that it describes one accepted path – that of embracing Jesus by faith for the forgiveness of sins.

I do not get upset when people passionately ask me, "What about all of those people in other faiths? What about the 1.3 billion Muslims, the 900 million Hindus, or the 376 million Buddhists? Surely they can't all be wrong!" I don't see those who ask these questions as attacking my faith as much as they are showing their compassion for these other people. I too am a compassionate person and I share their concerns.

As I write this section, I'm sitting in a food court in a shopping mall just outside Toronto. People from a dozen different ethnicities walk by me every minute, each with their own religious adherence. Trust me, if ever there was a place where touting the exclusivity of one's faith was politically incorrect, it's here in Toronto – one of the most multicultural cities in the world.

Even if I've managed to convince you that Jesus is inclusive and that his offer of salvation extends to all people groups, it is no less disconcerting to recognize that most people probably haven't embraced or followed Jesus on that narrow path in the way he described. Christians and non-Christians alike have tried to make sense of this over the centuries, asking "Why would God, if he wants a relationship with people so badly, offer a path that so few would be able to find?"

I will openly confess that this is a question that I don't feel I can answer, one that bothers me deeply. Many people simply haven't heard of Jesus. Of those who have, many have never clearly heard or understood what he has to say. Even a huge number of people who claim to be "Christian" and wear crosses around their necks are oblivious to the true message of the cross. [14.14] The majority of people in this world have grown up in cultures where they naturally absorbed the non-Christian faith of their parents. Should these people, by whatever means, learn about Jesus and want to follow him, they would suffer varying degrees of ostracism – if not outright threat of death – from their families and friends. I see this ostracism firsthand, even here in a tolerant city like Toronto.

Early on in this discussion I want to say that I have a great deal of respect for people of different faiths, particularly those who make significant sacrifices for their beliefs. My wife and I agree that we have more in common with some of our Muslim friends than we do with people who follow no faith tradition, simply because we share the camaraderie of swimming against the current of the culture. I respect any woman who wears a hijab, downplaying her feminine beauty and showing respect to her husband when she could be drawing attention to herself.

> *I respect people of all faiths who try to live by moral standards and give something back to their communities.*

I know that many Muslim women struggle to maintain the proper attitude, but at least the effort is there. I respect people of all faiths who try to live by moral standards and give something back to their communities.

I personally believe that all of these examples are evidence of God's existence and his influence on planet Earth. As the Apostle Paul has said,

God has not left himself without witness in the world.[14.15] When you take a moment to consider different world religions, it is fascinating to see just how much the different faiths have in common – despite the fact that we most often highlight the differences.

All faiths fall into one of two categories: authoritarian or non-authoritarian. Authoritarian faiths are those that follow a personal God of some form who has communicated his will for mankind in some way. Christians, Muslims and Jews all follow authoritarian faiths. Non-authoritarian faiths are those in which God is impersonal and where truth does not come from one single, authoritative source. Buddhists, Hindus and most Animists would fall into this category. (Sikhs are a fairly unique mixing of authoritarian and non-authoritarian, probably a little more of the latter despite their belief in a personal God.)

Of the three main authoritarian faiths, you may be interested to note that all of them revere Abraham as a founding father and draw upon the Law as given by Moses.[14.16] Most people have never taken the time to consider this. In other words, a majority of people in the world agree to a large extent on a basic set of laws that were given by a creator God, although each group has added their own belief structures and practices to this foundation.

My point here is that God has given to humanity a basic understanding of himself that has influenced people groups around the entire globe. Furthermore, we Christians will note that the Bible affirms that Jesus' appearance on the world stage was precisely timed by God.[14.17] Jesus came to earth at exactly the right time, and Christianity spread throughout the entire world in an amazingly short period of time because of a *lingua franca* (common language) and a comprehensive network of Roman roads. So powerful was the testimony of Jesus' existence that even our calendar came to be numbered around his life, the result being that his name has been known in every corner of the globe for centuries. No other person or faith can claim such broad exposure.

Again, this does nothing to change the fact that the majority of people in the world have not embraced Jesus. But it does, I believe, in some way demonstrate God's desire to make knowledge of himself available to mankind.

When we look at the Bible, we see three different categories of accountability before God. The *first* level of accountability is God's universal law written in the heart. You could call this a "conscience." According to the Bible, everyone has the law of God written in their heart.

> *Even Gentiles, who do not have God's written law, show that they know his law when they instinctively obey it, even without having heard it. They demonstrate that God's law is written in their hearts, for their own conscience and thoughts either accuse them or tell them they are doing right* (Romans 2:14-15, New Living Translation, ©2007).

This law, or what we might call God-consciousness, is buttressed by the testimony of nature itself, invoking a basic level of accountability to all mankind.

> *For since the creation of the world God's invisible qualities—his eternal power and divine nature—have been clearly seen, being understood from what has been made, so that people are without excuse.* (Romans 1:20).

The *second* level of accountability is the law of God as it was specifically revealed (through Moses) and consequently spread (via various groups).

> *All who sin apart from the law will also perish apart from the law, and all who sin under the law will be judged by the law* (Romans 2:12).

> *Now we know that whatever the law says, it says to those who are under the law, so that every mouth may be silenced and the whole world held accountable to God.* (Romans 3:19).

As you can see, exposure to God's specific law brings with it a higher level of accountability. This makes perfect sense; the more specific the instruction, the more precisely one is able to act upon it.

The *third* major level of accountability is knowledge of the person of Jesus himself.

> *The law of Moses was unable to save us because of the weakness of our sinful nature. So God did what the law could not do. He sent his own Son in a body like the bodies we sinners have. And in that body God declared an end to sin's control over us by giving his Son as a sacrifice for our sins. He did this so that the just requirement of the law would be fully satisfied for us, who no longer follow our sinful nature but instead follow the Spirit* (Romans 8:3-4, New Living Translation, ©2007).

> *In the past God spoke to our ancestors through the prophets at many times and in various ways, but in these last days he has spoken to us by his Son...* (Hebrews 1:1-2).

According to the Apostle Paul, those who have been exposed to Jesus and the powerful testimony of his life will be held to account in the highest degree.

> *In the past God overlooked such ignorance, but now he commands all people everywhere to repent. 31 For he has set a day when he will judge the world with justice by the man he has appointed. He has given proof of this to everyone by raising him from the dead* (Acts 17:30-31).

These verses clearly indicate that the farther up the knowledge ladder you go, the more accountable you are before God. Those who only have the law of God in their hearts via human conscience bear some accountability. Those who have God's specific law, a higher level. The ultimate level of accountability lies with those who have heard of Jesus Christ and understood his message. Their accountability is higher because they have the testimony of Jesus' identity and have heard the stories of his miracles, which bore witness to his divinity – most notably, the miracle of his resurrection.

The Apostle Peter was clear in reminding people of this strong accountability.

> *"Fellow Israelites, listen to this: Jesus of Nazareth was a man accredited by God to you by miracles, wonders and signs, which God did among you through him, as you yourselves know"* (Acts 2:22).

I am soberly aware of this fact when I share the good news about Jesus with anyone, for as I do, not only am I bringing good news, but a higher degree of responsibility. If this is indeed true, then the fact that you are reading this book and entering into a deeper understanding of God is not to be taken lightly. (I don't claim to be a source of God's truth, I only aspire to clarify what the Bible already teaches about God.) Each of us is responsible for responding to the light we have been given.

It is only with this understanding that I am able to sleep at night. I know that God is merciful, and that he loves people of all religions more than I do; he gave his own Son to die for them. I take unfeeling Christians to task who make blanket statements about where certain people will spend eternity, [14.18] because I truly believe that God is the only judge, and that he is going to surprise all of us on the day of judgment. For now, I believe God has given us some amazingly good news that I am compelled to share with everyone I know from any walk of life. I cannot allow my many questions to keep me from acting on what I am convinced to be true.

It could be significant that the only people who I've ever heard raise this question of *What about all the other religions?* are western Christians.

People of other faiths seem to understand and accept the fact that choosing a certain path will have its consequences. I'm increasingly convinced that most people who raise the "what about all the other religions" question are merely trying to avoid answering the Jesus question for themselves.

I confess that questions of such magnitude can be paralyzing. With so much information to digest, at some point we simply need to go with our gut. To say that a choice is too difficult to make because of too many options is simply not a very good excuse. (It's a bit like saying you can't choose a spouse because there are too many people to choose from.) Let's face it, we make big decisions with our gut all throughout life – what job offer to accept, what car to buy, who to marry, what house to purchase, and whether or not to have children. The success of any of these decisions cannot be guaranteed. As American property developer Trammel Crow once said, "There's as much risk in doing nothing as in doing something." And this statement is certainly true of those who try to decide which world religion to follow.

> *People of other faiths seem to understand and accept the fact that choosing a certain path will have its consequences.*

I still have a lot of questions about who will make it to heaven someday. But I'm content to let God be God; I don't need to have all the answers. According to Revelation 5:9, someday in heaven there will be individuals from every *people*, *tribe* and *nation* worshipping God together in perfect unity. I'm taking God's word on that, and, frankly, very much looking forward to it.

GOD ALLOWS SUCH SUFFERING

Whether you are a person of faith or not, one of the most difficult questions you've likely wrestled with is how God (if indeed he exists) could allow such pain and suffering in the world. Disease, premature death, poverty, starvation, disability, murder, child abuse, and accidents all make people question the goodness of God. Add to that list horrific events such as wars, earthquakes, tsunamis, hurricanes and grotesque acts of terrorism, and you're left scratching your head along with the rest of us. On the surface, the suffering question is a formidable argument against faith in a personal and loving God.

While the Bible actually has a lot of good insight for us, it is maddening to see how often professing Christians have offered stupid and hurtful reasons for why people suffer. I nearly popped a vein in 2005 when I heard Pat Robertson connect hurricane Katrina with America's abortion policy. How arrogant does someone have to be to claim that they understand something so profound? Yet people of faith have been notorious in offering oversimplified and thoughtless explanations for life's deepest hurts. So beware of religious zealots and the advice they offer in your times of suffering.

As a pastor, I've seen more than my share of pain and suffering firsthand. When it comes to helping people through these times, I've tried to adopt the policy of being present, supportive, and mostly *quiet* – speaking only when asked to do so. I'm not threatened by my lack of understanding, and I certainly want to be careful not to open my mouth at the wrong time and demonstrate that lack of understanding. Rather than be discouraged about my lack of insight, I've repeatedly been encouraged to discover that people who reference pain and suffering when they address their doubts about God are actually demonstrating their deep-seated, instinctive belief that God exists.

When we suffer, we get frustrated because we somehow expect the Great Someone to do something about it. How interesting that we've been taught in our schools that the universe is run by impersonal, random events, and yet we somehow instinctively expect justice and fairness. More on that later on.

The common argument as it relates to God's silence in our suffering goes something like this:

The fact that evil and suffering exist in the world suggests one of 3 things:

a) There is no God.
b) If God exists, he is incapable of eliminating evil and suffering (he is weak).
c) If God exists, he is unwilling to eliminate evil and suffering (he doesn't care).

It's a popular argument, but maybe not as complete an argument as is often assumed.

I think you'll be encouraged to know that the Bible doesn't avoid the topic of suffering. Students of the Bible know it is brutally honest when it comes to referencing pain and suffering in history as it records every terrible aspect of the human condition – murder, war, slavery, genocide, abuse – you name it. Furthermore, no Bible character we read about is exempt from suffering. And there are two characters in particular who shed significant light on the subject.

The first character is Job. The story of Job is one of the oldest in the entire Bible and fittingly deals with the preeminent dilemma of the human condition – that of suffering. The first chapter of the book describes how on a certain fateful day, Satan comes to speak with God. Like a Chris DeBurgh song, the writer recounts the epic conversation that leads to God permitting Satan to torment God's special servant, Job. The chapters that follow have become classic literature and must-read material for anyone going through the fire of suffering.

A few salient lessons come through pretty clearly:

a) *Suffering is complicated.* Forty-two long chapters of discussion confirm that suffering is very messy, and debating the reason for its existence leads to much misunderstanding. Even Job's closest friends offer up half-baked explanations for his plight, only to make his burden heavier.

b) *There are evil forces at work in the world.* While few people here in the West look first to the spiritual realm to explain their plight, the book of Job substantiates the existence of evil spiritual forces.

c) *God is sovereign.* The fact that God must give Satan permission to harm Job demonstrates that God is ultimately in control of this world (not to mention the fact that he reserves the right to do what he wishes with Job's life).

d) *God isn't ready to explain the reasons for suffering yet.* After 42 chapters of wrestling and anguish and confusion, God finally brings restoration to Job, but what many people miss is that God never does explain the reason for putting Job through these trials. Despite this glaring omission, Job gains a new perspective on God's sovereignty and apologizes for getting his back up.

Then Job replied to the Lord:

> *I know that you can do anything,*
> *and no one can stop you.*
> *You asked, 'Who is this that questions my*
> *wisdom with such ignorance?'*
> *It is I—and I was talking about things I knew nothing about,*
> *things far too wonderful for me.*

–Job 42:1-2 (New Living Translation, ©2007)

The word "wonderful" here is the Hebrew word *pala*, meaning "marvelous" or "extraordinary." [14.19] Ultimately, Job recognized that God's ways were higher than his and that God owed him no explanation.

e) *Some realities are apparently too complex for us to completely understand.*

Many of us refer to God as the heavenly Father, but often we are unwilling to let him be a true father – that is, one who is far beyond us in wisdom and experience, having answers that we are not yet able to understand.

Just this week one of our kids was very frustrated and questioned my wife about why she did something. There were reasons why she handled matters the way she did, and they were directly connected to some unspoken situations that have been taking place in our larger family – things we simply cannot talk about with our kids. They are complex, adult issues and the simple truth is that we may never be able to talk with our kids about them. If we are going to allow God to be our heavenly Father, we have to at least acknowledge that this same dynamic could be at play when it comes to God's silence during our suffering.

The second character who gives us insight on suffering is none other than Jesus. The Old Testament prophet Isaiah predicted that the Messiah would be "a man of sorrows, familiar with grief" and the New Testament record confirms it. Jesus was misunderstood by his family, falsely accused by religious people, and eventually tried in a kangaroo court. The apex of his suffering came at the cross, where he was subjected to the brutal Roman torture of crucifixion. He was tried and executed as a criminal although he had done nothing wrong.

It is in this theme of suffering that the Christian narrative is unique from all other faiths. While other religions depict God as distant and detached from human suffering, only the Christian narrative places God right alongside of us in the middle of our suffering and helplessness.

> *While other religions depict God as distant and detached from human suffering, only the Christian narrative places God right alongside of us in the middle of our suffering and helplessness.*

As Pastor Tim Keller describes in his book *The Reason for God*, Christ's participation in our suffering is very significant. While it doesn't explain what the reason for suffering *is*, it does explain what the reason is *not*: it cannot be because he doesn't love us.

> *But God demonstrates his own love for us in this: While we were still sinners, Christ died for us* (Romans 5:8).

You may not be convinced of the gospel narrative, but if it is true, Jesus suffered to the point of death, and he did it for you and me. So whatever the reason for suffering might be, it's not because God doesn't love us, and he wanted that to be very clear.

> *For God so loved the world that he gave his one and only Son...* (John 3:16).

So we know what the reason for suffering is not. But are there any palatable explanations for why God allows it? There is obviously no hard evidence, so could there be any right-brained, philosophical explanations for the existence of suffering that might allow us to see God in a more favorable light? Here are some that I've considered over the years.

1. *Suffering may be a natural by-product of free will and the fall.*

It may not be the greatest consolation, but many theologians would agree that the degree of suffering we experience in the world is in direct correlation to the amount of freedom we have. When mankind chose to sin and brought pain and suffering into the world, God, as any good parent does, simply allowed us to face the natural consequences of our actions. The ancient narrative doesn't tell us just how clearly Adam and Eve understood what the consequences of their rebellion would be – pain in childbearing, mosquitos, weeds, war, tsunamis, hurricanes... even death. One might argue that the punishment was too severe, but the argument that our suffering is in correlation with our freedom is a legitimate concept. Let's keep going.

2. *Suffering may be for a purpose, for a time.*

The common argument that God either doesn't exist, or that he is weak, or that he is uncaring is compelling. But philosophically, this argument is unsound in that it offers an incomplete list of options. One of those omitted options is that it is very possible that suffering has a purpose and that God permits it for a set period of time. As a matter of fact, the Bible supports this notion repeatedly. When you read to the end of the New Testament, this is the exact scenario we see being envisioned in the future.

> *And I heard a loud voice from the throne saying, "Look! God's dwelling place is now among the people, and he will dwell with them. They will be his people, and God himself will be with them and be their God. 'He will wipe every tear from their eyes. There will be no more death or mourning or crying or pain, for the old order of things has passed away"* (Revelation 21:3-4).

Furthermore, the idea of suffering being temporary seemed to be commonly accepted knowledge among the apostles. Twice in Peter's second epistle he refers to our suffering as being for "a little while":

> *And the God of all grace, who called you to his eternal glory in Christ, after you have suffered a little while, will himself restore you and make you strong, firm and steadfast* (1 Peter 5:10).

We may not understand the purpose right now, so faith is definitely required. But there's more.

3. *Suffering may be designed to provide mankind with the proper perspective.*

As a kid in church, I had a lot of time to let my mind wander. On rare occasions a brilliant speaker would capture my attention for an entire forty minutes, but usually, when I wasn't thinking about hockey or how hungry I was or the girl down the row, I found myself pondering deep theological questions while the preacher expounded doctrine I had already learned.

One of the questions I often considered was, why did God even allow human history to play out? After all, I figured, if the end goal is to end up in heaven with God, why was human history, with all of its horrific suffering, even necessary? Adam and Eve already had an intimate relationship with God in paradise. So why did he allow them to exercise their free will, knowing the intense, global distress that first sin would lead to?

Somehow, in God's great mind, something about the human experience was necessary. There has to be some perspective that we are gaining from the heartache of human history that will somehow benefit our experience on the other side. Maybe we will have a greater appreciation for the relationship we will enjoy with God in eternity – an appreciation so valuable that it merits the suffering we face in the here and now.

4. *Suffering may very well enrich our future experience.*

How difficult realities such as holocausts and tsunamis will enhance our future experience is a mystery for sure, but we can't rule out this possibility. The apostles, who lived with and learned from Jesus, all had the perspective that the suffering we endure on earth gives us an opportunity to experience greater glory in eternity. As the Apostle Paul said:

> *I consider that our present sufferings are not worth comparing with the glory that will be revealed in us* (Romans 8:18).

I can't think of anything better than the Stanley Cup Playoffs to illustrate this point.

I may be biased (okay, no "may be" about it), but no sporting playoffs are as grueling as the NHL playoffs. It takes sixteen victories over four series of best-of-seven matches to be immortalized on Lord Stanley's holy grail. Games are scheduled for 60 minutes, but regularly go into overtime, double overtime and even triple overtime. It is not uncommon to see upwards of 100 hits thrown per game, dozens of blocked shots and multiple injuries of various sorts. After a team gives everything they have to win one series, they somehow dig deeper and find a new gear to play an even better opponent the next round. It is awesome.

Throughout the entire ordeal, players feign invincibility. Just as their unshaven beards hide their faces, they refuse to show weakness to their opponent, no matter their circumstances. They disregard cheap shots and cover up their injuries. But when the final seconds finally count down on the realization of their lifelong dream, hardened men turn into little boys once again. Tears flow down their faces as they take turns hoisting the 35-pound trophy over their head. Only after the win do reports begin to emerge about how many players were playing with broken hands, ribs, and even legs. Yes, legs! [14.20]

Why do athletes pay such a high price? What could possibly be worth the pain and agony that winning the ultimate prize requires? One word: *glory*.

Do you know what happens when a team wins the Stanley Cup? The players form an eternal bond. They turn into brothers. It is not uncommon for them to move into the same neighborhoods and raise their families together. And rarely is there a neighborhood barbecue that goes by where stories aren't told about the greatest series in the history of the NHL.

Do you know what these players talk about? They talk about the hits, the cheap shots, and how badly those blocked shots really hurt. Their faces gleam and their chests puff out as they show each other their scars and replacement teeth. It is a ritual that gets repeated again and again until the warriors are old and frail and gray.

And every time a fan asks them to tell that story one more time, do you know how it feels? It feels freakin' awesome.

But rejoice inasmuch as you participate in the sufferings of Christ, so that you may be overjoyed when his glory is revealed (1 Peter 4:13).

Never discount the possibility that suffering may somehow enrich our future experience. What appears now to be God's greatest injustice may eventually, in fact, turn out to be his greatest gift.

MOST OF THE TROUBLE IN THE WORLD HAS BEEN CAUSED BY RELIGION

I will take just a moment to discuss this statement, one that is oft-repeated but not really believed by most who use it. It is the kind of rash and absolute statement that people make in frustration, akin to statements like "you *never* put the toothpaste cap back on," or "you can't do *anything* right."

Having lived long enough to witness some of the evils of religion, I understand very well the passion with which such statements are made. For the past decade or so, the evils of religion have covered the front pages of our newspapers on a daily basis: 9/11, Al-Qaeda and Osama Bin Laden, the Taliban and their repression in places like Afghanistan and their treatment of women (among other things), the eternal battle between Jews and Muslims in the Middle East, the political agendas of fundamentalist Christians in America… the list goes on.

Add to this media coverage the climate of fear in a world where cultures are increasingly colliding, and you have an environment where ideas like "most of the trouble in the world is caused by religion" are good eating. For dessert, atheists like to serve us some additional tasties – like "religion interferes with scientific advancement" or "religion imposes outdated controls on society."

In his book, *God is Not Great*, Christopher Hitchens rehearses some of the typical accusations against religion – the Crusades, religious discrimination in Ireland, Bosnian Muslims facing extermination in the Christian Balkans, and Shias being put to death by Sunni jihadists in Afghanistan and Iraq. He also describes firsthand experience with religious violence in Belfast, Beirut, Bombay, Belgrade and Bethlehem. In cases where religious leaders have spoken out against such violence, Hitchens is quick to call it "a compliment to humanism, not to religion." [14.21] Why, then, isn't the violence accredited to humanity's depravity in the first place, instead of to religion? Hitchens is hell-bent on seeing religion in a negative light.

Hitchens is too educated a man to believe his own claim that religion poisons everything. Was the AIDS epidemic in Africa caused by religion? If the African continent had adhered to more religiously influenced sexual parameters, we can say with confidence that they wouldn't have the epidemic they now do. Hitchens argues that resistance among the religious relief groups to use modern methods available for fighting AIDS (i.e. birth control) is perpetuating the misery in Africa. However, he completely ignores the well-known fact that Christian mission and medical groups are, and have long been, some of the most dedicated and effective in bringing real help to that region.

Was Hitler driven by religion? A few atheists have tried to convince us that he was, but even Hitchens has to balance Hitler's statements connecting him with Christianity with others that blatantly demonstrate evidence to the contrary. What does seem incontrovertible is that Hitler was driven by the scientific beliefs of the day in regard to eugenics, formulated by Sir Francis Galton, who drew on the work of his cousin, Charles Darwin. According to Ben Stein, producer of the movie *Expelled*,

Darwinism, perhaps mixed with Imperialism, gave us Social Darwinism, a form of racism so vicious that it countenanced the Holocaust against the Jews and mass murder of many other groups in the name of speeding along the evolutionary process. [14.22]

The great wars of the world were not caused by religion, but by unbridled human greed. On the exact opposite end of the scale, many of our renowned hospitals and universities in North America have been established by of religious organizations trying to make a positive difference in the world. The fact that most have long since been secularized doesn't change the fact that religion played a huge part in developing the environment of freedom and prosperity that we enjoy in North America today. A journalist like Christopher Hitchens does himself no favors by failing to balance his bombastic rants with truth of which he is well aware. (But I have come to expect as much from a man who has the dignity to refer to Mother Teresa as a "Sacred Cow," among other things.) [14.23]

We could go on. The genocide of 1.7 million Cambodians between 1975 and 1979 wasn't caused by any religious group, but by the anti-religious Khmer Rouge (a.k.a. the Communist Party of Kampuchea). The same is true of the Soviet invasion of Afghanistan between 1979 and 1989 and the long history of human rights violations in Communist China. Keep in mind that these are all groups who not only opposed religion, but forbade its practice altogether.

The genocide of the Tutsis in Rwanda was not the result of religion; rather, this was the result of pure hatred and racism. It certainly saddens me that such a horror could take place in a country where over two-thirds its citizens claimed to be Christian. (It doesn't say much for the power of their faith.) But I'm not trying to defend religion on this point; I've already stated that I'm not a religious person. My goal is simply to bring balance to the argument, as many are using it as an excuse not to embrace faith of any kind. [14.24]

Clearly, people commit horrific acts against one another because they are *human*, not because they are *religious*. The fact that people seem to be innately religious means that everywhere humans mess up, religion will be in the mix. Often, religion holds people in check from doing even worse. Sometimes it doesn't; sometimes religion fuels the hatred. This is why people need a personal transformation – a relationship with God, not a religion. My point here is simply to demonstrate that most of the trouble in the world has *not* been caused by religion.

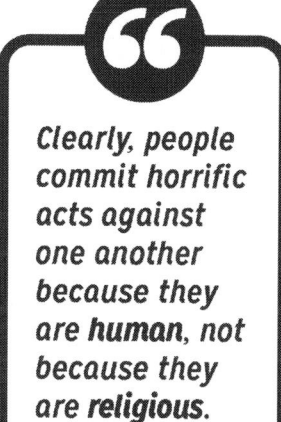

> *Clearly, people commit horrific acts against one another because they are **human**, not because they are **religious**.*

CHRISTIANITY IS OUT OF TOUCH

My wife and I met at a small Bible college in the Maritimes. The school drew students from all over Eastern Canada and New England, and had a reputation for imparting good Bible training at a very low cost. Every student worked on campus to reduce their board and tuition costs, and still many of us struggled to pay our bills on time. Stories of last minute, anonymous donors making up the difference for needy students were common (I benefited from these as well). I liked the emphasis the school placed on faith and dependence on God to provide for our needs.

I remember that periodically the school would receive large shipments of used clothing – dozens of garbage bags full of garments from local churches that were destined for Goodwill stores. The students got the first crack at sifting through the clothing before the remnants were repacked and forwarded to their final destination. As you might imagine, the arrival of these clothes were a big hit in the girls' dorms. We heard shrieks of delight across campus as they pulled the most ridiculous items from the bags and tried them on. They took pictures for posterity. The guilty pleasure seemed to be justified by the fact that most everyone found a little something they could actually keep and wear.[14.25]

If people are referring to fashion when they say Christians are out of touch, then they certainly have some corroborating evidence. Having grown up in a number of churches, I've seen some pretty scary things. Heck, I've *worn* some pretty scary things. I guess this is what happens in communities that value the interior person as opposed to the exterior. *God looketh on the heart!* Lucky for us. Things got really spooky when missionaries would come home on furlough – meaning that their backward styles were four *more* years out of date as they stood in front of churches to tell their stories..

Personally, I like to look good, but to this day I continually remind myself that the exterior is insignificant compared to the interior. Although I don't share the same fashion sense as some of my Christian brothers and sisters, I have no problem at all with those who couldn't care less about outward appearance. Clothes aren't what make a person beautiful. Some of the coolest people I know are terrible dressers.

Fashion is just one admittedly minor concern. Christians are often criticized for not keeping up with a variety of cultural norms. I'm not referring here to technology; those who take the time to notice will realize that very few Christians resist technological advances: I don't know many Christians who don't own cars or TV's or computers or cellphones. Rather, I'm referring to cultural norms that have overt moral implications. As our society has become less and less "Christian" in its perspectives, certain abstinences have become increasingly peculiar to people outside of the church. They just don't get why we Christians wouldn't participate in or do certain things.

For example, I know some Christians who will not enter a movie theater. Even though the odd movie might meet their strictest criteria, these Christians choose not to support an industry that they see as predominantly negative in its influence. Other Christians are strict in the styles that they wear. Many abstain entirely from alcohol, tobacco and recreational drug use. To people outside of faith, these Christians sometimes appear confusing, like Ned Flanders, who "resists all major urges." (I might add that some Christians would never watch the *Simpsons*. *D'oh!*)

> *To people outside of faith, [strict] Christians sometimes appear confusing, like Ned Flanders, who "resists all major urges."*

I don't need to outline or comment on all of the convictions that different Christians hold. We've discussed already (in the chapter on Grace) that not everyone makes the same decisions in the gray areas. I simply raise the subject to say that Christians are often labeled as being "out of touch" in relation to how they interact with popular culture.

Unfortunately, some people never recognize that many Christians are not really out of touch as much as they simply *disagree* with and decline to participate in or support certain elements of the culture. In a society where blending with the popular culture has become so important, abstaining Christians consistently come across as wet blankets, or at least curiously detached. This is most unfortunate, because I firmly believe that nothing is more relevant to today's real issues than true Christian faith.

True Christianity provides answers to life's nagging questions, showing us why we are here and what our purpose is. It teaches us the meaning of life.

True Christianity sheds light on the human condition. It explains why we do the things we do, why we struggle as a race and as individuals to be the kind of people we know we should be. And it gives us guidelines that move us in the right direction.

True Christianity helps us to maximize what's most important to us – our relationships. It teaches us to forgive and to pursue reconciliation. It tells us how to make our families functional and enjoyable. Most importantly, it tells us how to have a relationship with God himself.

True Christianity is concerned with justice. It helps us understand what justice really is and how to bring it to others. It is concerned with the well-being of people, and helps bring relief to those who suffer. Allow me one example. A few years ago while at our denomination's national conference, the speaker challenged the two to three hundred people gathered to do something for AIDS orphans in Africa. In a matter of 15 minutes, the unprepared congregation had donated over $30,000. And these are people who already give at least 10% of their income to their local church.) Christian charities and churches have always been on the cutting edge of bringing relief to those who most need help.

True Christianity is concerned about peace. We follow Jesus, the "Prince of Peace," and ask him to bring his peace into our hearts, personal relationships, and the world around us. As a result, we become agents of peace.

True Christianity is about happiness and joy. It shows us the secret to being happy in this fallen world.

True Christianity even cares about the environment. We believe that we have been entrusted as stewards of our planet, and as such we must make responsible decisions in regard to our plants and animals, oceans and forests.

True Christianity gives people hope, as it gives us a glimpse of what the future has in store and how to make the most of our time while we're here on the earth.

As you can see, true Christianity is anything but out of touch. On the contrary, it is thoroughly relevant. It deals with all of the things that are most important to us! In the final analysis, the time and energy that many people spend on keeping up with the latest styles, movies, music and so on isn't worth a whole lot. These are not the things that tend toward significant improvement in our lives or in our world.

That being said, I don't believe that becoming a follower of Jesus means that you need to turn into a cultural recluse. I have many Christian friends who enjoy elements of pop culture and who like to stay current with what's going on around them. While I hold to certain standards in what types of entertainment I will engage in, I too like to keep an eye on what's hot in the culture. By taking the time to know what TV shows and movies are popular and what lyrics are being sung over the airwaves, I keep a pulse on what people are talking about. This gives me connection points with people.

The Apostle Paul did the same thing, quoting from popular poets and philosophers as he engaged people in spiritual discussions. As a pastor who longs to change the perceptions that people have of Christians, I encourage my congregation to learn the language of the culture and engage it. Only then will many people ever arrive at a place where they can see how powerfully relevant our faith really is.

§

This brings us to the end of the chapter. I hope you'll agree that these common arguments against faith aren't as strong as you've been told. Christians certainly don't have all of the answers, but those of us who have taken the time to contemplate our faith at a deeper level have wrestled with some of the most popularly cited roadblocks. If I were not able to reach a certain level of peace on these matters, my right brain would never permit me to call myself a Christian.

Chapter 15

JUSTICE MUST BE HAD

If you tremble with indignation at every injustice then you are a comrade of mine.

—Ernesto Che Guevara

You know, the courts may not be working any more, but as long as everyone is videotaping everyone else, justice will be done.

—Marge Simpson

I met today with a man who is dying. His son, Ron, is a member of my church. He approached me last week to ask if I'd mind paying a visit. I was happy to. There was an additional request, however. Ron asked if we could first meet alone so that he could share some of the reasons why his father might be resistant to God, even in the face of his short time to live. I thought it was a wise decision.

When Ron and I met, he gave me a snapshot of his father's life. Wendell (or *Windy*, as his friends call him) was born and raised in

New Argyle, Prince Edward Island. By the age of 14 he was pulled from school to help his father, Jack, a struggling lobster fisherman, thus ending any hope for a promising education. Shortly thereafter he left home to live with his Aunt in Boston, and from there moved to Streetsville, Ontario.

In July 1953 he married the girl who used to live across the street from him in PEI. Without two cents to rub together, the couple lived on love. The birth of two healthy baby boys was followed by a miscarriage, and then a son born prematurely who had cerebral palsy. The couple adjusted and continued to be hospitable to friends and family who needed a place to stay – sometimes for months and even years on end.

In 1969 Wendell received shocking news that his brother had died at a young age. His spirit was crushed, but he moved on. Wendell's sons married and began to have children of their own.

Then in February 1993 an impaired driver robbed Wendell of his oldest son. (By this point in Ron's story, I just sat there with a blank look, wondering if the nickname "Windy" came from Wendell getting the wind knocked out of him so frequently.) The family was devastated. If that wasn't enough, later that year Wendell's mother passed away. But there wasn't much time to mourn.

In January, 1994, the son who had cerebral palsy (who had just made the entire family proud a few months earlier by graduating from the University of Toronto) was involved in a life-changing accident that left him brain-damaged. Right at the point where Wendell and his wife should have been looking forward to retirement, their lives became dedicated to caring for their adult son. Amazingly, through everything, Ron never remembers his father ever once complaining about the hand he had been dealt.

Finally, after a few years, life started to settle into a rhythm. Windy managed to get out and golf regularly with some close friends, only to be diagnosed with terminal cancer in 2006. He was already feeling his strength begin to fail when I met him. As I talked with him I was blown away by his faith. He was broken, but not bitter. He was confident somehow that there was a reason for everything and that justice would ultimately prevail.[15.1]

Truth be told, apart from the Bible and other religious writings, there's nothing in life that tells us that justice *must* be had. And yet most people, even those who adhere to no particular religion, agree that everything happens for a reason. Even people who have been turned off to religion like Ron's dad (who had been turned off to religion by hellfire-and-brimstone preachers as a kid) still hold onto the fact that somehow, some way, justice will be had. You would think with so many people experiencing injustice, somewhere the sense that right will prevail would decline, or even be lost. But it isn't. Instead, it seems to be as strong as any intuition I've ever witnessed.

"Life is not fair." [15.2] "Justice will prevail." The very fact that both of these contradictory axioms are quoted as timeless truths attests to mankind's proclivity for faith. Think of the implications of these two statements in juxtaposition: If justice can't be had in the here and now, then it stands to reason that it must somehow come in the afterlife, where the concept of an all-knowing, completely righteous judge must then also come into play. Moreover, this rationale points toward some sort of objective right and wrong, something new-age moralists have been downplaying for decades now.

As you can see, the innate belief in ultimate justice is central to religious discussion. Jesus

> **"Life is not fair." "Justice will prevail." The very fact that both of these contradictory axioms are quoted as timeless truths attests to mankind's proclivity for faith.**

talked a lot about justice. In the Beatitudes[15.3] he highlighted the unfairness of life, but also promised blessings to those who endured unfairness for good reasons.

In talking about issues of faith with literally thousands of people over the years, I know that the first conception most people hold about God is that of a judge. Somehow humans have a sense that everything we do really is recorded somewhere beyond the videotape of our own minds. As much as we try to rid ourselves of guilt, trying to make ourselves believe that guilt is nothing more than our consciences wrestling with irrational and manipulative restrictions placed upon us by religion, we just can't fully shake the idea that we will have to give account for our actions someday. We innately understand that there's more to the game than just not getting caught.

True Christian faith is all about justice. It begins with a God who is intrinsically just, and who made people to be the same way. When we humans chose to violate God's laws, we brought God's judgment against ourselves, and God could not simply ignore our crimes. (To do so would have been to deny his own holy and perfect character; God cannot live in harmony with sin.) So God was in a jam – his justice demanded judgment, but his love couldn't bear to see us suffer eternal separation from him.

Then, in the most poetic twist history has ever seen, God surprised everyone, including the powers of darkness, by coming to us in human form to pay the penalty for our wrongdoing.

If God would go to such extremes to ensure that justice was carried out properly; that is, if the Father would allow the suffering and death of his own Son, then I have great confidence that God will also mete out justice, by one means or another, at the end of time. Indeed, justice will be had.

I am a bit confused sometimes when I think about the number of people today who try to build a worldview without a personal God who stands as the ultimate judge of the universe. Even if these people convince themselves that man came to exist without God and that God has no part in what happens on the earth, doesn't the question of ultimate justice leave a gaping hole in their reasoning? How do they account for poverty, untimely death, and the molestation of little children? Isn't there some force that will call to account those whose actions cause such horrible things to happen? Nearly every person I have discussed this matter with thinks so.

My innate belief in ultimate justice makes me a believer. It is an entirely intuitive, right-brained response to life, but one that the huge majority of people share, regardless of the faith they follow or the place where they were born.

Chapter 16

THE BIBLE IS THE MOST RESONANT BOOK OF ALL TIME

"The existence of the Bible, as a book for the people, is the greatest benefit which the human race has ever experienced. Every attempt to belittle it is a crime against humanity."

–Immanuel Kant

I've never been a Rolling Stones fan. Why not – I can't say for sure. I like rock, especially blues rock, but the Stones have never really grabbed my attention. Maybe they were considered passé when I was a teen in the 80's, so they never hit my radar. To be honest, I've come to know their music better in recent years since moving here to Toronto, one of their favorite stomping grounds.

Regardless of what you think of the Stones' music, you have to admire their staying power. Sure, the band members have changed over the years, but Mick Jagger and Keith Richards have stuck it out and the heart of the

Stones has remained the same for almost half a century now. (Guitarist Ronnie Wood began playing with the group in 1975.)

In an industry that relentlessly favors youth and vitality over age and experience, the Stones have somehow made being a sexagenarian sexy. (I'd swear some people watch their shows today just for the spectacle of seeing if they'll all still be standing by the end of the 3-hour show.) Regardless, when a band or artist succeeds in resonating with people for over four decades, whether or not the band is "good" is a moot point.

> ...when a band or artist succeeds in resonating with people for over four decades, whether or not the band is "good" is a moot point.

As far as resonance goes, I see the Bible in much the same light. For how supposedly antiquated and irrelevant it has become, it sure does garner a lot of attention. No matter how much people may despise it and its influence on the human race, no one can deny that it's a classic. It is by far the best-selling book of the year, every single year. It is the most read, most quoted, most loved and most controversial book in history. Like the Stones, the Bible is not the work of one man alone, but a work that has evolved over many years with contributions from many different vantage points. Yet the spirit and theme of the work has remained remarkably uniform throughout the ages.

There's no denying that the Bible is a complex and book. Because it is open to differences of interpretation, it has been misquoted, misinterpreted and misused over the centuries. Religious and political leaders have employed it as a tool to control the masses or gain an advantage. Philosophers have decried its effect on the millions, while evangelists have relentlessly promoted it to more millions.

Some people feel guilty for not knowing it well enough while others study it every single day and look to it to inform their actions and attitudes throughout the day. No other book in history can claim that on the scale of the Bible.

It's a massive collection of ancient writings and some of its contents are just plain confusing. Because of this, well-meaning believers over the years have codified and canonized its teaching to the degree that many would-be fans have given up trying to chew on its "lyrics", assuming that there is nothing original left to discover about the book on a personal level.[16.1]

I find this last point to be most disappointing. How can believers fail to recognize that God is primarily the "Creator," a title that assumes *creativity*? God is first and foremost an artist, and the Bible one of his greatest masterpieces.

Perhaps you noticed the epigraph from the group U2 as you opened the cover of my book. I'm actually not a huge U2 fan, but I've quoted lead singer Bono because I feel that more than any other artist over the past few decades, he has succeeded at engaging the right side of his listeners' brains. One might expect someone as socially motivated as he is to take direct shots at the ills in society in his songs, but instead, Bono taps into listeners' emotions with nuanced sounds and lyrics that resonate with his audience. It is hard not to respect his artistry.

As an artist, can you imagine how ticked off a musician like Bono would be if someone published a book attempting to understand and explain every lyric that U2 ever wrote? Who could claim to understand every line, every inference, every nuance from every album? Such a claim would be extremely ignorant and highly insulting to the band. Lyrics, while usually designd to render some kind of unified message, always leave some room for subjectivity and interpretation.

For far too long, pastors and commentators have reduced the Bible to a how-to manual, raping it of its in-depth artistic value. In my mind, such a surgical dismantling of its meaning demonstrates profound ignorance of the author himself. It overlooks the fact that God is an artist who leaves varying degrees of imagination and interpretation in his work.

Allow me to illustrate. I know that U2's song, *Pride (In the Name of Love)* is about the power that is unleashed when one person acts out of love. Some of the references are undeniably clear. No one argues that the shots ringing out in a Memphis sky on April 4th were the bullets that killed Martin Luther King, Jr. But other images are not so clear. The man caught on a barbed wire fence could be a soldier in any one of a number of wars. This does not mean that the message of the song is unclear. Nor is the message of the Bible unclear; it's just not always as cut-and-dried as some people attempt to make it.

Like U2's music, the Bible resonates with people who take the time to read and study it. It deals with themes that have enthralled the human spirit since the beginning of time. It talks about the human condition, and why we act the way we do. It talks about reconciliation and justice. It talks about redemption and sacrificial atonement. These and other themes have dominated our art and literature for centuries, and also more recent artistic expressions such as movies.

Just take a minute and think about the number of classic movies that deal with self-sacrifice. *Braveheart, Gandhi, Chariots of Fire, Spiderman, The Lion King, Cinderella Man, The Wrath of Khan, Lord of the Rings, Saving Private Ryan, Schindler's List, It's a Wonderful Life, The Dark Knight, Avatar…* the list is essentially endless. Not to mention stories that have been purposefully crafted to make us think of Christ's ultimate sacrifice – *The Passion of the Christ, The Chronicles of Narnia,* and the like. True Christianity is the only world faith that has this most powerful and pervasive theme at its heart. And this is only the beginning.

The theme of self-sacrifice is intertwined with that of redemption – another powerful theme in classic and contemporary art and literature. Having studied the Bible my entire life, I can attest that the theme of redemption runs through every book. Add to that the themes of perseverance and reconciliation and you can see why the Bible has inspired so many people for so many years. While many faiths recognize these powerful spiritual realities, no other holy writings deal with them as thoroughly as the Bible, which interweaves them together from cover to cover.

SYNOPSIS

The story begins as sin enters the world and ends when it is destroyed. As soon as sin enters the world God promises that a Messiah will come to make things right. The rest of the story revolves around God bringing that Messiah to mankind and redeeming the world through him. God institutes the requirement of animal sacrifice as a constant reminder that sin must be paid for with blood and death,[16.2] a very tangible and consistent reminder that the Messiah will do the same.

God chooses a nation to keep the hope of the Messiah alive. He gives the law to Moses to keep people in check until the time when the Messiah will arrive.[16.3] God weeps over the failure of his nation to share his light with the world, but his plan is not thwarted. At precisely the right time, after most of the world had forgotten the prophecies of old, God stuns mankind by taking on human form himself and being born as a baby.

The Messiah amazes the crowds. Even the demons can't help but testify to his divinity. Satan incites the crowds against the Messiah, working overtime until they finally crucify him on a cruel cross. The shrieks of delight can still be heard from hell when God then responds with the greatest plot twist history has ever witnessed.

By allowing his Son to die on the cross, God purchases mankind's freedom, and then raises Jesus from the dead to secure his victory over sin, death and the devil for all time. Moreover, he begins the Church, a new light through which he will offer the gift of salvation procured by Jesus on the cross. Like Israel, the Church will meet limited success in the world, but it waits along with all of creation for the day when God will come back to earth and set things right once and for all.

The biblical narrative encapsulates the greatest, most resonant themes of all of history. What makes the story even more impressive the scope of the project. Peter Jackson, director of the *Lord of the Rings* cinematic trilogy, spent over 6 years with a production team of 2400 people and a cast of 500 actors (plus 200 background players and some 26,000 extras) to produce the most impressive movie experience ever witnessed to that time. But God's story has been unfolding for over 6000 years now. The action has been recorded by some 40 writers over a period of 1600 years. And we are among the billions of cast members who have been playing out the story for all these thousands of years. Over 110 million people worldwide lined up to see *The Return of the King*, but every person who has ever lived on planet Earth will witness the return of the King of kings:

> "Look, he is coming with the clouds," and "every eye will see him, even those who pierced him"; and all peoples on earth "will mourn because of him." So shall it be! Amen" (Revelation 1:7).

When you consider the poetic masterpiece of human history as told by scripture, I trust you can see why I derive so much confidence from the right side of my brain. No other faith resonates with the artist in me like true Christianity. Only the biblical account provides a consistent narrative to history – one with movement that builds to a climax and final dénouement in the book of Revelation. Its rhythms match the human experience on every level – our stories, our aging process, our sports and even our sex.

The power of the Bible's intense and panoramic metaphors resonate so strongly with me that I do not get overwhelmed by the details that trip up so many people today. The arguments raised against God (many of which I have treated in this book) fade into the fabric of the story.

I've never heard anyone complain that too many Orcs, or humans for that matter, die in the *Lord of the Rings*. Somehow people accept that this is J.R.R. Tolkien's story.[16.4] In the same way, I accept the biblical account of history as God's story. He is the author and the director. I've read the script, and I'm playing my tiny little part in the production. It doesn't all make sense to me right now, but someday, when the final work goes to celluloid, I'm pretty sure I'll sit back and watch in awe at the work God has wrought.

With any luck it will be on an iMax screen and accompanied by a massive bucket of popcorn.

Chapter 17

CERTAIN BIBLE PROPHECIES PIQUE MY INTEREST

"Science has not yet mastered prophecy. We predict too much for the next year and far too little for the next ten."

–Neil Armstrong

"Don't ever prophesy; for if you prophesy wrong, nobody will forget it; and if you prophesy right, nobody will remember it."

–Josh Billings (American humourist and lecturer)

One of the unique aspects of the Bible is its willingness to wade into matters of prophecy. Compared to the Judeo-Christian scriptures, other holy writings have relatively little to say on the subject. The Bible dedicates large portions of its text to this type of literature, and I have to say, some of the prophecies I have studied make a believer out of me. The poetic quality of prophetic literature is enjoyable in its own rite – many people enjoy reading predictions like those made by Nostradamus. But when you examine the predictions that were made and fulfilled in the Bible, as well as the predictions for our ultimate future, and you consider the likelihood of their fulfillment, the exercise becomes more than mere entertainment.

The big question, of course, is how much of what was predicted in the Bible was a clear and risky prognostication versus simple retroactive clairvoyance – accrediting accuracy after the fact. Some Christians try to prove the mathematical improbability of certain fulfillments of prophecy in an attempt to make them seem more amazing, but to be honest, they make a lot of assumptions in favor of their claims. Such "evidence" is counterproductive in my thinking. And God doesn't need help in the amazing department.

A few biblical predictions do hold particular interest for me, however, and I'll just throw them out for your own consideration. (Forgive me if I wax a little left-brained for a moment.) The first is the prophecy of the advent of the Messiah. Micah 5:2 clearly predicts that he will be born in Bethlehem, an unlikely choice for the birth of the Messiah. Seven centuries later, Matthew and Luke both state that Jesus was born in Bethlehem, explaining in detail why it happened in this way. Both men also confirm Old Testament prophecies that Jesus grew up in Nazareth, and numerous scriptures allude to the humble nature of this Messiah, with Zechariah (chapter 9 verse 9) even predicting the arrival of this gentle king into Jerusalem on a donkey. This last event is described in detail by the Apostle John (John chapter 12).

Either Jesus' life was carefully arranged to fit Old Testament prophecies (including much effort by his own parents to birth him in a specific place) or there is something more to the story.

A second prophecy that I like to ponder is Jesus' prediction of the destruction of the Jewish temple.

> *Jesus left the temple and was walking away when his disciples came up to him to call his attention to its buildings. "Do you see all these things?" he asked. "Truly I tell you, not one stone here will be left on another; every one will be thrown down"* (Matthew 24:1-2).

The fact that the temple was destroyed in AD 70 under Roman emperor Titus is one thing. The fact that stones were literally pried apart in order to reclaim the gold leaf that melted from the roof when the temple was set on fire is another. In 1968, archaeological excavations unearthed large numbers of these stones.

Jesus made other bold predictions. The greatest, and my third example of prophecies that make you go "huh? is Jesus' prediction of his own death.

> *Jesus answered them, "Destroy this temple, and I will raise it again in three days."*
>
> *They replied, "It has taken forty-six years to build this temple, and you are going to raise it in three days?" But the temple he had spoken of was his body. After he was raised from the dead, his disciples recalled what he had said. Then they believed the scripture and the words that Jesus had spoken* (John 2:19-22).

While this acknowledgement by Jesus' disciples is unabashedly after-the-fact, numerous other passages record that Jesus predicted his own death and resurrection. That's bizarre.

Maybe you've checked out some of Criss Angel's illusions on *A&E*. You have to give the guy credit – he's entertaining! He even likes to mess with Christians by performing illusions that parallel those of Jesus – walking on water, floating up in the air, and even turning water into beer. (I love the contextualization of that one.) Fortunately for Criss Angel, he has the advantage of video cameras and pre-arranged venues. Despite all this, his performances still leave you scratching your head – like the one where he walks through a glass window. Staged or not, you have to give him his props.

If Criss Angel really wants to pull a mindfreak, though, he should do the "death and resurrection" trick. Now, I realize that many people place no more faith in Jesus' resurrection than they do in Criss Angel's performances. After all, we can't absolutely prove that the resurrection wasn't a grand hoax, the result of a vast conspiracy led by the disciples and numerous unbelievers alike. But if that were true, even the hoax would be inexplicable. Try to explain how Jesus orchestrated his entire arrest, conviction and crucifixion in a way that it specifically, down to the last detail, fulfilled Old Testament prophecy.

These predictions and their fulfillment, since the discovery of the Dead Seas Scrolls between 1947 and 1956 in Qumran in the West Bank, are undeniable; experts have confirmed that some of these scrolls were last copied between 335 and 107 BC, long before Jesus walked the earth. One of the greatest portions of the Old Testament text that was preserved was the entire book of Isaiah. So how convincing are the prophecies made about the Messiah's death?

> *He grew up before him like a tender shoot, and like a root out of dry ground. He had no beauty or majesty to attract us to him, nothing in his appearance that we should desire him. He was despised and rejected by mankind, a man of suffering, and familiar with pain. Like one from whom people hide their faces he was despised, and we held him in low esteem. Surely he took up our pain and bore our suffering, yet we considered him punished by God, stricken by him, and afflicted. But he was pierced for our transgressions, he was crushed for our iniquities; the punishment that brought us peace was on him, and by his wounds we are healed* (Isaiah 53:2-5).

This prophecy was written some 600 years before Jesus' birth. If this messianic imagery isn't convincing enough, look at Psalm 22, written four centuries *earlier* than the Isaiah account by King David, from whose line the Messiah was promised to come.

> *My God, my God, why have you forsaken me? Why are you so far from saving me, so far from my cries of anguish?*
>
> *But I am a worm and not a man, scorned by everyone, despised by the people. All who see me mock me; they hurl insults, shaking their heads. "He trusts in the Lord," they say, "let the Lord rescue him. Let him deliver him, since he delights in him..."*
>
> *Roaring lions that tear their prey open their mouths wide against me. I am poured out like water, and all my bones are out of joint. My heart has turned to wax; it has melted within me. My mouth is dried up like a potsherd, and my tongue sticks to the roof of my mouth; you lay me in the dust of death. Dogs surround me, a pack of villains encircles me; they pierce my hands and my feet. All my bones are on display; people stare and gloat over me. They divide my clothes among them and cast lots for my garment* (Psalm 22:1, 6-8, 13-18).

Anyone who knows the details of the crucifixion account as presented in the New Testament has to be fascinated by the amazing parallels to Jesus' death on the cross. The opening question was uttered by Jesus as he hung on the cross. The insults hurled at him are word-for-word those hurled at him while he was dying. Jesus attested to his thirst on the cross (a well-documented affect of death by crucifixion), and even the incongruous mention of people gambling over his clothing is dead-on with the New Testament crucifixion account.

What is most strange, however, is the allusion to his hands and feet being pierced. So problematic for Jews who reject Jesus as the Messiah, recent Hebrew translations of the word for "pierced" have often been awkwardly rendered as "lion." This despite the fact that all of the earliest translations, including the Septuagint (an early translation of the Hebrew scripture into Greek, overseen by 72 *Jewish* scholars) render the word as *pierced*. What makes the predictions surrounding Jesus' crucifixion so problematic for those who deny Jesus as the Messiah is that crucifixion wasn't even developed as a form of torture until it was used centuries later by the Roman government as a form of capital punishment.

There simply is no easy way to explain away these uncanny statements and their astounding fulfillments.

If things like this stimulate your imagination, there are many other prophecies that you should check into. The Bible is full of them. Try to ignore the Christian bias that touts some of them as being much more convincing than they really are, but give some open-minded consideration to what you find. It's pretty interesting.

> **What makes the predictions surrounding Jesus' crucifixion so problematic for those who deny Jesus as the Messiah is that crucifixion wasn't even developed as a form of torture until it was used centuries later by the Roman government as a form of capital punishment.**

Chapter 18

THE BIBLE'S DEPICTION OF END-TIME EVENTS IS EERILY BELIEVABLE

Don't worry about the world coming to an end today. It is already tomorrow in Australia.

– Charles M. Schulz

I can't profess to understand God's plan, but when Christ promised a resurrection of the dead, I just thought he had something a little different in mind.

– Hershel, *The Walking Dead*

I think everyone has at least a passing interest in future events. Most of my readers will remember the hype surrounding Y2K and how much angst led up to the turning of the millennium. Whether or not you're the type to go overboard in your reaction to apocalyptic predictions, I think everyone hypothesizes over what the future will be like – the technology, the customs, the cultures. Ever since the beginning of recorded history doomsday prophets have adding their warnings to the collage of end-time predictions. Frankly, forecasting general human hurt and suffering is a pretty safe game, and doesn't pique our interest a great deal.

But then there are other predictions that capture our imagination. Once again, more than any other major religious book, the Bible makes bold and specific prognostications about the future here on planet Earth. Some have garnered enough attention as to become elements of pop culture, such as the number 666.

As a pastor, when I poll new Christians on what book of the Bible interests them most, Revelation is consistently the number one answer. Why? Because inquiring minds want to know what the future holds. As confusing as some of the imagery is, certain elements in the timeline of Bible prophecy are generally agreed upon and accepted by the larger Christian community, even across denominational divides. Let me share a few that might resonate with you. I find them to be eerily believable.

SIGNS OF THE TIMES

Various signs are specified as warnings that the end is approaching.

> *But mark this: There will be terrible times in the last days. People will be lovers of themselves, lovers of money, boastful, proud, abusive, disobedient to their parents, ungrateful, unholy, without love, unforgiving, slanderous, without self-control, brutal, not lovers of the good, treacherous, rash, conceited, lovers of pleasure rather than lovers of God— having a form of godliness but denying its power. Have nothing to do with such people* (2 Timothy 3:1-5).

> *The Spirit clearly says that in later times some will abandon the faith and follow deceiving spirits and things taught by demons. Such teachings*

come through hypocritical liars, whose consciences have been seared as with a hot iron (1 Timothy 4:1-2).

Jesus answered: "Watch out that no one deceives you. For many will come in my name, claiming, 'I am the Messiah,' and will deceive many. You will hear of wars and rumors of wars, but see to it that you are not alarmed. Such things must happen, but the end is still to come. Nation will rise against nation, and kingdom against kingdom. There will be famines and earthquakes in various places. All these are the beginning of birth pains.

"Then you will be handed over to be persecuted and put to death, and you will be hated by all nations because of me. At that time many will turn away from the faith and will betray and hate each other, and many false prophets will appear and deceive many people. Because of the increase of wickedness, the love of most will grow cold, but the one who stands firm to the end will be saved. And this gospel of the kingdom will be preached in the whole world as a testimony to all nations, and then the end will come (Matthew 24:4-14).

Obviously, none of these individual prophecies would impress a skeptic to the point of spontaneously igniting belief in the divine, but when combined together they form an intriguing picture of days and events that seem (to me at least) to be more and more familiar. War has risen pretty steadily over the past six centuries. [18.1] Every generation has had its share of disobedient children and cult leaders, so that may be harder to quantify, but North Americans would probably agree that our kids are increasingly disrespectful toward authority, but that may be a local phenomenon. According to Samaria Garrett, who writes for the Borgen Project, natural disasters worldwide are definitely on the rise.[18.2] The depersonalization of society through the growing use of social media could be connected to the prediction of "love growing cold." It's all pretty interesting.

ANTICHRIST AND THE MARK OF THE BEAST

After these initial "signs" come some more specific events. One is the rise of a worldwide leader and a ten-nation confederacy from which he will rule the earth. His early reign will be marked by peace, something the world has long been searching for. I think most secular people today would agree that our growing globalization has us on track for such a scenario – world peace, which will only be achieved through a single world ruler. According to the Bible, this peace will be superficial and short-lived. Sounds pretty believable to me.

> *I think most secular people today would agree that our growing globalization has us on track for such a scenario – world peace, which will only be achieved through a single world ruler.*

The Bible goes so far as to predict that under this rule, everyone will be required to receive a mark in their right hand or forehead in order to buy or sell (see Revelation 13). While interpreters have attributed many explanations to this description, news articles today consistently chart the development of microchip technology. Chips are already being inserted into pets and even, in some countries, into criminals. Heightened security concerns since September 11, 2001, have made this type of technology – once considered invasive – an increasingly palatable option. The growing use of smart cards and debit cards (along with the huge load of fraud cases these companies handle every day) make the idea of a permanent, all-purpose, subcutaneous chip a convenient solution. It seems to me to be only a matter of time before this form of identification becomes a reality.

As our society becomes increasingly reliant on technology, many of the predictions in the book of Revelation are, to many observers, becoming much more realistic. For instance, consider the Bible's prediction of the global vision of Jesus' return. How realistic did that seem before the advent of the Internet and global news organizations such as CNN? In a day when smartphone technology is the prevailing method of global information access, it doesn't take much thought to imagine how such a thing might happen. Global events are reported and witnessed every single day on a scale previously unheard of a mere 20 years ago.

But let's get back to the mark of the Beast. According to the Bible, this measure (whether a microchip or not) will be marketed as a form of allegiance to the one-world ruler (as opposed to God) and many who remain faithful to God will choose to abstain and suffer the consequences of their actions.[18.3] The text goes as far as to identify the required number as "666." How's that for going out on a limb?

I'm not always sure how specific to be in my belief in these prophecies; again, there is ample for interpretation. But the events described are definitely something to watch out for.[18.4]

THE PROMINENCE OF ISRAEL

The Book of Revelation depicts the nations of the world eventually converging militarily on the nation of Israel in an attempt to finally rid the world of God's influence.[18.5] Many times in both ancient and modern history, Jews have been targeted for extinction. One has to ask if the attention this small nation has garnered over the years is coincidental, or if in fact it is evidence that the Jews have been chosen by God for special purposes. Many of the end-time events described in the Bible center on the nation of Israel, an astounding thing in and of itself, considering not only its tiny size but the fact that it only received nationhood in 1948 in an unprecedented move by the United Nations. The very existence and survival of the Jewish nation over many thousands of years is a whole discussion in itself that fortifies my strength in God and the Bible.

ANTI-GOD SENTIMENT

Also interesting to me is how the one-world ruler (a.k.a. Antichrist) will clearly posture himself against God. [18.6] The very concept of rebelling against a singular "God" must have seemed absurd to people of the first century, when the Book of Revelation was penned by the Apostle John. Although atheistic, materialistic thought had been popularized five or six centuries earlier in India and Greece, the Roman world of John's day recognized many gods. Monotheism, while practiced by certain groups, was by no means pervasive, so for John to depict a future world ruler fighting against "God" (in the singular) is quite an unanticipated prediction.

And yet today there is a very real anti-God movement afoot. Atheism is the "new black," and people everywhere feel compelled to denounce God while at the same time saying they don't believe in the one they are denouncing. Authors like Richard Dawkins, Sam Harris and Christopher Hitchens have been scathing in their relentless attacks on God and on those who choose to believe in and follow him. [18.7] Organizations like the American Atheists are just as militant, and you may have heard of the challenge offered a few years back by the Rational Response Squad and Beyond Belief Media – inviting people to go to their website (blasphemychallenge.com) and "blaspheme against the Holy Spirit." I'm incredibly intrigued that John could have predicted that people would rebel against God in such an outright manner. Whether or not we're in the end times, we surely can't deny that the type of boldfaced rebellion predicted in the Bible is very possible, if not part of our cultural experience already.

If you are into prophetic literature, I think you'll find Revelation an interesting read. The persecution of Christians, the revival and fall of "Babylon" (whose true identity is much debated), the crash of world financial markets... it's all there. Much of John's vision is blurry, but many people find it fuels their belief.

Chapter 19

MY CHRISTIAN FAITH GIVES ME HOPE

Nature's first green is gold,
Her hardest hue to hold.
Her early leaf's a flower;
But only so an hour.
Then leaf subsides to leaf.
So Eden sank to grief,
So dawn goes down to day.
Nothing gold can stay.

–Robert Frost

Whence come I and whither go I? That is the great unfathomable question, the same for every one of us. Science has no answer to it.

–Max Planck (German theoretical Physicist who originated quantum theory)

I'm a helpless idealist. Fed by my perfectionism, my idealism keeps me in a constant state of dissatisfaction. The story of my life has been that of setting unrealistic expectations only to fail to attain to my goals. I read somewhere once that leaders are highly dissatisfied people, so whenever I'm doubting my leadership ability I hold onto that one. I never just see something for what it is; I always imagine what it could be.

As much as this perspective annoys me and colors my world blue, somewhere inside I believe there is something divine to it. I'm positive that God has no trouble managing his emotions like I wish I could, but down deep I know that he isn't satisfied with the way things are either.

God can't possibly be satisfied with the world we know. If the biblical account is accurate, he made the world perfect, and we humans screwed it up. I can just imagine how ticked off I'd be if someone came along and defaced—or *mutilated* – the greatest masterpiece I'd ever painted. Only God's immense and perfect patience must keep him from kicking butt. If he's omniscient, as the Bible describes him to be, he is also thoroughly aware of all the crap that this world churns out minute by minute. (It's worse than having CNN on 24-7.) As much as God's magnificent creation amazes me, I am equally dumbfounded by his ability to tolerate the ugliness and pain of our planet.

A few years ago my wife and I were on vacation in California. After some sea kayaking in La Jolla and our first try at surfing on Mission Beach we decided to spend the night in San Diego. It was late by the time we got cleaned up and made our way over to the Gaslamp Quarter – a charming and vibrant nightlife area. Unfortunately, the kitchens in most of the bars and restaurants were closing, so my wife spied what I could tell was a pricey establishment that was going to put a serious hit on my wallet. I insisted that we try a few other places first and I could sense her temperature rising as I made her follow me around in her high heels. By the time we found a more reasonably-priced spot that was still making flatbread pizzas, she was pretty miffed. As our drinks arrive she says, "Let's go sit at the bar," which was her way of saying, "I don't feel like talking to you; let's go find some people I might want to talk to."[19.1]

As we sat at the corner of the bar we got chatting with a couple named Dan and Karen who were not "together" but were attending a restaurateurs' convention together in San Diego. [19.2] Dan in particular was very personable and engaging, and we were all enjoying each others' company. The conversation soon revealed that Dan had been snorting cocaine for a good part of the afternoon, and he was drinking pretty enthusiastically at the bar as well. "A round of Fireballs!" he shouted. (It soon became apparent that Karen was watching out for him.)

Soon they suggested that we check out a hookah lounge a few blocks away. (My wife had long wanted to try it, so she was game; me – not so much, but I was along for the ride.) The lounge was closed so they suggested another establishment. I leaned over and whispered to my wife, "I think we're bar hopping." She laughed. A few blocks away we filed into a buzzing little hotspot with a rockabilly band jamming in one corner. The girls split up from me and Dan for a while as we all got to know one another better. As we stood next to the bar, Dan started telling me that he had recently returned from Iraq.

And then it happened.

By "it" I mean what happens every time Sarah and I make new friends out of complete strangers like this. Dan left for a minute to chat with Karen, and when he returned he had a look of shock on his face. He glared at me as he shouted out over the din of the tightly packed bar, "You never told me you're an f---ing *pastor*!" I held my breath awaiting the words that would follow...

"You're the coolest pastor *ever*! Another round of Fireballs!"

Exhale.

And then the dams opened. Through a haze of cocaine and alcohol Dan started pouring out his heart over what had taken place in Iraq. Tears ran down his face as he described how he saw his best friend get blown apart in front of his own eyes. He mentioned something about shooting a kid, but it was loud and part of me was afraid to ask for clarification. I just let him talk. He was a broken man, and he was doing his very best to drown all of the powerful emotion that refused to stay below the surface. My heart was breaking for him.

I drew close to his ear. "Dan, you're a good person," I said. "I've only just met you and I can see that. God loves you and he forgives. He hasn't given up on you." I tried to help him see that life was still worth living, that God offers real hope to us. Through the noise and tears and alcohol I could see a little bit of peace come back into his soul, and around 2 am when it was time to part ways we all gave each other big hugs and agreed on what an amazing evening it had been. I've never been able to locate Dan on Facebook, but I still pray for him whenever I think of him.

A big part of what makes me a believer is my need to hope. I've already shared how I like being a person of faith because it helps me to be more optimistic on a day-to-day basis. But I also find that faith makes me more optimistic about my life, and the human race. Without faith in God I would quickly become overwhelmed by all of the pain and brokenness, but with him I am somehow able to engage the ugliness. Jesus gives me a model to follow in bringing redemption and hope to those around me. And when I can't see a hopeful ending for some of life's problems, I look forward to heaven, a place where everything will be perfect, a place that the Bible talks a lot about.

SO MUCH TO HATE

When I see litter and graffiti trashing up my city, I get angry. One time when I saw someone chuck a plastic bottle from their car window going through a McDonald's drive-thru, I got out, picked up the bottle and threw it back in their window, saying, "Hey, I think you dropped something." (Not until hours later when I cooled off did it dawn on me how badly something like that could have gone down.) I hate the fact that many of our rivers are too polluted for fish to live in and that many of our beaches here in Toronto are unfit for swimming.

I get angry when I see people hurting – whether by wars, poverty, famine, or government repression. In a world as rich in wisdom and resources as ours, there is simply no need for all of the suffering we witness, and when I see people intentionally hurt or take advantage of others, I burn with righteous indignation. I believe God planted in me that part of my personality that responds so passionately to these matters, and I have full confidence that there will come a time and place where God will act to set everything right.

I hate to see people suffering through sickness. I hate to see people die and leave loved ones behind. Every time I preside over a funeral it breaks my heart, and I get angry inside that we live in a place where little children need to have death explained to them. I hate seeing all of the hideous results of sin's curse upon humankind as well – birth defects, accidents, war and disease. I loathe the shame and indignity of the entire human experience. Something inside me tells me that we were meant for so much more.

I hate seeing what aging does to a human body. While sometimes we're tempted to mock people who get plastic surgery, more often I find myself sympathizing with those who do. I get sad and angry at the same time when I see a woman fighting against the tide, trying in vain to hold onto her youth. Something inside me admires her spirit despite the hopelessness of her efforts. I don't cherish the thought of getting old either (and I'm beginning to see signs of it).

I hate the pain that ravages the human spirit, the selfishness that brings people to take advantage of others and the unforgiveness that perpetuates the hurt. I hate the emptiness I see in people's eyes – that look that emerges after they have tried everything and have still come up empty. It's the same look that drives people to bury themselves in sex or drink or drugs long before their actual burial.

If there is not a place, somewhere, sometime, when all of these things are made right, then we're all royally screwed, because we know that this place isn't it. Short of God working his magic in our midst, we have no hope as a species. As Christopher Hitchens astutely asserted: "The awareness that our death is coming and will be succeeded by the death of the species and the heat death of the universe is scant comfort." [19.3]

Some, like Richard Dawkins, would say that my dilemma has led me to embrace the "God Delusion." If that's what he chooses to call it, then so be it. Like Abraham, the ancient father of the faithful, I'm looking forward to something far better.

> *If there is not a place, somewhere, sometime, when all of these things are made right, then we're all royally screwed, because we know that this place isn't it.*

For he was looking forward to the city with foundations, whose architect and builder is God (Hebrews 11:10).

I believe that God is creating a place where I will finally be able to catch up with old friends. A place where time is no longer the enemy. A place where work is no longer a curse. A place of peace for the human spirit. We all long for eternal life, and I believe we can have it. As English writer and philosopher Harriet Martineau said, "We do not believe in immortality because we can prove it, but we try to prove it because we cannot help believing it."

My confidence that such a place exists is what helps me make it through the day. I have no confidence in evolution or in the intelligence of the human race; I'm staking it all on God. In this world, nothing gold can stay, but someday, the gold will be restored. My Christian faith gives me this kind of hope.

> *"He will wipe every tear from their eyes. There will be no more death' or mourning or crying or pain, for the old order of things has passed away"* (Revelation 21:4).

Chapter 20

THE TEACHINGS AND LIFE OF JESUS INSPIRE ME LIKE NONE OTHER

*If Christians would really live according to
the teachings of Christ, as found in the Bible,
all of India would be Christian today.*

–Mahatma Gandhi

*Even those who have renounced Christianity and attack
it, in their inmost being still follow the Christian ideal,
for hitherto neither their subtlety nor the ardour of
their hearts has been able to create a higher ideal of man
and of virtue than the ideal given by Christ of old.*

–Fyodor Dostoyevsky

There's nothing like the power of paradox. We love to discover truths that contradict common understanding – truths that aren't supposed to be true. Moral paradox is particularly pleasing to the right brain, because it requires experimentation; we have no choice but to test the paradox in order to verify its veracity for ourselves.

Take, for example, Jesus' words in Matthew 20:16: "So the last will be first, and the first will be last." As you can see from this simple statement, verifying moral paradox always requires personal experimentation, which in turn requires faith. You simply cannot stand back and rationally analyze paradoxical statements and discover if they are true or not. An experiential approach is required. In the case of Matthew 20:16, a person must be willing to be "last" in order to understand in what sense this will make him "first."

> *You simply cannot stand back and rationally analyze paradoxical statements and discover if they are true or not. An experiential approach is required.*

It may never have occurred to you, but much of Jesus' teaching was in the form of paradox. He loved to turn commonly held knowledge on its head. This approach made his teaching engaging, because it shocked and surprised those who listened. Jesus' famous Sermon on the Mount (in truth, a number of different topics that Jesus repeated on numerous occasions) includes several different paradoxes, and is my absolute favorite section of the entire Bible. All four gospels contain numerous examples of the many paradoxes Jesus taught. Consider these popular examples...

- that he was human and divine at the same time – "I and the Father are one" (John 10:30).
- that internal transformation (rebirth) was necessary for external reformation; Jesus thoroughly confused Nicodemus, a religious leader, when he insisted, "You must born again" (John 3:7).
- the call to lose one's life in order to find it – "Whoever finds their life will lose it, and whoever loses their life for my sake will find it" (Matthew 10:39).

- "It is more blessed to give than to receive" (Acts 20:35).
- "Do unto others as you would have them do unto you" (Matthew 7:12).
- the invitation to a higher level of living – "Love your enemies," "Pray for those who persecute you" (Matthew 5:43-45), "If anyone slaps you on the right cheek, turn to them the other cheek also" (Matthew 5:39).
- the necessity of humility – "The first will be last, the last will be first" (Matthew 20:16). I call this "the great reversal," taught in detail in Luke 16.
- that the law and grace can exist at the same time (John 1:17)
- that we can find blessing in suffering, poverty and persecution (Matthew 5:11-12)
- that private worship of God results in public blessing (Matthew 6:6)
- that you can "gain the whole world but lose your own soul" (Luke 9:25)
- that the road to exaltation is humility – "For those who exalt themselves will be humbled, and those who humble themselves will be exalted" (Matthew 23:12)
- that needs are met, not by worrying, but by trusting (Matthew 6:25-34)
- that people improve when they are loved, not when they are judged (Luke 6:37)

As you can see, the bulk of Jesus' teaching was paradox! No other teacher or religious leader had the insight that Jesus had. His teaching provides me with a lifetime of paradoxes to examine – a lifetime of experimentation to undertake. So far, every one of the paradoxes of Jesus that I've tested has proven to be true. Contrast that to the emptiness I've found from my experience with the world's so-called "wisdom" and it just further strengthens my belief.

Now, I'm sure that many a reader will silently ask, "Aren't the right-brained reasons for faith presented in this book attainable through the teachings of a variety of religious leaders?" Of course, many leaders in the past and the present spoke of faith, love, humility and morality. So much so that common wisdom today figures that all religious systems are basically the same at the core and that all great religious leaders have contributed something to the grand religious think tank from which we ought to drink.

This line of thinking is convenient in that it appears to spare the individual from choosing one specific teacher or path, allowing that person to avoid the flack that such a choice might attract. But as we discussed in an earlier chapter on inclusiveness, not choosing really isn't an option. Jesus, wise teacher that he was, reminded us of this fact: "No one can serve two masters. Either you will hate the one and love the other, or you will be devoted to the one and despise the other" (Matthew 6:24). Another paradox that must be tested experientially!

For those of you who are still resistant to embracing Jesus as your faith solution, I would ask you to consider three things. First, compare the thoroughness of Jesus' teaching with that of any other teacher. Whose complete teachings best appeal to your sense of truth?

Second, compare the life that he lived with the lives of other great teachers. As James C. Hefley, Christian author and founder of Hannibal Books remarks:

> *"Here is a man who was born in an obscure village, the Child of a peasant woman. He worked in a carpenter shop until He was thirty, and then for three years He was an itinerant preacher. He never wrote a book. He never held an office. He never owned a home. He never had a family. He never went to college. He never put His foot inside a big city. He never traveled two hundred miles from the place where He was born. He never did one of the things that usually accompany greatness. He had no credentials but Himself. He had nothing to do with this world except*

the naked power of His Divine manhood. While still a young man, the tide of popular opinion turned against Him. He was turned over to His enemies. He went through the mockery of a trial. He was nailed to a Cross between two thieves. His executioners gambled for the only piece of property He had on earth while He was dying—and that was His coat. When He was dead He was taken down and laid in a borrowed grave through the pity of a friend. Such was His human life—He rises from the dead. Nineteen wide centuries have come and gone and today He is the Centerpiece of the human race and the Leader of the column of progress. I am within the mark when I say that all the armies that ever marched, and all the navies that ever were built, and all the parliaments that ever sat, and all the kings that ever reigned, put together, have not affected the life of man upon this earth as powerfully as has that One Solitary Life."

When you compare the life of Jesus to the lives of other great teachers, which inspires you the most? Which most captures your imagination? Whose life was the most beautiful, the most poetic? Learn everything you can about Siddhartha Guatama, Confucius, Mohammed, Gandhi, Martin Luther King, Jr. – whomever you want to, and then compare them with Jesus. We all choose to emulate someone. Who will *you* pattern *your* life after?

Third and finally, consider Jesus' claims to deity. We could embrace Jesus as a formidable teacher if that was all he alleged to be. Many faiths and individuals take just such a position. But Jesus claimed much more. His claim to deity, reinforced by the performance of the miracles that even secular history records, forces our hand.

"Buddha never claimed to be God. Moses never claimed to be Jehovah. Mohammed never claimed to be Allah. Yet Jesus Christ claimed to be the true and living God. Buddha simply said, "I am a teacher in search of the truth." Jesus said, "I am the Truth." Confucius said, "I never

claimed to be holy." Jesus said, "Who convicts me of sin?" Mohammed said, "Unless God throws his cloak of mercy over me, I have no hope." Jesus said, "Unless you believe in me, you will die in your sins."

–Author Unknown

I agree with C. S. Lewis' conviction that to simply call Jesus a great teacher is "patronizing nonsense." Either he was who he claimed to be or his entire reputation was shot.

If you find someone whose life and teaching inspire you more than Jesus, then I would encourage you to follow them. If you find someone who was more convincingly divine, then I would encourage you to follow that person.

It's really not that complicated.

> **If you find someone whose life and teaching inspire you more than Jesus, then I would encourage you to follow them.**

Chapter 21

I NEED GOD

I am not in danger, Skyler. I am the danger!

–Walter White, *Breaking Bad*

I'm not normally a praying man, but if you're up there, please save me, Superman!

–Homer Simpson

They say we are normally most comfortable with what we grew up with. If this is true, I should be more than comfortable with traditional North American Christianity. Few people have experienced it from any closer vantage point than I have.

I became a "follower of Jesus" just prior to my fifth birthday. (In retrospect, I actually became a follower of the church culture I was presented. Truly following Jesus came much later.) I was baptized at age nine. My father was a pastor. When I was twelve my family joined with a seasoned pastor and his wife to start a church. As a boy and as a teenager I participated in every imaginable aspect of church life. By Grade 12 I knew the Bible as well as many Bible-college graduates. After graduating from high school I went on to attend three different schools, darkening the doors of numerous churches from a wide variety of denominations in the process.

And yet, with all of this exposure, some things that I learned never did become comfortable for me. I am thankful today that they never did.

NO MAN'S LAND

Not until I became a pastor myself did I fully wrestle through some of the issues that had long created tension in my spirit in regard to the church. Like many other people that I came to know as an adult, I discovered that I loved Jesus a lot more than I loved his followers. Sadly, I appreciated the Bible a lot more than I appreciated many of the people who taught it to me.

From the time I was a teenager I resisted certain elements of the Christian scene that others unthinkingly embraced – the unwritten church rules, the slick preachers, the aggressive proselytization, the political posturing. I couldn't even bring myself to watch Christian TV or listen to Christian radio (and to this day people look at me funny for not knowing some of the big names in Christian media). I made friends with non-Christians as easily as I did with Christians (and oftentimes, more easily).

With all of my frustrations, however, I never did swing the pendulum to the other side.[21.1] I never rebelled against my parents or the church or its leaders. I never got into drugs or alcohol or wild living. I never sowed my wild oats (or any other wild grains, for that matter). I never rejected God in favor of science or nihilism. I simply embraced the truth that I couldn't deny and continued to live as I thought a true Christian should.

As a result of this choice, I have spent a good part of my life in no man's land – never really feeling at home in the church or the world. I've always loved the message of Jesus, but I've often preferred the authentic company of the "heathen." It was probably inevitable that I would become a church planter – that I would eventually take a crack at redefining the church experience.

Over the years I have worked to identify those elements of North American Christianity that have perturbed me, and I have tried to help my congregation understand these perceived failures within the church. I've come to realize that it is only because I care about the church so deeply that I even bother to try. To my surprise (and delight), many people outside the church have resonated with these discoveries and have cautiously embraced Jesus as well.

MORE THAN ENOUGH DETRACTIONS

Here's the deal. Most Christians in North America (which is what I refer to here throughout my discussion) have never properly grasped Jesus' simple message of love. When asked what it means to be a Christian, many people will tell you about going to heaven someday, not about being on a mission of love like Jesus described.

Many Christians haven't understood the message of grace – the reality that only broken, humble people can truly connect with Jesus. Instead, they are trying to impress God by how well they follow rules – like people who lived in the Old Testament era – and as a result are judgmental and obsessed with exterior performance (just like the religious leaders whom Jesus criticized the most). Overall, our judgmental posture makes us very uptight. Not only does this render us an unpopular invitation to parties, [21.2] it sets us up for insincerity, pride and hypocrisy, which do not go unnoticed.

A disturbing number of Christians are protectionistic. They are living their lives in a way that protects a lifestyle they have come to enjoy.

(Strange, because Jesus never talked about living a safe, protected life. He risked everything to introduce people to a God they didn't understand.) Many Christians today avoid "sinful" people and tend to be very narrow-minded. Like Jesus' own mistaken disciples, they want their Jesus to create a political arrangement that will support their lifestyle.

Relatively few Christians truly understand God's final word to mankind (that is, Jesus). Consequently, the average Christian's understanding of their faith is only about ankle deep. We avoid intellectual debate, oversimplify our positions, and in general deserve the reputation we have for being non-thinkers.

If all of that's not enough, I am convinced that Christians are the most clueless lot on the planet when it comes to knowing how other people perceive them. In fact, sometimes we're just plain cheesy. I can't stomach most televangelists or Christian TV hosts. It seems we're either judgmental bigots or we're such nauseatingly sweet, "plastic" people, that turn people off completely.

> ...the truth I have come to discover is powerful enough to overcome all of these detractions.

My point in sharing all of this is simple: I want you to understand that *the truth I have come to discover is powerful enough to overcome all of these detractions*. If the decision to follow Jesus was based on the winsomeness of his followers (myself included), then I'd have abandoned my faith in Jesus a long time ago.

FAITH IN GOD FEELS RIGHT

I am a believer because of a handful of converging realities – my inability to deny a creator God, the wisdom that has (allegedly) emanated from God, and the person and teaching of Jesus Christ. Combined, they form for me a complete, satisfying and stalwart certainty that nothing to date has been able to shake – be it the discoveries of science, public opinion, competing philosophies or faiths, or even the repugnance I feel toward many who claim to share my views. My conviction is not merely intellectual, as I've tried to demonstrate throughout this book; it's largely intuitive.

I need God. I believe that you do too, but your discovery of this fact (if indeed it is fact) will be a personal one. When you do a quick scan of humanity, you recognize that people everywhere have a need for someone greater to guide and inspire them. As kids we latch onto our parents, then superheroes and then movie stars.

I need God to be my object of worship. I have come to discover, most absolutely, that I am going to give my devotion to something in my life. I cannot agree more with Emerson on this:

> "A person will worship something, have no doubt about that. We may think our tribute is paid in secret in the dark recesses of our hearts, but it will out. That which dominates our imaginations and our thoughts will determine our lives, and our character. Therefore, it behooves us to be careful what we worship, for what we are worshipping we are becoming."

I will inevitably latch onto something greater than me: an image, entity or ideal, be it right or wrong, healthy or destructive. It may be my wife, or a teacher, or a friend, or even a sports figure. It may be a more noble object, such as my career or a good cause. It could even be myself. But if I direct my worship toward anything short of God himself, I will be missing the mark. I have a desire to be one with the great mind of the universe. I desire to find his intended place for my life in his grand scheme of things. My right brain tells me that this is where satisfaction will be found.

I need God to inspire my imagination. I believe it is the Creator who bestows creativity. Remove God, or even just the idea of God, from my mind and I am convinced that I would lose all desire to create. Maybe this is where I differ from left-brained people. In my life I have never been motivated to create simply to solve a problem. I create because when I do I feel connected to my purpose. I feel like Eric Liddell in *Chariots of Fire*:

> *"I believe that God made me for a purpose... but He also made me fast, and when I run, I feel His pleasure."*

I don't want to mislead anyone – when *I* run, I usually just feel nauseous. But when I sit at the piano or in front of a blank canvas or at my laptop, I feel connected to my source. I get the same feeling when I sit next to the ocean. God meets me in these places.

It could be argued that life itself is full of inspiration, but life as we know it will only inspire for a time. The older I get, the more I acknowledge that there is only so much to discover on planet Earth. Remembering that there is a God who is not contained within this world breathes new hope into my soul.

I need God to keep me moral. While I dedicated a chapter in this book to confessing that I like doing right more than wrong, the confession was incomplete. Although I like doing good, I know that I lack the strength in and of myself to be good on a consistent basis. Atheists may claim they have no need of God to be moral and good. I cannot speak for them. For me, without the belief that God watches me and that I will one day give account to him, I would fall headfirst into selfish and destructive hedonism. Not only do I find I need God to keep me from falling, but when I do fall, I need his forgiveness and love to help me get back on track. I need him to free me from the nagging guilt I feel when I hurt other people.

I need God to present me with more noble aspirations than those that surround me day after day. The themes of love, redemption, grace and forgiveness that I find in God's Word are the most noble I've found, and ones to which I aspire. I believe they are divine and that they find their root in God, who has consequently become the focus of my devotion.

LET'S KEEP WRESTLING

I have a real fear that some will interpret my writing as a statement that I have all the answers. Nothing could be further from the truth. I am still on the pathway of discovery, but I like the path that I am on. Everything inside me says it's the right path.

While I disagree with some of today's most prominent thinkers, I respect the fact that they are bothered enough by life's big questions to wrestle with them and share their thoughts with others. In this matter I feel a certain kinship with my opponents. Strong left-brainers will surely find these people more convincing than me, and I do not argue their intellectual prowess. I have embraced the reality that living as a person of faith comes with labels. Sometimes it hurts my pride, but I have learned to be comfortable with the discomfort.

If being a person of faith makes me ignorant, deluded, or irrational in your eyes, I cannot help that. I am – and as far as I can tell, always will be – a person of faith. I am not too proud to walk with a crutch, if that is how you perceive my belief in God. Having engaged in hundreds of spiritual conversations over the years, I understand that you may feel no need whatsoever for God in your life right now. But someday if that changes, I hope you'll pick up my book again and reconsider.

ONE LAST STORY

On a flight home from board meetings a few years ago I watched a movie I would otherwise never have taken the time to see. It was *Shall We Dance*, starring Jennifer Lopez and Richard Gere, an actor that makes every guy's "chick flick" radar scream. But there I was with a couple of hours to kill, so I bit the bullet.

The story is about a man in midlife crisis who decides to throw caution to the wind and take a dance class. In the process, he falls in love with his instructor. I hated to admit it, but the film had a potent humanness to it that I hadn't experienced in a long time.

One poignant scene made the entire film one I will never forget. It was razor-sharp. Richard Gere's character speaks with his wife (played by Susan Sarandon) at a key moment when their marriage seems to be crumbling around them. She asks him, "Why is it that people get married?" Gere's character is silent as she continues:

> *We need a witness to our lives. There's a billion people on the planet... I mean, what does any one life really mean? But in a marriage, you're promising to care about everything. The good things, the bad things, the terrible things, the mundane things... all of it, all of the time, every day. You're saying 'Your life will not go unnoticed because I will notice it. Your life will not go un-witnessed because I will be your witness'."*

The scene left my right brain humming like a tuning fork.

I need God because I need a witness to my life. Without a witness, life is meaningless. So much of our lives is lived out of sight or below the surface. The small amount we do share is often misunderstood or disconnected. As a person who embraced God early in life, I simply cannot imagine a life without a constant, loving witness. I don't think I'm egocentric in this regard; I just think I'm human – made in the image of God to love and enjoy him forever.[21.3]

> **I need God because I need a witness to my life. Without a witness, life is meaningless.**

I recognize very well that there is no rational basis for needing a witness for my life, and that simply feeling a need for God does nothing to satisfy the questions of my left brain. But don't you get it? Doesn't it make sense?

Don't you need a witness to your life as well?

CONCLUSION

*Love the Lord your God with all your heart and
with all your soul and with all your mind.*

—Jesus (Matthew 22:37)

Duality is everywhere. Body and mind. Darkness and light. Yin and Yang. Masculine and feminine. Matter and spirit. Right and wrong. Theory and experience. Life and death. North and south. Left and right. We understand the universe around us in contrasts and comparisons. Trying to understand darkness without light is impossible, as is trying to understand any of the words above without its opposite.

When it comes to understanding the nuances of life, duality is essential. We hear sound in stereo with two ears. We see things in focus with two eyes. Left-brain and right-brain. Facts and feeling. Logic and emotion.

When it comes to making sense of life's deeper questions, we are better served to employ a balance of our opposing dualities. My goal in writing this book has been to bring balance to the faculties we bring to bear on issues of faith. Far too often in our scientific age, we are guilty of basing our faith decisions solely on facts and logic.

Ironically, we do this in no other area of life. When choosing a spouse, a car, an apartment, or even a piece of clothing, we always engage our right brain in the process, and we are happier with our decisions as a result.

Think about it. There is no purely scientific way to choose a spouse. You can run all the personality tests you want, make checklists for desired traits and frequent the highest probability hangouts. None of these controls would be able to account for the timing or circumstances of your first romantic encounter, let alone the millions of other factors that would influence your decision – the way the light hit their eye, the warmth of the wind on your skin, the subconscious memories connected to their smell, the tilt of the earth. And yet, with such a myriad of variables in play, complex human beings regularly join their lives with other complex human beings. Every day on our lonely planet people find love. Commitments are made when millions of ethereal questions are somehow satisfied but while millions more remain unanswered.

> **When choosing a spouse, a car, an apartment, or even a piece of clothing, we always engage our right brain in the process, and we are happier with our decisions as a result.**

At times, we all wish we could understand life like a computer program and then just run the application. But life doesn't work like that. As Kierkegaard lamented, "Life can only be understood backwards; but it must be lived forwards." Fortunately, we can live by faith with unanswered questions when the object of our faith is a person, a person who in love and generosity of spirit makes up the difference for everything that we lack. The beauty of this arrangement is that it leaves life full of mystery, discovery and emotion.

For all our complaints, I don't think we'd want our relationship with God to be any different.

A FINAL WORD TO FELLOW TRAVELERS

I understand that I have probably raised more questions than I have answered in this book. That's okay; in fact, it's a good thing. If I've stirred up any creative thoughts at all, then I've engaged the right brain, which has been my goal.

I don't profess to be a scientist. My training is in theology, and I'm a recreational philosopher at best. But I'm not dumb, and I'm guessing neither is the one holding this book in their hands. So while I've tried to give you something to chew on, I celebrate the fact that one of the beauties of faith in Jesus is that it is a personal decision – the decision of one person to embrace another. I believe God intended that decision to be free from the coercion and control of outside forces, be they religion, science, politics, or one's next-door neighbor. Choosing to embrace Jesus is a choice that anyone can make, even a helpless left-brainer.

> What I'm saying is that God made us with two sides of our brain. He does not expect us to deny our left brain with all of its questions, but neither will he permit us to deny our right brain with all of its intuition.

What I'm saying is that God made us with two sides of our brain. He does not expect us to deny our left brain with all of its questions, but neither will he permit us to deny our right brain with all of its intuition. Jesus told us to love the Lord our God with *all* of our mind, not just half of it. Faith, contrary to popular opinion, is a dynamic that requires both sides of the brain to act in harmony. It's facts and feelings, logic and emotion. Together.

That being said, in my years of experience with faith I have witnessed repeatedly that there is a "leap" element to faith that frightens left-brainers. This "leap" is not the abandonment of reason, but the willingness to embrace more than reason alone. Admittedly, this kind of duality creates a certain tension inside, but I have found it to be a most healthy tension.

Even people who are rich in faith must continually confront new leaps of faith. Faith is by no means a one-time event; it takes courage for any of us to embrace it day by day. In my experience, it is in these leaps of faith that real life itself is found – rich, exciting, invigorating life. In our quest for answers, we mustn't miss out on life.

I appreciate your willingness to consider some new ideas. As a fellow traveler, I wish you the best on your faith journey. I hope that your pursuit of faith will not be a half-brained affair. Don't just be logical; be smart. In your gut, I suspect you hold more reasons for faith than you may acknowledge.

ABOUT THE AUTHOR

Bartley Sawatsky is the co-founder and Lead Pastor of Renew Church, a multisite church in the Toronto area (www.renewchurch.ca). He grew up in Nova Scotia, Canada, and received his Masters of Divinity degree from Capital Bible Seminary in Washington, D.C., graduating *magna cum laude*. It was there that he first connected with the Grace Brethren Fellowship, with which he now associates. He serves on two different church planting boards, one in the U.S. and one in Canada, and has a keen interest in starting new churches that will reintroduce Christian faith to people in a post-Christian culture. In 2013, he was elected Executive Director of the Fellowship of Grace Brethren Churches. Bartley has been married to his wife, Sarah, for 23 years and they have four children.

ENDNOTES

0.1 Postmodernity is one of the most ambiguous cultural movements you'll ever study and not even considered a legitimate historical era by some. It is thus no surprise that dates for it are all over the map. Although the movement really began in the early part of the 20th century, historians who try to pinpoint the decline of modernity usually find it coinciding with events like the Hippie Revolution (Summer of Love, 1967) and student movements which began in 1968. The pervasive spirit of the age was a rejection of modern conveniences, ideals and mores.

In *The Condition of Postmodernity* David Harvey sees the origins of postmodernity in the cultural Sixties, the period which he dates as 1968-1972 (www.interpretingpostmodernity.net). The exhibition *Postmodernism: Style and Subversion 1970–1990* at the Victoria and Albert Museum in London (September 24, 2011 – January 15, 2012) was billed as the first show to document postmodernism as a historical movement. The dates used to bookend the era are noteworthy.

Postmodernity as an identifiable cultural shift tends to be dated around 1970, as you can see from the quotes below:

"The term *postmodern* may first have been coined in the 1930s to refer to a major historical transition already under way and as the designation for certain developments in the arts. But postmodernism did not gain widespread attention until the 1970s." (Stanley J. Grenz, *A Primer on Postmodernism*, ©1996 Wm. B. Eerdmans Publishing Co., P. 2)

"I will here distinguish four different stages in the development of postmodernism: accumulation; synthesis; autonomy; and dissipation. In the first stage, which extends through the 1970s and the early part of the 1980s, the hypothesis of postmodernism was under development on a number of different fronts." (Steven Connor, *The Cambridge Companion to Postmodernism*, ©2004 Cambridge University Press, P. 1)

For the sake of this book, when I use the term postmodern I am generally using it loosely to refer to everyone since the decline of modernity – some of Generation X, Generation Y (a.k.a. Millennials), Generation Z and beyond.

0.2   Today we understand that right-brained and left-brained thinking is more about the way in which individuals process information and less about which hemisphere of the brain is at work, although there is some correlation. (Check out "Lateralization of brain function" on Wikipedia.) There are various self-tests you can do online to determine whether you are more left-brained or right-brained in your "wiring." A controversial one you may have seen doesn't even use questions, but merely asks you to indicate which way you see the silhouette of a dancer turning. (I saw it turning clockwise, suggesting that I am predominantly right-brained.) In a couple of brief moments I saw it turn in the opposite direction, but I couldn't control when. I can't really believe that such a simple test (more like an optical illusion) can really tell if someone is right or left-brained, but I find it fascinating that some people can only see the image turn in one direction, no matter how hard they try to see the other. It makes me think about how some people have a hard time exercising faith, no matter how hard they try. Here's the URL if you've got a few minutes to kill: http://braintest.sommer-sommer.com

1.1   The transfiguration is recorded in Matthew 17:1-13, Mark 2:9-13, and Luke 9:28-36. According to Matthew 17:2, Jesus' "face shone like the sun, and his clothes became as white as the light."

1.2 Matthew 9:20-22 and 14:34-36, Mark 6:53-56, and Luke 8:43-48. Jesus said he actually felt power going out of him when people touched the hem of his garment in faith.

1.3 Wired Magazine, Issue 14.11, November, 2006, *The Church of the Non-Believers*, by Gary Wolf.

1.4 Baruch A. Shalev, *100 Years of Nobel Prizes* (2003), Atlantic Publishers & Distributors, P. 57

1.5 So much for reputable journalism. I'm quoting Wikipedia as a reliable source! (Be honest – don't you trust it all the time?) Oh yes, the reference... they've updated it, but take a look anyway. Look up *Coelacanth* and read the paragraph under *Fossil record*.

1.6 The Darwinian model relies on minute changes in organisms which slowly take place over very long periods of time, meaning we should see an innumerable number of intermediary life forms in the fossil record. But we simply don't see them. (Some Christian scientists are emboldened enough to say that we don't see any!) Even Darwin acknowledged the problem in this: *Geology assuredly does not reveal any such finely-graduated organic chain; and this, perhaps, is the most obvious and serious objection which can be urged against the theory.* (Charles Darwin, *The Origin of Species*)

1.7 In her April 23, 2015 Huffington Post article, Catherine Taibi reminds us of 7 products that Dr. Oz has "peddled". Have you used all of your "garcinia cambogia" yet?

1.8 Larry King once said: "I would like to ask [Jesus] if He was indeed virgin born, because the answer to that question would define history."

1.9   2 Peter 3:3-4 – *First of all, you must understand that in the last days scoffers will come, scoffing and following their own evil desires. They will say, "Where is this 'coming' he promised? Ever since our fathers died, everything goes on as it has since the beginning of creation."*

1.10   Even most Christians are surprised to learn that miracles are actually very rare in Bible history. Apart from a few brief periods of time, miracles are mostly absent from the human experience. For me, it's an observation that makes the dearth of miracles we experience today less discouraging.

1.11   Hebrews 11:1 (King James Version)

2.1   I should clarify that at the time of writing this section, my three oldest children who watch the show are 20, 18 and 16. Some portions of this book were written when my kids were much younger, and I didn't want to leave you with the impression that my preschoolers were watching the show.

2.2   Here's a tangible application of trigonometry I just found on the internet: *At 57 feet from the base of a building you need to look up at 55° to see the top of a building. What is the height of the building?*

Can you believe that I can't remember being given a single real-life scenario like this from high school? Not one. I'm so angry right now; this could have made all the difference for me. Let's be honest though – wouldn't you just as soon find the building plans before actually finding a way to measure your viewing angle of some building that you can't get closer than 57 feet to? For those who care, the height = $57 \times \tan(55°) = 81.4$ feet.

2.3   Tim Keller, in his book *The Reason for God*, does a great job in demonstrating that unless someone is open to the concept of a miracle in the first place, there is no way that they would ever be able to say they witnessed one. Their naturalist presupposition of the universe would not allow them to acknowledge it. Rather, it would force them to look for some explanation based on natural laws.

I once remember reading such a person's desperate theory of how Moses crossed the Red Sea. He proposed that an extremely improbably weather incident resulted in a flash freezing of the Red Sea, allowing Moses and the children of Israel to walk across. (I'm not even kidding.) At a certain point, the attempt to explain away the miracle becomes more absurd than the miracle itself.

2.4   G.K. Chesterton, *Introduction to the Book of Job*, 1907.

3.1   *For now we see only a reflection as in a mirror; then we shall see face to face. Now I know in part; then I shall know fully, even as I am fully known.* (1 Corinthians 13:12)

4.1   G.K. Chesterton, *Orthodoxy*

4.2   Why is "front yard" two words and "backyard" only one word?

4.3   Google "city patterns" (images) and get a feel for how the divine instinct to create order and patterns has found its way into our DNA.

5.1   Cue cards never hurt either, like in the *Subterranean Homesick Blues* video. Sickest song title *ever*.

5.2   1 John 4:16

5.3   According to Wikipedia, "the 1971 TV commercial featured young people from around the world singing on a hilltop outside

Rome, Italy, and was so popular that the song (without the Coke references) became a hit in its own right."

5.4 *Dear friends, let us love one another, for love comes from God. Everyone who loves has been born of God and knows God. Whoever does not love does not know God, because God is love.* (1 John 4:7-8)

5.5 *God is love. Whoever lives in love lives in God, and God in them.* (1 John 4:16)

5.6 John 13:35; Christians should find it convicting that Jesus said his followers would be recognizable – not by their impeccable doctrine or by their many abstinences – but by their love for other people. Ouch.

5.7 *"My prayer is not for them alone. I pray also for those who will believe in me through their message, that all of them may be one, Father, just as you are in me and I am in you. May they also be in us so that the world may believe that you have sent me. I have given them the glory that you gave me, that they may be one as we are one— I in them and you in me—so that they may be brought to complete unity. Then the world will know that you sent me and have loved them even as you have loved me."* (John 17:20-23)

5.8 *"So now I am giving you a new commandment: Love each other. Just as I have loved you, you should love each other. Your love for one another will prove to the world that you are my disciples."* (John 13:34-35, New Living Translation)

6.1 How's my punctuation, Mr. Penny? (Blame my editor.) Thanks for giving us the tools for success. I honestly wouldn't have had the guts to even attempt writing were it not for the confidence I gained from your classes.

6.2 John 6:28-29.

6.3 Matthew 5:1-12.

7.1 I visited a Sikh gurdwara in Vancouver a few years ago. It was a fascinating experience. In my study of the Sikh religion I was interested to learn that Sikhs profess to believe that all roads lead to God. Yet at the same time, I have heard numerous stories of Sikh family members who tried to depart from the faith and were violently threatened. It is a conundrum that I'd like to investigate further. I have seen similar things in many faiths, including Christianity.

One other sidebar here. I mentioned that people of *all* faiths are shy to pronounce the exclusivity of their faith. I should have said, "everyone except atheists," who are most undiplomatic in pronouncing the need for everyone to bow to their views.

7.2 Christ's disciples were called Christians first in Antioch. See Acts 11:26.

7.3 Perhaps you've been taught that Jesus never really claimed to be God. Check it out for yourself:

Jesus answered, "I did tell you, but you do not believe. The miracles I do in my Father's name speak for me, but you do not believe because you are not my sheep. My sheep listen to my voice; I know them, and they follow me. I give them eternal life, and they shall never perish; no one can snatch them out of my hand. My Father, who has given them to me, is greater than all; no one can snatch them out of my Father's hand. I and the Father are one."

Again the Jews picked up stones to stone him, but Jesus said to them, "I have shown you many great miracles from the Father. For which of these do you stone me?"

"We are not stoning you for any of these," replied the Jews, "but for blasphemy, because you, a mere man, claim to be God" (John 10:25-33).

(Some say Jesus didn't make his point clearly enough. Yet he nearly got stoned for the same thing in John chapter 8 as well, so you'd think he would have toned down the language if he didn't mean to say he was God.)

7.4 John 3:16 – Look it up and you'll finally know what those nuts behind home plate have been holding up on signs for so long.

7.5 I want to make an important footnote at this point. Many people come to North America from a different part of the world, having been taught that America is a "Christian" nation. In turn, they interpret the immoral entertainment and music, along with all of the abuses that come with freedom, as the product of Christian faith. I would encourage these folk to understand that in more recent decades North Americans have largely abandoned Christian faith. We enjoy the freedom that finds its roots in the Christian faith that built our formidable society, but to our own detriment we have abandoned God's ways and the selfless love of Christ. We have already begun to pay the price. My hope is that North America and readers like you will rediscover *true* Christian faith.

7.6 John 6:51

7.7 Acts 17:16-34

7.8 John 8:24

8.1 I hesitated to use Mr. Derrick's name, but those who knew him would have identified him easily by my description anyway. He passed away many years ago, and I wouldn't want to say anything to detract from his memory. As a grown man now, I understand how words said without much thought can take on a life of their own. I'm simply reporting on how the words impacted me. Mr. Derrick was an amazing educator and I only want to honor his memory. We need more teachers like him.

8.2 My Canadian readers may remember how during the Canadian federal election of autumn 2000, our nation's most respected news magazine, *Maclean's*, published a cover story on Stockwell Day, the openly Christian leader of the then Canadian Alliance party. The caption "How Scary?" donned the cover, and Day was virtually mocked over his belief in creationism. Even non-Christians who had no interest in Day's party were offended by the disrespect he received.

Mr. Day did his fair share to bumble the election in ways that had nothing to do with his Christian faith. Google "Stockwell Day," "wetsuit," "Sea-Doo" and you'll get the picture.

8.3 The negative portrayal of Christians in popular entertainment continues today. Respected American public radio personality Ira Glass, himself an atheist, acknowledges this very clearly, stating that "Christians get a really bad rap in the media" and that contrary to the way they are often depicted in pop-culture, the Christians he knew "were all incredibly wonderful and thoughtful." You can read the entire article in the June 3, 2013 edition of Relevant Magazine: *Christians Are Horribly Covered by the Media*.

I am well aware that there are strains of Christianity in North America that are very narrow-minded, wacky, unscientific, ignorant – you name it. But Christianity is a global movement that should be evaluated on a much grander scale. Most of all, it should be evaluated on the merits of its founder and original intent.

8.4 For a break from your standard reading, try *Life After Life* by Raymond A. Moody, Jr. and Elisabeth Kubler-Ross and *The Afterlife Experiments* by Gary Schwartz and William Simon. I wouldn't dive headfirst into their findings, but there's definitely some interesting stuff to chew on. These and other books recount numerous tales of people who have had out of body experiences after flatlining. Upon reviving, they were able to give clear details of things they saw in other rooms of the hospital or on the hospital rooftop that they witnessed while out of body. A stunning number describe the beginnings of heaven or hell experiences strikingly similar to the descriptions given in the Bible.

8.5 The Bible supports this notion (1 Corinthians 8:1): "Knowledge puffs up while love builds up."

8.6 There are literally thousands of studies defending the health benefits of faith, but if you're helplessly left-brained you might need one more article to convince you, so check out the online article by the irreligious Tom Knox: *The tantalising proof that belief in God makes you happier and healthier*, published on www.dailymail.co.uk, February 18, 2011.

8.7 One example would be Albert Einstein's highly intuitive "thought experiments" which led him to formulate the theory of relativity. The types of frontiers Einstein broke through required not only logic, but imagination.

9.1 Matthew 27:46, uttered by Jesus just before expiring on the cross. The question of how Jesus' full deity interplayed with his full humanity is a question that stumps the best theologians even today. In many passages Jesus demonstrates that he understands that he will die on the cross for mankind, and yet in this verse his humanity seems to be surprised by the intensity of the separation he felt from the Father as he bore the world's sin in his body. Deep questions like this add a richness to my faith.

9.2　From where I sit today, I have no regrets about not pursuing hockey further. Very few make it through to the NHL. One guy who played on our team that year did – Glen Murray of the Boston Bruins. Everyone from Bridgewater, Nova Scotia, is very proud of Glen. He was an all-around athlete, better at soccer than hockey when I first knew him.

9.3　I realize that many Christians in North America are deistic determinists (often self-identified as Calvinists). They see God as controlling every single, minute action in the universe; in fact, they reason, God could not be God if he did not exercise such control. I disagree. Pushing God's sovereignty to such an extreme leads to (in my humble opinion) ridiculous statements like we find even in some of our most popular worship songs:

> *Who has told every lightning bolt where it should go*
> *Or seen heavenly storehouses laden with snow?*
>
> (Chris Tomlin, *Indescribable*)

Chris Tomlin is one of my favorite Christian artists, but really? God actively decrees for lightning bolts to strike certain people? That'd be a cheery angle to share at the funeral of someone who was so fortunate to be struck by lightning.

If I'm reading scripture right, we live in a world where chaos reigns. This does not negate God's sovereignty; he still has the power to do as he wishes. But he has chosen to let the effects of sin run their ugly course. Hence the existence of birth defects, tsunamis and even rogue lightning bolts.

9.4 Check out Christopher Hitchens, *God is Not Great*, P. 17.

10.1 As I'm editing my work, I am sitting in a café in Trois-Rivières, Québec. It's New Year's Eve, and I have joined my father-in-law and brother-in-law in quitting the house for a bit so I can work on my book. Unfortunately, the public library is closed, so we came to this grubby but charming little café called *Mosaïque*. It's owned by some guys from Tunisia. There's Arabic music playing and soccer on a big screen in the corner. My father-in-law and brother-in-law decided to try smoking from this bizarre vaporizer they call a *shisha*. (Commonly called a *hookah* in other parts of the world; it looks like a glorified bong to me.) Neither smoke cigarettes, but they enjoy the occasional cigar or pipe. Any minute they're going to be bugging me to try their new toy, and I'm really not interested – even though it's probably harmless. Anyway, I just thought this was an interesting aside to add to our "grace" discussion.

10.2 I should inform you that as a kid, despite being leery of this black-and-white mentality, I had a strong desire to show respect to my spiritual authorities. As a result I never used "bad" words (even when kids in the lunch room would surround me and try to get me to), I never played hockey on Sundays (even though I was the goalie), I never touched alcohol, and I never went to dances – not even my prom. When I got older and free from these authorities, I began to reevaluate my values according to the Bible as opposed to the church culture I was raised in. I can tell you that it took all of the courage and determination I could muster, but unless you've walked a similar path, you have no idea just how much courage and determination I'm talking about.

10.3 John 1:14

10.4 As a new writer, I never considered the implications of writing time-based illustrations. I fear Josef may be 22 *years* old by the time I get this finished.

11.1 My younger readers may not be aware of just how brash Agassi was when he turned pro and took the tennis world by storm at just 16 years of age. Topping his list of infamous exploits was his snubbing of tennis' most sacred establishment, Wimbledon, from 1988 to 1990 because he didn't want to conform to their all-white dress code.

11.2 OK, for you language buffs… I tried to use a hipper word for "feed," but I used a hipper word for "eat" instead. "Daniel a *bouffé* les lions" instead of "Daniel a *nourri* les lions." The teens were gracious; they considered me free entertainment.

11.3 Which positions am I referring to? Too many to mention, but divorce and remarriage, gambling, dancing, drug and alcohol use to name a few.

11.4 You may be surprised that a pastor, someone who is only supposed to be concerned with being God's servant, could get caught up in the whole "success" thing. And what's up with comparing? Aren't we all on the same team? It has taken some time for God to work these truths from my head down to my heart.

11.5 Have you ever considered what it would be like to be the creator of everything in the world and then refraining from experiencing some of the world's greatest pleasures? Jesus created sex, yet he never was intimate with a woman. Wow. That's like creating the world's best video game and then never getting to play it. Incredibly weak example, but you get the point.

12.1 Evolutionists would have us believe not only that the universe has built-in intelligence and designs itself, but also that emotion and morality emerged from impersonal material. This takes a lot of imagination. Sort of like imagining a rock developing feelings and wanting to care for other hurting rocks.

12.2 *But love your enemies, do good to them, and lend to them without expecting to get anything back. Then your reward will be great, and you will be children of the Most High, because he is kind to the ungrateful and wicked. Be merciful, just as your Father is merciful* (Luke 6:35-36).

(Throughout the Bible, the term "to be a son or child of" was often used to describe "one after the kind of." When we do good to people we follow in God's pattern.)

12.3 Check out Romans 2:12-16.

13.1 By microevolution I am referring to variation and adaptation within a species. (It's the change from one species to another different one that I'm having a hard time swallowing.)

13.2 We've been able to create amino acids and other organic compounds, but not life. In 2002, scientists succeeded in creating an artificial Polio virus, but scientists agree that viruses do not meet the biological criteria of life. Biogenesis (the concept that life arises only from life) has been an accepted law since the time of Louis Pasteur. Abiogenesis (the concept that life arises from non-life) is at best a theory, but the more we test the theory to no avail, the more it loses credibility.

13.3 Leading atheist Richard Dawkins contests that there are also vampire myths the world over. A weak comparison in my opinion. For those interested in reading many different flood myths (and comparing their details) go to www.talkorigins.org/faqs/flood-myths.html. I have no reason to doubt the research.

13.4 Richard Dawkins, *The God Delusion*, Houghton Mifflin Company, P. 4.

13.5 Richard Dawkins, *The God Delusion*, Houghton Mifflin Company, P. 375.

13.6 Even feminists are divided on this issue. Some argue that allowing women to use their sexuality to their advantage is empowering. Others see that a few beautiful and "uninhibited" women are placing incredible image pressure on their fellow woman that results in poor self-image and a willingness to succumb to male demands in the area of dress and sexual expression. In essence, women are enslaving other women with their sexual freedom.

While I believe that God made women beautiful and able to use their beauty to their advantage, I think many of the pop stars our little girls are being exposed to are abusing this God-given advantage.

13.7 Benjamin Franklin once said, "Beer is proof that God loves us and wants us to be happy." I'd have to say the same thing about sex.

13.8 Abraham H. Maslow, *The Maslow Business Reader*, Edited by Deborah C. Stevens, Published by John Wiley & Sons, 2000, P. 12.

13.9 Jesus did tell the rich young man of Matthew 19 to go and sell all his possessions, but this appears to be an isolated incident designed to get to the heart of the young man's issue – his unwillingness to put God before his possessions. So long as people are able to "put first the kingdom of God," Jesus doesn't seem to give them a hard time.

13.10 I can't leave this topic without acknowledging that many Christians are caught up in a "prosperity gospel" and have become very materialistic. Some high profile "Christians" also take advantage of the sick and disadvantaged by promising them miracles and physical blessings. These charlatans will have some answering to do to God someday.

13.11 I got excited when I first heard about CBS's new show, *Kid Nation*, thinking it might resemble an experiment à la *Lord of the Flies*. I was most disappointed.

13.12 Don't let your faith get derailed when you see professing Christians, even prominent ones with great followings, who don't seem to be overcoming their own selfishness. Jesus said, *"Not everyone who says to me, 'Lord, Lord,' will enter the kingdom of heaven, but only the one who does the will of my Father who is in heaven. Many will say to me on that day, 'Lord, Lord, did we not prophesy in your name and in your name drive out demons and in your name perform many miracles?' Then I will tell them plainly, 'I never knew you. Away from me, you evildoers!'"* (Matthew 7:21-23)

13.13 One day on a total whim, the Boys and I made a picture book, complete with glossy photos and sturdy binding. (Isn't this what all the teenage boys do when they're bored?) It was called *All Roads Lead to Ritchie Rentals*, and contained elements of various children's stories. Besides being terribly politically incorrect (we were still in the 80's), all of the characters end up dying a gory death. If I can convince the others, maybe someday I'll post it online. You may find it amusing. (You may also think we're a bunch of idiots.)

13.14 1 John 2:2

13.15 *For since the creation of the world God's invisible qualities—his eternal power and divine nature—have been clearly seen, being understood from what has been made, so that people are without excuse* (Romans 1:20).

13.16 Spock's quote for the ages is actually a one-phrase summary of utilitarian philosophy. Men like Jeremy Bentham and John Stuart Mill spent much time developing the concept in the 19th Century.

13.17 I even took a selfie with William Shatner's star on the *Walk of Fame* in Hollywood, but let's keep that a secret too. The way Shatner pimps himself nowadays in TV commercials makes me feel awkward just to watch him. Maybe he's just manly enough to laugh at himself and I should cut him some slack.

13.18 I believe that there are legitimate grounds for divorce, but I cringe at the classic response that is given: *Our children will be better off without all of the fighting.* Here's an idea – how about the parents learning to love one another! Children are given no option when it comes to learning how to get along with their siblings. What are we teaching our children about how to deal with difficulty? What are we teaching them about keeping their commitments? Again, personal pleasure trumps all, and parents have more power than kids. Bottom line.

13.19 *"In the beginning, Lord, you laid the foundations of the earth, and the heavens are the work of your hands. They will perish, but you remain; they will all wear out like a garment. You will roll them up like a robe; like a garment they will be changed. But you remain the same, and your years will never end."* (Hebrews 1:10-12).

Although I'm not sure there is sufficient scientific data to confirm that humans are causing it, the concept of climate change is consistent with the Bible's rendition of future events.

14.1 For one, the sun wasn't created until the fourth day, while plants and vegetation were created on day 3. A thousand years is a long time for plants to go without sunlight for photosynthesis. True, the light provided by God in day 1 could have sustained them. But Genesis 1 continually uses the phrase, "and there was evening and there was morning" to describe each day. The writer seemed to be determined to present the days in the way we normally understand them.

14.2   See Matthew 19:4-5, as well as Jesus' genealogy in Luke 3. The Apostle Paul, who wrote most of the New Testament, also treated the creation story and the fall of Adam & Eve as factual. (See Romans 5.)

14.3   In *God is Not Great,* Christopher Hitchens devotes an entire chapter to debunking arguments from design and yet never mentions the affects of the curse even *once*. A tip for Mr. Hitchens: If you're trying to convince theists in North America (many of whom believe the Bible) you should at least make mention of the curse, even if you regard it as mythical nonsense.

14.4   Matthew 25:41

14.5   Revelation 20:10-15

14.6   Tim Keller, *The Reason for God: Belief in an Age of Skepticism*, P. 79.

14.7   "*Therefore since we are God's offspring, we should not think that the divine being is like gold or silver or stone—an image made by human design and skill. In the past God overlooked such ignorance, but now he commands all people everywhere to repent. For he has set a day when he will judge the world with justice by the man he has appointed. He has given proof of this to everyone by raising him from the dead*" (Acts 17:29-31).

Even though I was once a blasphemer and a persecutor and a violent man, I was shown mercy because I acted in ignorance and unbelief (1 Timothy 1:13).

14.8 A Christian once told me about a children's puppet play he witnessed at a vacation Bible school. In the play, in order to drive home the seriousness of hell, a puppet was lit on fire as it flailed and screamed on the stage. I was dumbfounded at the story, but sadly, had no doubt that it was true. As far as I'm concerned, this is child abuse. We often see Jesus warning wayward adults and religious leaders about the danger of hell, but whenever we see him with children, he takes them in his arms and pours love on them. People who try to scare the hell out of children distort their perspective on God, often irreparably, in which case other teachings of Jesus apply: *But if you give them a hard time, bullying or taking advantage of their simple trust, you'll soon wish you hadn't. You'd be better off dropped in the middle of the lake with a millstone around your neck. Doom to the world for giving these God-believing children a hard time!* (Matthew 18:6-7, The Message) There is a time and a way to introduce the subject of hell to children. This is not it.

14.9 Richard Dawkins, in his book *The God Delusion*, has leveled the harshest criticism I've ever heard against God. I thought you might be interested in hearing it: "The God of the Old Testament is arguably the most unpleasant character in all fiction: jealous and proud of it; a petty, unjust, unforgiving control-freak; a vindictive, bloodthirsty ethnic cleanser; a misogynistic, homophobic, racist, infanticidal, genocidal, filicidal, pestilential, megalomaniacal, sadomasochistic, capriciously malevolent bully." (*The God Delusion*, P. 31)

14.10 *When you enter the land the Lord your God is giving you, be very careful not to imitate the detestable customs of the nations living there. For example, never sacrifice your son or daughter as a burnt offering. And do not let your people practice fortune-telling, or use sorcery, or interpret omens, or engage in witchcraft, or cast spells, or function as mediums or psychics, or call forth the spirits of the dead. Anyone who does these things is detestable to the Lord.*

It is because the other nations have done these detestable things that the Lord your God will drive them out ahead of you. But you must be blameless before the Lord your God. The nations you are about to displace consult sorcerers and fortune-tellers, but the Lord your God forbids you to do such things (Deuteronomy 8:9-14, New Living Translation, ©2007).

14.11　I'm sure the name George W. Bush flashed trough many readers' minds. We see from the Bible that God certainly can use one leader or nation to bring justice to another. When Moses received a command from the Lord, people didn't doubt, because they already believed he had given them the Law from God. Let's just say that Bush didn't have the same credibility. I'll let God be the judge of Dubya. He took heat for invading Iraq. Few will argue that Saddam Hussein didn't deserve what he got, but people have the right to disagree with how it was all carried out.

14.12　Atheists tend to lead the cry that God is bloodthirsty. Funny, because a God who doesn't exist can't lead anyone to hurt anybody. To be fair, atheists will argue that it is the *belief in God* that causes people to engage in bloodthirsty acts. I would argue that it's more about what kind of God people believe in.

14.13　I have long believed that God has treated humanity just like a parent treats their child. When the child is young, the parent lays down the law and enforces the rules. As the child ages, he or she discovers the heart that was behind the rules. The enforcement of the rules becomes less necessary because the laws have become embedded in the heart.

14.14　Matthew 7:21-23

14.15　*In the past, [God] let all nations go their own way. Yet he has not left himself without testimony: He has shown kindness by giving you rain from heaven and crops in their seasons; he provides you with plenty of food and fills your hearts with joy* (Acts 14:16-17).

14.16   It should be noted that Sikhs follow the teaching of their 10 gurus, who at points drew upon concepts from the Law of Moses through their Muslim roots. Their adherence, however, is more to a divine law imparted by their gurus.

14.17   Galatians 4:4-5

14.18   This infuriating arrogance is not limited to people in local churches. Certain high-profile Christians have claimed to speak on God's behalf on all types of matters. They should read their Bibles more: *As you do not know the path of the wind, or how the body is formed in a mother's womb, so you cannot understand the work of God, the Maker of all things* (Ecclesiastes 11:5).

14.19   Job wasn't saying that his suffering was "wonderful" as we understand the word. That would be stupid.

14.20   No one could state it any better than sports reporter Nate Scott, when he reported on Bruins' center Gregory Campbell's heroics in the 2013 playoffs...

During the second period of last night's Game 3 of the NHL Eastern Conference Finals, Bruins center Gregory Campbell dove to the ice to get in front of a shot taken by Penguins star Evgeni Malkin. The shot broke Campbell's leg, specifically the right fibula. He stayed on the ice for 10 seconds, clearly in pain. Then he did something only a hockey player would do.

He got up and killed the rest of the penalty off.

14.21   Christopher Hitchens, *God is Not Great*, P. 27.

14.22   This quote appeared on Stein's blog, www.expelledthemovie.com on October 31, 2007: *Darwinism: The Imperialism of Biology?*

14.23   Hitchens has demonstrated repeatedly that his distaste for certain individuals either clouds his thinking or causes him to speak out of turn. I heard him in a radio interview in 2007 with John Moore from CFRB Toronto. In it, he referred to the late Jerry Falwell as a "carcass" and gloated that upon suffering his heart attack his body wasn't "raptured" but rather found slumped on the floor. If Hitchens is so ignorant of a Christian doctrine as basic as the rapture (which no one believes happens upon an individual's death) he'd do himself a favor by not broaching the subject at all. (Just for the record, I've never been a Jerry Falwell fan either; but that's not the point here.)

14.24   It would be a most enlightening exercise to list all of the atrocities committed through the ages by people who *didn't* believe in God, but I have neither the time nor the interest for such an endeavour. I originally suggested that Hitchens compile such a list, but since the time of my writing these words Mr. Hitchens has passed away.

14.25   For the record, two decades later and Goodwill is my wife's favorite shopping excursion. She finds some amazing stuff.

15.1   Wendell died on May 23, 2007. I had the privilege of visiting him in the hospital and also of performing his funeral. In my message I highlighted the power of Wendell's faith. Most who were in attendance knew of his difficult life, and there wasn't a dry eye in the place. Mine included.

15.2   My good friend, Paul MacKinnon (whom I've mentioned in these pages), paid me the favour of reading through my book before I had it published. Upon contemplation of the truism, "Life is not fair," he was struck with a great thought that demonstrates that his right-brain is well at work:

> Even the saying "life is not fair" implies that there is some expectation that life *should* be fair. Why is that? Surely from a naturalist's point of view, this should not be an expectation. And as Christians we know life is not fair (the Bible tells us so). Yet, in our souls, we *want* it to be. How do we even know what is fair? This sense, like all morality, must come from somewhere outside of ourselves.

15.3 Jesus' teachings in Matthew 5. The word, not found in the Bible, comes from Latin word for happiness, *beatitudo*. You may recall the Jesus started each line in this message with "Blessed (or happy) is the man who..."

16.1 I can understand why early Christians wanted to develop official positions on certain Bible teachings, but I have long believed that the doctrine of the inspiration of scripture has been oversimplified by many Christians. I would guess that a majority of us ignorantly believe that "inspiration" means God zapped every scripture writer into a trance and had them robotically scribe his precise words. While God did dictate his exact words on a few occasions, this is the exception, not the norm. Much of what we now call "scripture" was recorded history or stories passed down by a rich verbal tradition. Other parts were regally funded collections of wise human sayings (such as the Proverbs). Other sections were popular songs. This does not mean that God could not have specially "inspired" these writers in a greater way than a modern day poet is "inspired." It simply means that Christians need to broaden their understanding of inspiration, recognizing that the standard Bible (or canon) was disputed hotly for some 400 years before anyone settled into a general agreement of which books should be included. (Catholics and Protestants still disagree on the authority of the Deuterocanonical or Apocryphal books.) Anyone who explains the inspiration of scripture without accounting for God's guidance through the collection and acceptance processes (both of which drew upon human wisdom) is uninformed or in denial.

When the Apostle John finished the book of Revelation, he did give a warning to anyone who would add or take away from the words of his book. Many believe that because he was the last living apostle (and knew it) that he was referring not merely to his book, but to all of the New Testament scripture. But this is next to impossible given that the canon of the New Testament wouldn't even be agreed upon for another 300 years. I would agree, as would many Christians today, that the end of John's life serves as a good marker for the end of scripture being written. I believe this based on the fact that Jesus was God's final word to man (Hebrews 1:1-2) and John was the last living disciple who could give us firsthand account of it.

In questioning the common view of inspiration I am in no way suggesting that the Bible we have isn't accurate or even the precise record God wanted us to have. Nor am I lobbying for other books to be contained in it. I am simply saying that God has always been faithful to give mankind ample information to pursue him and he is not afraid to work in partnership with human beings. "Inspiration" is much messier an affair than most Christians want to admit, but it is consistent with how God works in this fallen planet. He uses broken people, systems and methods to accomplish his work.

The purpose of a canon is to allow us to get beyond the debate of *What is scripture?* to the more important debate of *What does scripture say and how should I apply it to my life?* I am thankful for the way God used people not only to write scripture, but also to combine human wisdom with divine guidance in deciding which books are worthy to be called scripture.

16.2   Interesting that cultures all over the world have practiced animal sacrifice. Where do you suppose that came from?

16.3   *Before the coming of this faith, we were held in custody under the law, locked up until the faith that was to come would be revealed. So the law was our guardian until Christ came that we might be justified by faith. Now that this faith has come, we are no longer under a guardian* (Galatians 3:23-25).

The original Greek actually says that the law was our *paidagogos*, a family slave who was in charge of children, particularly escorting them to and from school each day. Similarly, the Law kept mankind out of trouble until Jesus came.

16.4   You probably know that Tolkien was indeed a Christian who derived much of his imagery from the biblical narrative. A friend of C.S. Lewis, Tolkien was more subtle in his use of the biblical metaphors and messages than his well-known contemporary.

18.1   Max Roser published an amazing graphic in the Washington Post entitled, "Global deaths in conflicts since the year 1400" that shows deaths by war in relation to world population. Google it. It shows a steady increase until World War 2 with a slight decline since then. Optimists have suggested war is on the decline. Others say we are merely in a short lull. You be the judge.

18.2   Samaria Garrett writes a blog for the Borgen Project, a respected non-profit that is fighting global poverty and hunger. Go to www.borgenproject.org and look up her June 14, 2015 article: *Are Natural Disasters Increasing?* Among other things, she cites: "In

1970, the average of natural disasters that were reported was 78; in 2004, this number jumped to 348." Also... "From 1980 to 2009 there was an 80 percent increase in the growth of climate-related disasters."

18.3   Revelation 13:16

18.4   Many people have seen the use of the number 666 in our UPC's (bar codes). I'll let you look into it for yourself. I am always leery about things like this and think it's wise to reserve comment. One thing that it does demonstrate is that the technology is already in place for such a development.

18.5   Revelation 19:19

18.6   Revelation 13:6

18.7   Understandably, these men all clarify that they are railing against those who believe in God, as opposed to God himself.

19.1   My wife, Sarah, is a passionate French Canadian. She is my soulmate and sparring partner, and our loving and fighting reach equal heights of intensity – sometimes blending into one another. We totally get one another and it's not uncommon for our fights to end in laughter as we recognize how we are just using each other to blow off steam. She's awesome.

19.2   Not their real names.

19.3   Christopher Hitchens, *God is Not Great*, P. 91.

21.1   Many have and will continue. Billy Graham's companion Charles Templeton lost his faith decades ago and wrote about it in his book, *Farewell to God*. More recently I learned about a 56-year old Lutheran minister named James McAllister who lost his as well. Check it out in the February 2008 edition of Psychology Today, *An Atheist in the Pulpit*, P. 78.

21.2   Jesus, on the contrary, was often invited to parties. See John 2:1-11 and Matthew 9:9-13.

21.3   The Westminster Shorter Catechism asks "What is our chief end?" The answer: "To glorify God and enjoy him forever." I Like that a lot!

Made in the USA
Columbia, SC
18 April 2018